THE
LIBERATION
LINE

Also by Christian Wolmar

THE
LIBERATION
LINE

THE UNTOLD STORY OF HOW AMERICAN ENGINEERING
AND INGENUITY WON WORLD WAR II

CHRISTIAN WOLMAR

 hachette
BOOKS
NEW YORK

Hachette Books
Hachette Book Group
1290 Avenue of the Americas
New York, NY 10104
HachetteBooks.com
Twitter.com/HachetteBooks
Instagram.com/HachetteBooks

First Edition: May 2024

Published by Hachette Books, an imprint of Hachette Book Group, Inc. The Hachette
Books name and logo are trademarks of the Hachette Book Group.

The Hachette Speakers Bureau provides a wide range of authors for speaking
events. To find out more, go to hachettespeakersbureau.com or email
HachetteSpeakers@hbgusa.com.

Books by Hachette Books may be purchased in bulk for business, educational, or
promotional use. For information, please contact your local bookseller or email the
Hachette Book Group Special Markets Department at special.markets@hbgusa.com.

The publisher is not responsible for websites (or their content) that are not owned by the
publisher.

Print book interior design by Bart Dawson

Library of Congress Cataloging-in-Publication Data

Name: Wolmar, Christian, author.
Title: The Liberation Line: the untold story of how American engineering
    and ingenuity won World War II / Christian Wolmar.
Other titles: Untold story of how American engineering and ingenuity won
    World War II
Description: First edition. | New York: Hachette Books, 2024. |
    Includes bibliographical references and index.
Identifiers: LCCN 2023058297 | ISBN 9780306831980 (hardcover) |
    ISBN 9780306831997 (trade paperback) | ISBN 9780306832000 (ebook)
Subjects: LCSH: World War, 1939–1945—Transportation—Europe. |
    Military railroads—Europe—History—20th century. | World War,
    1939–1945—Campaigns—Western Front. | United States. Army.
    Military Railway Service. | Military engineering—United States—History—
    20th century. | World War, 1939–1945—Europe—Engineering and construction.
Classification: LCC D639.T8 W65 2024 | DDC 940.54/1273—dc23/eng/20240102
LC record available at https://lccn.loc.gov/2023058297

ISBNs: 9780306831980 (hardcover); 9780306832000 (ebook)

Printed in the United States of America

LSC-C

Printing 1, 2024

Dedicated to the thousands of unknown railwaymen who served from both sides of the Atlantic and who deserve far more recognition than they have ever received.

CONTENTS

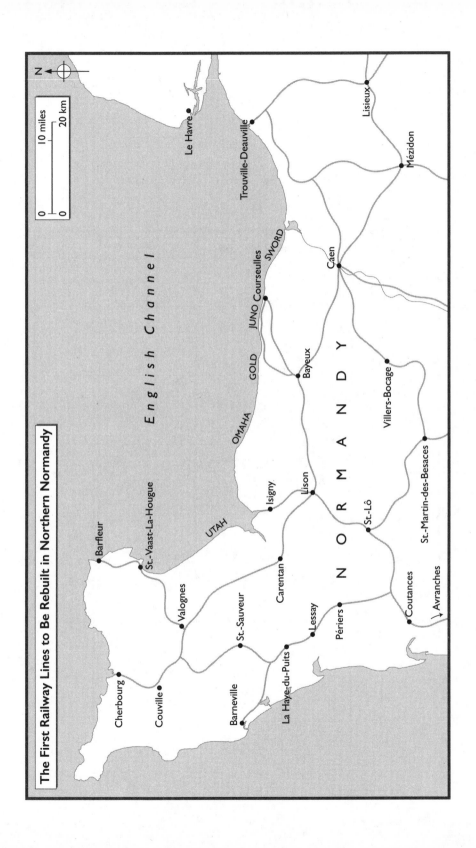

The First Railway Lines to Be Rebuilt in Northern Normandy

N

10 miles
20 km

English Channel

Le Havre
Trouville-Deauville
Lisieux
Mézidon

SWORD
JUNO Courseulles
GOLD
Caen
OMAHA
Bayeux
Villers-Bocage

Isigny
Lison
St.-Lô
St.-Martin-des-Besaces

UTAH
Carentan
Coutances
Avranches

St.-Vaast-La-Hougue
Barfleur
Valognes
St.-Sauveur
Lessay
Périers

Cherbourg
Couville
Barneville
La Haye-du-Puits

N O R M A N D Y

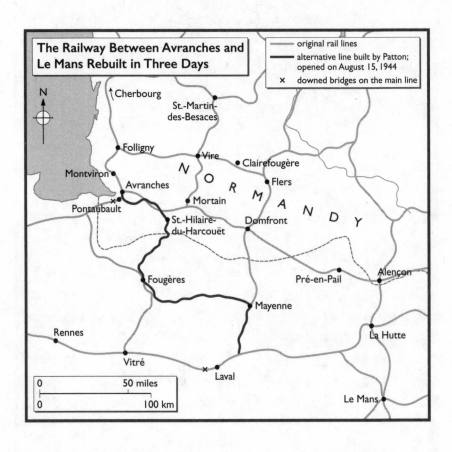

The Railway Between Avranches and Le Mans Rebuilt in Three Days

original rail lines
alternative line built by Patton; opened on August 15, 1944
× downed bridges on the main line

N

↑ Cherbourg

St.-Martin-des-Besaces

Folligny

Montviron

Avranches

Pontaubault

Vire

Clairefougère

Flers

Mortain

St.-Hilaire-du-Harcouët

Domfront

N O R M A N D Y

Fougères

Pré-en-Pail

Alençon

Mayenne

Rennes

La Hutte

Vitré

Laval

Le Mans

0   50 miles
0   100 km

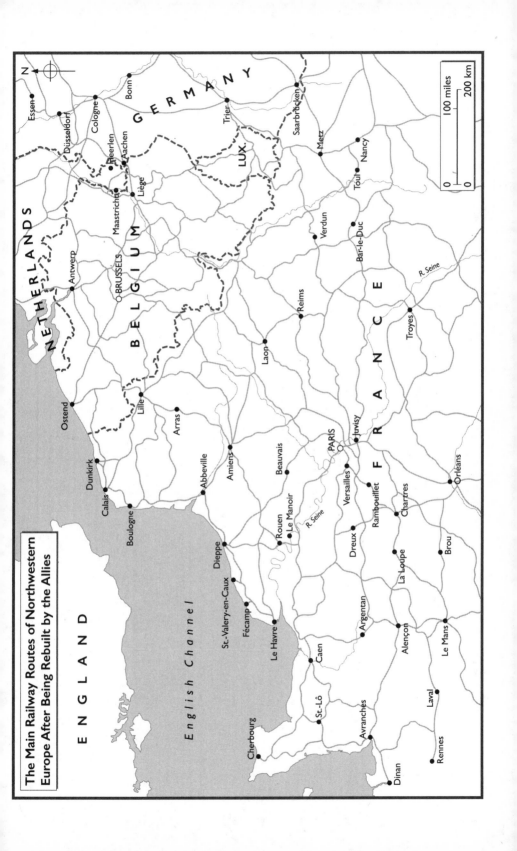

The Main Railway Routes of Northwestern Europe After Being Rebuilt by the Allies

FOREWORD

As it is now 80 years since D-Day, one might ask if there is anything new to be said, given the voluminous and ever-expanding literature on the subject. Yet British railway historian Christian Wolmar has unearthed the last untold story of the Battle of Normandy and the subsequent campaign in northwest Europe of 1944–1945. *The Liberation Line* reveals the critical role played by railways and railwaymen in propelling and sustaining the Allied war effort, and ultimately defeating Nazi Germany.

Any army that fights in intense combat against a determined and well-equipped opponent depends critically on its logistics for the transportation of critical matériel such as ammunition, equipment, fuel, and food. In large-scale continental warfare, only the railways have the capacity to meet the huge and relentless demands of military supply over long distances and durations. Without them, the war could not have been fought, let alone won. But all this effort was as much about the men involved as it was about their machinery. In his fast-paced account, drawing on a host of previously unpublished sources, Christian Wolmar narrates a series of remarkable experiences of British and American railway troops in overcoming a host of challenges in rebuilding and running railways from the Normandy coast through France and the Low Countries into the heart of Germany. As he skillfully explains, whether repairing damaged bridges, signals, or track, and on many occasions under enemy fire, the railwaymen performed their duties with a combination of expertise and hard grit.

But they received remarkably little recognition. At the end of the conflict, most returned to their civilian rail companies in the UK and the United States, and their extraordinary work was quietly forgotten. Now, some 80 years later, we can learn for the first time of their many and varied achievements.

As a historian of the Corps of Royal Engineers, which alongside its American counterpart played an enormous role in the wartime railway effort, and one who has studied, taught, and toured the campaign in Normandy for many years, I was honored when Christian asked if I might contribute the foreword to this essential new work. *The Liberation Line* deserves a prominent place in both military and railway histories. Although the book should belong in any serious reference collection, it also richly deserves to be enjoyed by a wide audience as a fascinating and absorbing read in its own right.

—Major General (Ret.) Mungo Melvin, CB OBE,
Historian of the Corps of Royal Engineers

INTRODUCTION

George Patton was not a happy man. His US Third Army, newly arrived in France a few weeks after the initial D-Day landings, was in danger of becoming bogged down. Patton had built his reputation on his ability to move and maneuver swiftly. Static armies, he believed, were useless. His Third Army had just fought its way to Le Mans—a mere 150 miles from Paris—surprisingly quickly, and he was keen to keep up the momentum. Capturing the French capital was his goal, and he reckoned that with the right support, he could reach Paris within a couple of weeks. The fact that his superiors in high command were concerned he was going too fast and would overstretch his supply line did not worry him. All he needed was enough gasoline to fuel his precious tanks and trucks.

Patton had just achieved the near miraculous feat of leading the Third Army out of the Cherbourg Peninsula on a narrow road under constant threat of air attack. He had been so anxious to get his troops moving that he spent a couple of hours personally acting as a traffic cop, directing the flow of military vehicles at a vital crossroads. Nothing was going to stop him heading toward Paris—except a shortage of fuel, and that was because the damned planners had failed to recognize how fast armies could move.

It was precisely Patton's military nous that had persuaded Dwight Eisenhower, the Supreme Commander of the Allied forces, to put the impetuous and impatient general in charge of the Third Army. Patton was the go-to man when the military high command wanted a rapid advance, and he had earned that reputation in two earlier major campaigns in the war. In Tunisia in early 1943, he had taken over the leadership of a demoralized invasion force and instilled a fighting spirit by boosting morale and paying attention to detail. The result, barely a month after he took over, was the important victory in the El Guettar battle, the first in North Africa in which the Americans overcame the German tanks. In Sicily, in the summer of that year, he led another invasion force with great success, making effective use of the new amphibious trucks that were to play a vital part in Normandy. In both cases, Patton took over armies that consisted largely of inexperienced and untried troops and turned them into effective fighting forces through inspiring leadership and improved morale.

Patton was a formidable leader who was proud to call himself a cavalryman in an age when horses were no longer at the spearhead of any attacking army. He deliberately cultivated a flashy, distinctive image to win over the men under him. He carried an ivory-handled Smith & Wesson Magnum, and on visits to the troops he invariably donned a perfectly polished helmet to go along with his riding pants and high cavalry boots. His jeep bore oversized placards displaying his rank on the front and back, as well as a Klaxon horn that would loudly announce his approach from afar, notably on visits to address his troops. His speeches, delivered without notes because of his dyslexia, were "simplistic, profane, [and] deeply offensive to some," but proved effective at motivating the troops even if some of his officers disapproved of his use of bad language.[1]

His enthusiasm, though, could rapidly transform into intolerance. After a shameful episode in Sicily during which Patton slapped a soldier in a field hospital who, today, would be recognized as suffering from post-traumatic stress disorder, it took Eisenhower's intervention to prevent Patton's dismissal from the army—though at the cost of being sidelined for a few months.

Eisenhower's faith in Patton never wavered. And so it was Eisenhower himself who, in January 1944, appointed Patton to lead the
American Third Army. This force was not to be part of the initial
Normandy invasion that began on June 6, 1944, but rather would
form a heavily armored mobile group that took advantage of an
embattled enemy and swept through France to the German frontier
and beyond. Patton's two previous campaigns, however, had been
short, both around a month long. Retaking continental Europe was
bound to require a much longer effort. Even so, Patton wanted to
make sure it took as little time as possible.

He did not waste those months of preparation in England. The
long delay before his army was sent abroad gave Patton the chance
to turn his troops, many of whom had only just arrived in the UK
a month or two before the Channel crossing, into what he called a
"hell on wheels" outfit, as battle-ready as possible, thanks to a grueling training program. And he did his homework. He read Edward A.
Freeman's book *The Norman Conquest* very carefully, focusing particularly on the sections describing the routes the king and his army
had used almost 900 years previously through Brittany and Normandy to reach the Channel.

Patton also played another role during his stay in England, one
that involved no work on his part but that was of vital importance to
the preparations for the landing. He was a decoy, set up to fool German intelligence. He was the supposed commander of a phantom
army group that appeared to be building up forces around Dover in
order to attack Calais and Boulogne in the Pas-de-Calais, the nearest
part of France to the English coast. This was part of a gigantic decep-
tion operation for the benefit of the German High Command,
persuading members that they needed to reinforce that part of the
coastline rather than Normandy, where all the Allied forces ultimately
were sent. The Germans would have perceived Patton, a successful

general with a proven record of success, as having a key role in any invasion force, which made him the perfect choice to lead this nonexistent army. The confidence trick worked, and the Germans massed forces around Calais in anticipation of an attack that never came.

Patton was a general who both loved and hated war, but, irrespective of the horrors he had seen all too often, he always wanted to be in the thick of the action, and it was with relief that, at last, he crossed to France on July 4. His men, who would constitute the Third Army, were arriving there, too, but would wait in camps behind the lines until the new army was officially brought into being. Bad weather caused delay, and progress was slower than expected in the face of German resistance. Consequently, the Third Army was not activated until August 1, and even then not publicly acknowledged until two weeks later in order to maintain the subterfuge that there would be an attack via Calais.

The Third Army was to be the Allies' secret weapon, the equivalent of the Germans' blitzkrieg, a force that would sweep through France in the same way the Germans had four years previously. From the outset, Patton deployed his troops with characteristic alacrity after the First Army's initial breakout of the Normandy bocage — the difficult territory of hedgerows and ditches in northern France that made it hard for tanks to move forward and where, consequently, the Allied invasion force had been stuck for weeks. After pushing through a bottleneck at Avranches, the crucial junction at the base of the Cotentin Peninsula, the Third Army split in two and advanced simultaneously southeast toward Paris and southwest toward Brittany. The latter had initially been a priority but was now seen as a secondary objective. The main thrust was to be toward Paris, and Patton's troops progressed remarkably quickly, reaching Le Mans, 110 miles by road from Avranches, on August 8.

Early on, the transport planners had expressed their doubts about the feasibility of Patton's endeavor, suggesting that moving so fast was impossible, but their fears had been largely ignored. Consequently, Patton faced an obstacle that risked stopping the Third Army in its tracks: it had overrun its supply line. Patton was not a man who would allow such base considerations as a lack of transportation to stop him—the planners be damned (though Patton's language would undoubtedly have been stronger). He needed to establish a line of communication to support his troops, notably to provide enough gasoline to enable him to keep moving toward the French capital. He knew there was only one way that sufficient supplies could be brought forward. Road transport was proving itself to be too slow. The key roads were in terrible condition and were heavily congested with military and civilian traffic. Moreover, there was a shortage of trucks and drivers. There was nowhere for planes to land, and in any case, they could not carry sufficient quantities of fuel. Only trains could provide sufficient supplies in good time.

Patton's demand was quite specific. He needed 31 trainloads of gasoline to be delivered to the yard at Le Mans. And quickly.

His problem was that the railways had been wrecked—by the Allies themselves. Earlier in the year, the Allies had successfully launched their so-called Transportation Plan, relentlessly bombing the French rail network to prevent the Germans from using it to bring up reinforcements that could repel the Allied forces arriving on the beaches. Although the authors of Operation Overlord, the Normandy invasion plan, had envisaged a key logistical role for railways, they had assumed that the scale of the damage wreaked on the system meant the railways would not be usable until much later, in the advance toward Germany.

That assumption, however, was a grave mistake. As it turned out, the railways were needed far more urgently than anticipated and therefore considerable forces would need to be allocated to repairing them.

Patton was furious that the planners had not addressed this issue. He contacted Colonel Emerson Itschner, the commander of the Corps of Engineers in northern France, about the need for a rail connection to Le Mans from Cherbourg, the port where most of the supplies were arriving. Itschner, although just 41, was the perfect man for the job because he knew about both engineering and the need for speed. He had trained as a civil engineer and previously worked on building roads in Alaska. As part of the war effort, he was responsible for the construction of a series of airfields across the United States, and his current role involved supporting the army by building and repairing a wide variety of civil engineering projects, including the railways. The instructions Itschner received from the Third Army headquarters near Bayeux, on Saturday, August 12, were unequivocal:

> General Patton has broken through and is striking rapidly for Paris. He says his men can get along without food, but his tanks and trucks won't run without gas. Therefore the railroad must be constructed to Le Mans by Tuesday midnight.[2]

That was just three days away.

Fortunately, the area had been well reconnoitered over the previous couple of days by an aerial photographic team led by the president's son, Colonel Elliot Roosevelt. On the basis of these pictures, Itschner devised a plan that used minor single-track lines through the forests and fields of the southern Normandy countryside; he quickly realized that a collapsed bridge at Laval on the main line could not possibly be repaired in time. But neither was Itschner's chosen route, mostly a rural single-track used by a few desultory local passenger services in peacetime, in functioning condition. Itschner flew over the route to check the state of the line and found that five bridges were down, three railroad yards had been wrecked by bombing, several miles of track had been damaged by bombs that left deep craters, and few, if any, watering and coaling facilities were available on the 135-mile-long railroad.

The task was to rebuild the line in 75 hours, a project that would normally take several months. It was later called "the most dramatic achievement of engineers in railroad reconstruction."[3] Yet, it is just one of the many amazing stories of how railwaymen, a truly forgotten group of soldiers, influenced the course of the Second World War.

This remarkable but forgotten feat of engineering is part of a much larger lacuna in even the most impressive accounts of this decisive phase of World War II. There is so much more to war than the dramatic aspects, such as weaponry and leadership, that are routinely highlighted in both historical accounts and fiction. Most notably, the fighting men depend on a wide range of support functions, from mechanics to mappers, and a key, often forgotten aspect is the need for engineering, which, appropriately, the French call *La Genie*. And none had a more important task in World War II than the railroaders brought over to ensure the lines of communication remained open for the advancing troops.

Yet, in the index of Max Hastings's brilliant reconstruction of D-Day, *Overlord*, there is no mention of either railways or trains.

Similarly, Anthony Beevor's *D-Day: The Battle for Normandy* contains nothing about the role the railways played in supporting the invasion. This is not to criticize these two excellent books but merely to emphasize that conventional histories of the conflict tend to neglect the key role the railways and the railwaymen played, especially in the final stages of the war.

It is not difficult, however, to find compelling evidence of the railways' importance in supporting the progress of the Allied forces as they swept—or sometimes stuttered—through France and Belgium, and indeed over the Rhine and right through Germany. In Cherbourg's maritime museum Cité de la Mer, the permanent exhibition on the Battle of Normandy includes a panel that provides a telling fact: after the Allies took Cherbourg in July 1944, 2.5 million tons of war matériel was carried through the town, of which 1.5 million tons was taken onward to the front by rail, leaving just 1 million tons carried by road. There were four phases to the invasion: the landings, the breakthrough, the passage through the Siegfried Line, and the crossing of the Rhine—in each one, the railways were an essential component of success.

Despite the omission of the railways' role from so many accounts of the retaking of Europe, it is difficult to dispute the notion that the railways were the key to the Allies' ultimate victory. A quote in a US military account of the conflict sums up brilliantly the role of transportation in war: "Objectives were set high. In war, transportation frequently has to try to do more than it can. Otherwise it will not do enough."[4] Transport is often the last consideration in military minds but is, in effect, the first requirement. "Nothing happens until something moves" is the apposite credo of the US Transportation Corps.

Moreover, even when transport logistics are considered, the roads and the trucks so often get the credit, despite the fact that railways can carry far greater loads more quickly and more efficiently with far less manpower. This bias is well reflected in 1952's film *Red Ball Express*, which celebrates the special truck route the US Army set up briefly to support General Patton's advance through northern France to Paris. The film highlights the trucks' role, which was, in reality, far less significant than the rebuilding of the rail line in southern Normandy mentioned previously. Maybe we should not be surprised that the film industry of the most car-dependent culture on the planet should draw the wrong conclusion in its analysis of the logistics or perpetuate a myth about the primacy of road transport.

A few lonely voices have pointed out the fallacy of this road-centric view. A 2019 article in *Classic Trains* expresses it best. In explaining how, just four months after D-Day, 20,000 freight cars, 37 ambulance trains, and 1,300 locomotives had been transported across the English Channel, the author notes that Hitler was bemused by the Allies' ability to supply their armies: "Hitler had said it couldn't be done—not inside of three years. Hitler forgot or overlooked the vital importance of railroads in war. The Allies did not."[5]

Hitler, as the author indicates, was obsessed with roads and built the world's first highways—*autobahnen*—paid for by the German national railway system, the Reichsbahn, on his orders. He ignored the evidence from the Luftwaffe's reconnaissance of the classification yards and railway sidings in southern England, which revealed that they "were full of locomotives and freight cars which the Allies apparently intended to use to penetrate his 'impenetrable' fortress." In contrast, Hitler's "own roads to victory became progressively useless as Allied planes bombed the Third Reich out of gasoline, and when he turned to his long-neglected railway system to help him out, it was unequal to the task."[6]

Indeed, the importance of the railways grew as the Allied troops headed toward Germany and the ports of Cherbourg and, later, Antwerp became fully operational. Without the ability of the railways to transport the vast quantities of supplies needed to maintain and continue the Allies' sweep eastward, the ultimate victory may well have been in 1946 rather than May 1945 — or perhaps never.

The work carried out by these railway soldiers encompassed every task needed to run train services in peacetime plus a few more. The introduction to *United States Military Railway Service* "acclaims the heroism of the G.I. railroaders in moving gargantuan amounts of freight and large numbers of troops, often under intense fire and bombardment, over impossible railroads, with motive power that in the United States would have been relegated to the scrap heap half a century before." The book rightly celebrates the wide variety of men involved in these tasks, which included many unsung heroes and countless actions of bravery: "Cited along with the clerks, telegraph operators, and others who outside normal lines of duty voluntarily manned switch engines to move cars of explosives and inflammables away from other cars that had been set ablaze by enemy action, are the managers who brilliantly planned and coordinated the services' daily operations."[7]

———————

One constant refrain of this story is the priority the military commanders gave to reopening the rail lines to restart rail services. As the forces advanced through France, just behind the front line the railwaymen were at work, taking over the lines left by the Germans and bringing them into use as soon as possible. Yet again, this is a story that has been missed in so many accounts of the Allies retaking Europe after D-Day. Moreover, this process continued across borders, from France into Belgium, Holland, and Germany. In all those countries, the high command's clear priority was reconstructing the railway lines to ensure the continued sweep of the Allied forces through Europe.

This book is about the role railways and trains played in the war after the Normandy landings and the men who rebuilt and operated them. Inevitably, therefore, it leaves out many other aspects of the conflict. Even so, I have attempted to provide a broad picture of events so that we might understand the precise role of the railways in a wider context. The advance through France and into Belgium, Holland, and Germany was a convoluted affair, requiring the transport over water of an army whose size and whose demands for supplies were totally unprecedented. Moreover, that army could not remain static and was forever on the move taking territory, with little time to consolidate its gains. The advance of the troops was not steady. For the first month, the Allies were confined to a small peninsula with Cherbourg, the principal port, at its northern tip. After the breakout in July, the advance was much faster and resulted in the capture of much of France, helped by the advent of another army moving northward after landing on the Mediterranean beaches. The sheer size of the Allied forces inevitably led to delays, most notably in the autumn of 1944 after a period of rapid advance. Then, finally, after the Germans' failed counterattack in December, the Allies were able to move into Germany, overcome the difficulties of crossing the Rhine, and bring about a stunning victory.

Throughout this process, the various tasks of bringing the railway back into use had to be undertaken at great pace, from rebuilding lines, repairing tunnels, and replacing bridges to laying out new signaling systems. This book combines the macro with the micro, outlining the strategic issues, setting out the importance of the railways in the context of the conflict, while relating stories of the railwaymen who enabled it all to happen. Great individual heroism and dedication were required to undertake these tasks.

Because of the sheer scale and numbers, I am bound to introduce an occasional error, for which I sincerely apologize. Accounts of particular events conflict and I have used the most reliable source, at times explaining that this is what I have done. But also, much of the primary material comes from army sources, and the requirement for optimism and positivity might have superseded the fundaments of accuracy.

Many other stories remain to be told about the achievements of these railwaymen turned soldiers. Hopefully, this book will prompt other efforts to uncover and tell the story of these forgotten brave men. As David Matthew Wilkins, author of a treatise on the 728th Railroad Operating Battalion, put it, "for all of the 'Saving Private Ryans' and Stephen Ambrose books, little attention is being given to those troops who served in a support capacity during the war. Even today [2002], little scholarly attention is being focused on the Transportation Corps or the Military Railway Service."[8]

I have eschewed technical terms for military and transport matters—the former because I am not competent to explain them, and the latter because I know how alienating they are for readers. Occasionally, this has meant simplifications that some more expert readers may take issue with but that are a necessity to ensure this book, which I am convinced will open many people's eyes to neglected aspects of the story of the Second World War, is read as widely as possible. Quibble over the detail, indeed. But the core thesis will, I hope, bear any in-depth scrutiny.

———

Some might initially consider this to be an unexciting story of communication lines and supply routes when compared with the tales of heroism of the men at the front lines and all the exciting hardware they deploy. However, it quickly becomes evident that the opposite is true. The waging of wars has always been a matter of logistics, and the Second World War is an example of where logistics played a particularly prominent and even decisive role. This book is not about the transport of goods and vehicles but rather the people who organized the supply, the strategies involved in enabling this huge movement of men and matériel, and the ways these processes contributed to the war effort. This tale is anything but dull. It includes amazing stories of courage and, too, tales of snipers killed with bayonets, attractive female spies trying to extract information from railway workers, and even the occasional romance and wedding.

Ultimately, the rebuilding of the railway line in Normandy over the space of three days is a microcosm of a far bigger story involving at least 50,000 US and British troops who were involved in reconstructing, maintaining, and operating railways across Europe after the Normandy landings. As such, this reframing is absolutely essential for understanding what happened in that decisive battle 80 years ago. As the author of a history of one army unit cited in this book puts it: "In comparison with the deeds of gallant air and ground force troops, and the attendant publicity given to them during the war, the role of the American Services of Supply may seem unspectacular and colorless. But those who served in forward areas realize how the combat and service forces were mixed together, often fighting side by side. There are 'foot-sloggers' who served in the European Theater of Operations who will never forget the job done by the men who sustained them."[9]

To understand the magnitude of their achievement, we have to consider the extent to which war and railways are anathema to each other, seemingly almost incompatible. Railways need stability, safety, and security. The very act of running a train at speed over tracks requires societal trust because nothing is easier than obstructing a railway or putting it out of action with an act of sabotage. Moreover, reinstating a broken railway is a complex and time-consuming process. Yet, as becomes increasingly evident over the course of this narrative, countless such rebuilding projects were achieved at great speed through teamwork and cooperation, often with minimal resources and tools. Again, this is the opposite of what railways need. Railways require constant maintenance and renewal, and invariably those take time and resources. Yet, in this case, engineers quick to adapt to novel situations brought railways back into productive and intensive use in unprecedented circumstances far more rapidly than ever was done in peacetime.

THE
LIBERATION
LINE

1

THE BIGGEST TASK

It is easy to forget, with the benefit of hindsight, that during much of World War II the outcome of the conflict was not inevitable.

Victory for the UK and its allies was by no means assured. As the eminent British historian Max Hastings writes, "For a year following the fall of France in 1940, Britain fought on without any rational prospect of final victory."[1] Even the entry of the United States into the war after Pearl Harbor provided no guarantee of success. Doubts remained even at the highest level. As the Normandy landings unfolded, Supreme Allied Commander Dwight Eisenhower famously carried a letter he'd written on the eve of D-Day that he intended to make public in the event of failure. It read: "Our landings in the Cherbourg-Havre area have failed to gain a satisfactory foothold and I have withdrawn the troops. My decision to attack at this time and place was based upon the best information available.... If any blame or fault attaches to the attempt it is mine alone." Fortunately, the letter remained in the Supreme Commander's pocket.

There had, of course, been previous setbacks. Perceiving the rescue of hundreds of thousands of troops from the beaches of Dunkirk in 1940 as a heroic adventure masked the fact that it was a major defeat that could have had a far worse outcome if the evacuation had been delayed any longer and the 338,000 returning troops had remained stranded. At the time, Britain was standing almost alone against the Nazi threat and, in the event, the entry of the United States into the war more than a year later proved to be decisive but only after some frightening reverses and numerous holdups. In fact, the Japanese attack on Pearl Harbor that precipitated US entry had followed another decisive instance of Axis overreach: Hitler's invasion of Russia in June 1941, described by Hastings as the "most demented of his [Hitler's] strategic decisions." After Pearl Harbor, the might of the US forces backing the UK and the other countries fighting alongside it ensured that the Allies were thereafter odds-on favorites to win the war. But as racegoers know, being favorite is no guarantee of victory. Even then, the road to victory was long.

On land in most of the key theaters, the railways were central to the transportation system in a way that seems improbable today. In fact, the railways were at the core of the UK's transport system. All long-distance freight transport was by rail, supported by coastal navigation for bulk products such as coal. There were no highways, and apart from the odd bypass and short four-lane sections, the roads were more suitable for the horses and carts they still carried than for large trucks. Although the reliability and size of trucks had improved since the First World War, when they were little used except for short journeys, after World War II broke out, carrying freight on roads remained a subsidiary form of transport and was principally confined to delivery to and from railheads.

Defense planners in the 1930s had long understood that the railways would remain key to the transport of goods across the UK and therefore mandated that all military depots and warehouses be accessible by rail. Even secret underground facilities needed to be rail connected, with tracks invariably running right into the tunnels, despite this being a telltale sign for hostile aircraft. It would, indeed, have been unthinkable to build a major storage facility without rail access.

A small but instructive example of the primacy of railway travel at the time is that when Dwight Eisenhower was appointed commander of the US forces in Europe in 1942—later becoming Supreme Allied Commander—he was allocated a train for his principal travel needs. His predecessor had used these railcars and had given them the rather strange name Alive. Rail travel was deemed far safer than road transport, especially because Alive was an armored train consisting of three coaches protected by bulletproof glass. Flatcars at each end offered further protection and carried jeeps that were deployed for short journeys from a railhead. In the five months running up to D-Day in 1944, Eisenhower's train was intensively used, covering just under 100,000 miles as preparations escalated.

Given the railways' importance, it was inevitable that the four main British railway companies, which provided nearly all the nation's train services, would quickly be nationalized when war broke out, replicating a similar move made at the onset of the First World War. As soon as news arrived of the German invasion of Poland on September 1, 1939, Britain's rail network came under the control of a Railway Executive Committee appointed by the Ministry of Transport and remained so throughout the conflict. By taking control, the UK government was able to commission extra services for major operations and ensure that the movement of military supplies and personnel was prioritized over civilian trains.

Long before Operation Overlord (the code name adopted in late 1943 for the Normandy landings) was conceived, the railways played a major role in several aspects of the war. For one, the railways were used by the ill-fated British Expeditionary Force, which crossed the Channel to France within days of the announcement of war, on September 3, 1939. Less than a week later, no fewer than 261 special trains carrying more than 100,000 troops ran from various parts of the country to Southampton on the South coast. The very busy network, in addition to normal demand, had to cope with the evacuation from major cities of all schoolchildren aged 3 to 13 and many adults deemed vulnerable. Ultimately, in the five months of the buildup of the Expeditionary Force, some 1,400 special trains carrying 420,000 men were deployed to the ports. Many of these soldiers traveled onward aboard ships owned by the rail companies, which at the time operated extensive fleets of ferries on routes to France, Ireland, and even further afield. Additional major railway operations supported the Anglo-French Expeditionary Force's failed attempt in April 1940 to prevent Norway being taken over by the Germans and then barely a month later transported the Dunkirk survivors of the retreating Expeditionary Force away from the Channel ports where they were landed.

The biggest of these operations was the Dunkirk evacuation, code-named Dynamo. It had to be undertaken nimbly because the timing of arrivals and the numbers involved were uncertain. The railways amassed a stock of 2,000 carriages and 186 locomotives, tucking them away in various nearby sidetracks and little-used branches near the ports in preparation for transporting the evacuees away from the coast. To keep these trains and, in particular, their steam locomotives ready for immediate use, many drivers worked 24 or even 36 hours continuously, supported by local volunteers who provided food and drink for them. The Southern Railway, one of the Big Four rail companies in the UK, bore the brunt of this traffic, a task made more difficult by the frequency of enemy attacks on its lines that ran closest to European shores. The Southern owned 42 of the ferries that were used in the Dunkirk evacuation, 5 of which were sunk during the operation. The railway authorities, therefore, were ready for the intensive use of the rail network in preparation for the Normandy landings, even though Operation Overlord would be on a far larger scale.

In fact, the logistics required for the success of Operation Overlord were of a scale that had never previously been considered, let alone implemented. Operation Overlord was in essence about the logistics on both sides of the Channel; all the planning and preparation were focused on the movement of men and materials after the initial landings. As the head of the US Army Transport Service later summed up: "Throughout the late war, the plans for the launching and subsequent maintenance of every campaign were conditioned to a large extent by the capacity of the transportation facilities that existed, or could be developed. Indeed, it is inconceivable that any commander would embark on an operation without considering transportation and its influence on the military situation."[2]

These episodes did much to reinforce the awareness among the American leadership that logistics would be a crucial factor in the ability to launch such an attack. Consequently, a new Transportation Corps, hived off from the Corps of Engineers, was set up in June 1942. The new corps was made explicitly responsible for managing the railways and equipment sent from the United States, and it became a vital part of Overlord planning. After all, this war was much more genuinely a world conflict, with battles on four continents, than the First World War had been, with its focus exclusively in Europe and the territory of its immediate neighbors. Robert P. Patterson, the US under secretary of war, described the task of the Transportation Corps as "entirely without precedent in the history of our country."[3] Indeed, it was without precedent in the history of the world.

Even though most historical accounts of D-Day and its aftermath ignore or minimize the role of the railways, the military planners of Operation Overlord were certainly aware of their importance. In February 1944, four months before D-Day, Field Marshal Bernard Montgomery addressed 400 staff of the London, Midland and

Scottish Railway at Euston in central London, stressing the critical role of the railways not just in the war effort generally but specifically in achieving the successful launch and execution of the second front in northwest Europe. As Lieutenant Colonel Clem Maginniss later reflected, "Sixty years on, with our reliance on the motor vehicle, it is almost impossible to appreciate that in 1944, the railways were fundamental to the existence of the United Kingdom and that without them, D-Day would never have been mounted."[4]

Overlord required a series of massive but discrete transport tasks. First, the team needed to ship vast amounts of matériel from the United States to the UK, where the supplies and equipment would sit idle for many months or years, followed by transport to bases, which presented another logistical headache. In addition, over a million men had to be brought to the UK and taken onward to their camps to await deployment across the Channel. Then, all the supplies had to be assembled at nine huge classification yards while ensuring that hundreds of thousands of men were battle-ready in the days before the assault. This was followed by the actual crossing of the Channel, not just on D-Day but also in the following weeks and months. Finally, there was the most complex movement: the heavily resisted sweep through Europe, which had to be backed up by lines of communication dependent on the railways.

––––––––––

During the months following Dunkirk, little thought was given to invading the Continent itself. On the contrary, Britain was on the defensive and the idea of retaking Europe from the Germans seemed inconceivable. Indeed, the main concern was shoring up the British rail network and preparing it for destruction in the event of an invasion. Explosive devices were preemptively fitted to all major bridges, including the famous Forth Bridge north of Edinburgh. Anti-tank ditches, some up to 20 miles long, were dug alongside main lines, which were also protected by miles of concrete blocks to help resist an invading force. Toward the end of 1941, British Joint Planners, under the aegis of the Ministry of Defence, drew up a rudimentary and half-hearted plan for an attack on German-occupied Europe, but its very name — Roundup — was a bit of a giveaway of its limited scope, implying that it would be some kind of mopping-up operation of a demoralized force. Nevertheless, even though Roundup was not taken seriously, some of the ideas it set out eventually found their way into the Overlord strategy.

Pearl Harbor ultimately proved to be Britain's salvation. The attack on the Hawaiian port by Japanese aircraft on December 7, 1941, followed by Hitler's declaration of war on the United States four days later, changed the entire course of the conflict. Now, the United States could reveal itself unequivocally as Britain's ally rather than merely surreptitiously offering support behind the scenes. Within a couple of weeks, a joint strategic meeting, code-named Arcadia, was held in Washington, during which the first ideas for an invasion force were set out.

In fact, the cooperation between the two nations, which shared a common language but differed greatly in history and culture, had been happening for some time. As the US official report into the Normandy landings revealed: "In the late spring of 1941, a few American officers in civilian clothes slipped into London and established a small headquarters in a building near the American embassy on Grosvenor Square. They might have been attachés of the embassy, as far as the general public could tell. Their name, Special Observer Group (SPOBS), like their attire, concealed rather than expressed their functions, for they had much more urgent business than to act as neutral observers of the military effort of a friendly nation at

war."[5] Indeed, their role was rather greater than their numbers—
initially just 18 officers and 11 enlisted men—might have suggested:
they formed the nucleus of a military organization encompassing all
aspects from intelligence gathering to logistics and supply. Initially
they identified possible sites for future US bases and camps, mostly in
Scotland and Northern Ireland.

Pearl Harbor, however, ensured this little task force played a key
role in the strategy for winning the war. The United States officially
entered the conflict and was determined to win. Crucially, despite the
fact that the United States had been attacked from the east by Japan,
President Franklin D. Roosevelt decided that the first strategic goal
would be to overcome Germany, leaving the resolution of the Pacific
theater to be decided at a future date. In effect, this guaranteed the
need for landings on the Continent; within a few weeks, plans were
being drawn up for a cross-Channel attack.

In April 1942, General George C. Marshall, US Army chief of
staff, and Harry Hopkins, President Roosevelt's personal represen-
tative, presented the initial plan, code-named Bolero, to the British
government. The idea was to "prepare plans and make administrative
preparations for the reception, accommodation and maintenance of
United States forces in the United Kingdom and for the development
of the United Kingdom in accordance with the requirements of the
Roundup plan."[6]

But the three-phase Bolero plan was conceived on a totally different scale from that of Roundup. It envisaged a massive buildup
of American forces and supplies in the UK, which would then be
followed by the seizure of beachheads and conclude with an advance
into German-occupied Europe to be carried out later that year.

However, in reality, an invasion in 1942 was impossible. Marshall's plan relied on considerable amounts of British shipping to
carry American men and supplies across the Atlantic, which was

never feasible. Neither was Marshall's suggestion that, to support Russia, the British—alone—should launch an invasion of northwest Europe as a sacrifice to attract German resources away from the Eastern Front. Not surprisingly, this idea did not go over well with the British command. To prevent a rift between the Allies, the British paid lip service to the possibility of an invasion in 1943. However, in July 1942, the decision to confront the Germans in North Africa meant that preparations for a cross-Channel invasion were put on hold.

If there were any lingering doubts about the difficulties of launching an invasion against such a well-entrenched enemy, an ill-fated attack on the French port of Dieppe on August 19, 1942, confirmed them and demonstrated the foolhardiness of such an undertaking without massive resources. The plan had been to capture the port, albeit briefly, before testing the German defenses and destroying key structures. The idea itself was conceived by Lord Louis Mountbatten, whose military performance had already been found wanting as commander of a fleet of ships that included *Javelin*, a destroyer that was torpedoed off the coast of Cornwall as a result of a mistaken maneuver. An initial attempt to attack Dieppe in early July had to be abandoned when the flotilla was spotted by German aircraft; nevertheless, Mountbatten persuaded Churchill, a personal friend, that the raid should go ahead, despite two previous test runs in Bridport having proved unsuccessful.

The raid was supposed to take place only during the 15 hours of daylight. Unfortunately, when it was launched the enemy was well prepared, probably as a result of information from French double agents. Though the Allies managed to land on four beaches, very little territory was gained but heavy losses were incurred. Within 10 hours, the force of 5,000 Canadian and 1,000 British commandos had been routed, with 3,600 killed, wounded, or taken prisoner. In contrast, German casualties amounted to just under 600, half of whom were killed. The Royal Air Force (RAF), too, lost 106 aircraft, more than twice the total of German losses.

In an analysis of the raid years after the fact, Joshua Schick, curator of the American National WWII Museum, concluded: "The raid was not intended as a practice run for the landings in Normandy, nor did it provide any new techniques or problems to overcome that guaranteed the success of Overlord."[7]

Despite the obvious failure of the Dieppe raid, the initial plan for an invasion — the large-scale transfer of American men and supplies to the United Kingdom — was still implemented, and Bolero went through numerous iterations. By the time the third version was produced at the end of 1942, any hope of launching an attack in 1943 had been extinguished given the sheer scale envisaged: 1.1 million US servicemen were to be accompanied across the Atlantic by almost unfathomable quantities of supplies, including no fewer than a thousand locomotives.

And the plans kept growing. After it was recognized that the invasion would have to be delayed until 1944, Bolero's fourth iteration published in the summer of 1943 required a further escalation in the number of men: upward of 1.5 million soldiers. An assessment of the supplies needed to maintain such a force suggested the need for 150 cargo ships per month to cross the Atlantic in addition to the troop ships, most of which were themselves hastily converted cargo ships. This involved an almost exponential rise in the capability of the US merchant fleet, particularly when it came to ships in the Atlantic defending themselves from attacks by German U-boats. In June 1942, Lieutenant General Brehon B. Somervell, commanding the Army Services of Supply, had warned: "The losses by submarine sinkings threaten failure of our war effort." A few months later, he reported, "Our plans to carry out a determined and effective offensive during 1943 and to strike further decisive blows in 1944 are measured almost entirely by the shipping which can be made available for military operations."[8]

Indeed, the early stages of Bolero were severely disrupted by these German U-boat attacks. Of 74 vessels earmarked by the British authorities for shipping material from the United States in the early summer of 1942, 17 were sunk before they even reached the United States. This rate of monthly losses could not continue because it surpassed the number of vessels that UK and US shipyards could build. Fortunately, things turned around at the beginning of 1943, thanks to improved strategies against the German submarines. New types of depth charges proved effective, and improved radar detection increased the effectiveness of air attacks on submarines. Moreover, ships were mostly sailing within convoys with navy protection, which made the submarines more vulnerable.

By early 1943, the number of new ships was finally exceeding losses. The ability of American shipyards to churn out ships was remarkable and largely the result of a fortuitous change in legislation governing the shipbuilding industry, introduced just before the war, that mandated new merchant ships be capable of military use. In May 1942, President Roosevelt, who personally backed this endeavor, wrote about the urgent need to increase shipbuilding production: "I cannot over-emphasize the necessity that this objective be met, as the success of our war effort must rest on our ability to provide the shipping required for the transportation of our troops and their supplies, and to continue the flow of essential military equipment to our associates in the United Nations."[9] At last, American industry was harnessed for the war effort, and shipbuilding was at the heart of the undertaking

The American shipbuilders' output more than doubled in 1943 to 20 million tons, up significantly from the previous year. This increase provided the capacity to move troops and matériel across the Atlantic, especially as the submarine threat receded. More than half of the tonnage completed during the war was of a basic freighter design known as the Liberty ship, a relatively small vessel at under 11,000 tons deadweight. The Liberty was an adaptation of a British coal-burning ship, fitted with oil-fired engines that were manufactured in unprecedented numbers. The ship was not universally welcomed because it was slow and had structural weaknesses, but the simplicity of its design and industrial production methods enabled 2,710 to be built during the war. By 1943, the shipbuilders also successfully reduced the completion time for such a vessel from a prewar total of 244 days to an average of just 42 days.

Though several other standard types were produced over the course of the conflict, their numbers were dwarfed by the huge number of Liberty ships. A measure of the scale of this operation, which ultimately underpinned the US effort in Operation Overlord and the subsequent sweep through western Europe, was the more than 10-fold increase in shipyard workers employed on the commission program; their numbers reached a peak of nearly 600,000 in July 1943.

Many of the troops were carried in markedly more pleasant accommodation than the cramped Liberty ships. The two liners, the *Queen Mary* and the *Queen Elizabeth* (named after the wives of George V and George VI, respectively, not the Elizabeth who reigned for 70 years until 2022), shuttled back and forth across the Atlantic at speeds of up to 30 knots, enabling them to outpace German submarines and therefore obviating the need for escorts. As such, both could make three round trips per month carrying 15,000 troops on every journey, and ultimately, these two ships alone brought 425,000 American troops to the United Kingdom, a quarter of the entire buildup.

The accumulation of supplies in response to the demands of Operation Overlord was similarly unprecedented. Around 60 percent of all supplies came across the Atlantic to supplement locally sourced matériel. This influx of American supplies depended heavily on the ability of the British to transport them around the country efficiently and rapidly, and it placed a huge burden on the wartime transport system.

All the men and matériel arriving from the United States had to be accommodated in the UK in existing facilities to limit the need for new construction. The buildup stretched over two years, so many men remained in the UK for a long period awaiting deployment. In order to build the barracks and warehouses needed for these men and supplies, 57,000 UK citizens were employed on US construction projects by the end of 1943.

The fact that the United States and UK were long-standing allies did not mean that relations were always cordial. At first, the strongly unionized British longshoremen refused to allow American personnel to handle goods, which mostly were physically carried off the ships, but as the volume became insurmountable, they relented and allowed the military stevedores to help discharge the supplies. Much of the arriving matériel was not properly marked and vast "sorting" sheds were created at the UK ports, where supplies were examined, identified, and dispatched. Though improvements in marking cargos were mandated, the problem of matériel sometimes taking 90 or even 120 days to reach its destination persisted right up to D-Day.

When in 1943 the focus of the European war shifted to the Mediterranean and North Africa, Britain for a time became a staging post for US troops and supplies on their way to those active theaters. Between October 1942 and April 1943, a staggering three-quarters of a million US and British troops, along with a huge quantity of supplies, were taken from the UK to North Africa to fight in the desert, with the result that the buildup for Bolero, Overlord's precursor, was all but halted.

It was not only the North African campaign that diverted men and supplies from Bolero. The Allies also agreed on a plan to attack Italy, with initial landings on Sicily scheduled for mid-July 1943. A major amphibious operation requiring simultaneous landings on several beaches, it was in some ways a dress rehearsal — on a smaller scale — for Overlord. Even so, the buildup for this operation was more complicated because it had to be planned from North Africa and Malta, much farther away from the eventual landing sites than the short cross-Channel journey between England and France would be for D-Day. Supplies not available locally had to be shipped from the United States, a process that could take three months. Inevitably, as the date of the landing approached and detailed logistical plans were drawn up, any focus on Bolero was lost.

In January 1943, the Allies gave Overlord a provisional green light at a crucial strategic conference held in Casablanca. However, despite this commitment, they still disagreed over both the timing and the nature of the assault. The Americans were increasingly impatient, wanting to see the rapid end of the conflict, whereas the British prevaricated. Indeed, behind the scenes, the Americans became progressively concerned that the British, fearing a high number of casualties and aware of the logistical constraints after four years of war, were trying to delay any invasion beyond even 1944.

These challenges did little to improve relations between the two powers. As Max Hastings writes in his account of the landings: "Throughout the autumn and winter of 1943, even as planning and preparation for Overlord gathered momentum, the British irked and angered the Americans by displaying their misgivings and fears as if Overlord were still a subject of debate, and might be postponed."[10] These doubts went right to the top. Churchill was committed to the plan, but he was fearful of both the outcome and the Allies' ability to sustain the attack. In a letter to Roosevelt, he wrote: "I am however deeply concerned with the situation that may arise between the thirtieth and sixtieth days."[11]

However, positive news from Italy bolstered British resolve. After a hard-fought campaign, the Allied forces overtook Sicily, and as they began working their way—with great difficulty—up the mainland of Italy, attention could at last be focused once again on Bolero. After a series of conferences in the later part of 1943, a firm decision was finalized for a landing on the French coast with a provisional date of May 1, 1944. Subsequently, Bolero became the Allies' top priority, and everything was done to ensure that sufficient men and supplies were available in the UK.

Though it was widely acknowledged that US and UK resources should be pooled in readiness for the invasion, this plan was fraught with difficulties because of contrasting expectations of soldiers from either side of the Atlantic. Most notably, US servicemen balked at eating British food, finding the bread tasteless, even though the rations were of equal nutritional value. Therefore, separate bakeries and kitchens were required for each camp. Although this may seem petty and trivial, in fact army commanders were greatly concerned that such disparity in rations would undermine morale. What's more, according to a US Army report on the logistical buildup, the Americans had to be careful about revealing their rather generous soap and candy rations. Language differences also caused considerable confusion, particularly on the railways, where British *sleepers*, *points*, and *brake vans* were in American English called *ties*, *switches*, and *cabooses*.

The weight of imports grew steadily throughout 1943 before increasing rapidly in 1944. Army equipment and ammunition made up much of these consignments. The demands of American troops

were far greater than those of their UK equivalents. Given the shortage of just about everything in the UK, an island overly dependent
on imports even in peacetime, equipment sent over from the United
States ranged from lumber and prefabricated sections of barracks to
millions of K rations, the staple for field troops, and medical supplies, including complete field hospitals. The proportion of supplies
per soldier had increased almost exponentially since the First World
War, including the amount of ammunition and mechanized equipment such as armored vehicles, motorcycles, and tanks provided.
Importantly, World War II was the first conflict in which the US
Army was largely motorized. In the First World War, there were 37
troops for every vehicle; in this conflict—barely a quarter of a century later—there were fewer than 5 men for every piece of motorized equipment. All this equipment required transport and, on many
occasions, rail was the only option.

The American troops had additional and quite specific demands
rooted in the need to keep up their spirits. As the author of the report
on the performance of the Transportation Corps noted, "The American youth is accustomed to a full quota of recreation, and supplies
for that purpose were provided at all Army stations—athletic goods,
motion picture equipment, theatrical properties, books, magazines,
soft drinks, ice cream, etc. The best builder of soldier morale—mail
from home—was encouraged, with only moderate restrictions on
the size of packages."[12]

All this soon became apparent as the first 4,000 troops deployed
under the Bolero plan left New York on January 15, 1942, and began
arriving at Belfast in Northern Ireland, their initial barracks. However, because Bolero was initially downgraded, it was not until more
than a year later, in the middle of 1943, that troops started arriving
in considerable numbers. In the period running up to D-Day, the
pace became more and more frenetic, and by May 1944, the planned

total of 1.5 million troops had finally arrived in the UK. The total amount of cargo discharged in those months, amounting to 2 million tons, also placed an enormous burden on the UK's transport system, because it all had to be discharged within eight days, the planned interval between convoys. This alone required the weekly running of 100 special freight trains encompassing 20,000 loaded railcars, many of them using routes already overburdened with other military and civilian traffic.

Fortunately, at the outbreak of the war, the British railway system had been reorganized to cope with such extra demands. In the early stages, when most of the men and supplies were arriving at Liverpool and Glasgow, the West Coast Main Line—by far the busiest main-line route—was cleared of local trains (which were shifted to the parallel East Coast Main Line) to ensure there was sufficient capacity for the American military traffic. The Railway Executive, the government agency that took over running the railways at the outbreak of war, embarked on a series of schemes to improve the capacity of the rail network, particularly in the South of England. Vast new sidetracks were built to accommodate the arrival of supplies, along with connections to new camps, double or quadruple tracking of key sections of line, and even the actual construction of short new routes. Bristol and Cardiff were increasingly used for supplies arriving from the United States to relieve the pressure on Liverpool. As the war progressed, several existing and new railways were allocated for purely military purposes, either for storing ammunition and dangerous chemicals or for training.

From the outset, a key component of Overlord planning was determining how the Allies would maintain the lines of communication once the lodgment—the initial small area to be taken over by the Allies—had been established. It was axiomatic that the railways would play a key role. Therefore, a crucial aspect of preparation in the UK was not only to figure out how to store railway equipment (such as locomotives and freight cars) but also to ensure enough trained men were available to rebuild and operate the railways. Lessons had been learned from the First World War. On the British side, many railway workers, notably those with specialized skills such as drivers and signalmen (known as blockmen in the army), were part of a "reserved occupation," exempt from being called up. Despite the intensive use of the railways in the First World War and the widespread recognition of their importance in conflicts, military organization for the railways in both the UK and the United States had been run down, with the consequent loss of expertise on how to operate them in wartime. The situation was made even worse in the UK when, in 1941, the railway resources that had been retained by the British Army were dispatched to the Middle East to reopen a line running from the coast at Basra through to Baghdad as part of the campaign to stop the Germans exploiting the vast oilfields of Persia (now Iran). Therefore, in late 1941, the British military authorities decided to create two new railway operating companies, the 164th and 181st, each around 350 men who would be responsible for running the railways on the Continent and could call on thousands of their army colleagues in the Royal Engineers and Pioneers to help carry out repairs.

Although most recruits to these companies had previously worked on the railways, they needed training at the Longmoor Military Railway to learn how to operate trains in military conditions. Former railway staff were much in demand during this time. Initially, many potential recruits were rejected because of minor medical issues, but as the authorities became more desperate for experienced railway personnel, the medical requirements were relaxed. Steve Hayes, a former railway booking clerk who wore spectacles and was flatfooted, was originally confined to clerical duties, but after a couple of years, he was transferred to active service and later worked as a blockman in France. The blockmen were taught French railway signaling methods and given some rudimentary language lessons. To broaden their experience in advance, many recruits were seconded to the civilian railway companies, which were always short of personnel during the war. A large group of 181st men, for example, worked on the narrow-gauge Romney, Hythe and Dymchurch Railway that, despite its miniature size, was used extensively to carry troops along the coast and later to haul the pipes for the construction of the cross-Channel oil pipeline known as Operation Pluto.

Whereas these men were essentially railway workers, they became aware of their military role when, a month before D-Day, the railway companies were confined to barracks in order not to compromise security. Although the men inevitably learned they were part of an invasion force, something that was still being kept from the public, they were not informed of the details of their role in France. The 181st was rather pleasantly accommodated in Guilsborough Hall, a spacious country house in Northamptonshire. The men were instructed to stay within three miles of their quarters, but they didn't always keep to the rules; some, such as Roy Jenkins, a privately educated blockman, had bicycles that enabled them to make far longer journeys and visit girlfriends.

The US military, too, had learned much from its experience in the First World War and was well aware of the need for experienced railway workers to serve in the army. After entering the war in April 1917, the Americans dispatched 33,000 soldier-railroaders to provide transport for the troops arriving in western France and to operate services right up to the Western Front. The Baldwin Locomotive Works, the biggest US manufacturer at the time, supplied 3,400 engines for the conflict in Europe using a very basic model specially developed for use overseas; several were found to still be in service 27 years later when the Allied troops arrived after D-Day. However, much of the expertise garnered then was lost as the Military Railway Service, which had been in charge of this huge operation, was reduced to a skeleton service in the interwar period before being revived in the aftermath of Pearl Harbor in December 1941.

After the United States entered the war, an agreement between the American railroad companies and the government established a series of units based around particular rail companies, which was seen as the most effective way of recruiting skilled railroad men. These battalions, each around 850 officers and men, were divided into four companies, essentially creating a self-standing railway organization that had the capacity to operate services in a particular geographical area. The headquarters unit was responsible for supplies and dispatching and oversaw the other three companies, which in turn dealt with track and maintenance, equipment (including rolling stock), and operations, including management of the crews. All the large railroad companies were asked to sponsor a battalion, while smaller ones banded together to create a joint one. On top of this structure, a series of Grand Divisions were in charge of managing both the maintenance and operation of the railways, effectively a kind of Fat Controller, with each being responsible for a handful of battalions under them. The men recruited into these units, both in the UK and the United States, would have the status of combatants, but in reality they were simply railway workers in military uniforms. They signed up to serve their country, but fighting was not their primary objective.

Considerable efforts were made to ensure that these men had the right railway skills. To help train railroad men in the United States, a 50-mile line called the Claiborne & Polk Military Railroad was constructed between two military camps in Louisiana. The line was built by troops of the 711th Engineer Battalion with support from a couple of all-black battalions starting in August 1941, and it was completed just under a year later. The military planners deliberately chose difficult railway territory with very hot weather, swampland, and hilly terrain through forests because they were intent on mirroring wartime conditions so that the men could learn how to build and rebuild railway lines in areas where fighting was still taking place. It was, in effect, a big practice train set with daily trains and even freight specials. The track was never very stable, which led to frequent derailments and a permanent 25 miles per hour speed restriction. The greatest threat, however, was posed by the local wildlife, which included alligators and venomous snakes. The alligators were a particular problem once the line opened because they enjoyed basking on the warm wooden railroad ties. Even the locomotives' loud whistles failed to dislodge the dozy reptiles, who had to be prodded off the tracks by the bravest of the trains' engineers. The difficulties of operating the railway in the harsh conditions of the Louisiana swamps led the soldiers to rename the C & P MRR the "Crime and Punishment Railroad." Nevertheless, the soldiers assumed all the basic functions of operating, maintaining, and signaling a railway, skills that would prove extremely useful in France. Importantly, during this time, the soldiers also learned how to sabotage a line using various types of explosive devices to ascertain which was the most effective.[13]

The first of these railway soldiers to be called into active service were men of the 727th Railway Operating Battalion, which had been sponsored by the Southern Railroad and therefore trained on its line around New Orleans. Next was the 713th, which worked on the Santa Fe, and within months virtually every major railroad and several smaller ones had sponsored a unit. Initial battalions were sent to the Middle East, later to Italy, but by far the greatest number went to the UK for transfer to France.

The learning process for these men continued after their arrival in the UK, and they were required to adapt to very different working conditions. In addition to learning how to repair and operate railways in the UK and Europe, the most demanding task for the railway troops was the reconstruction of bridges, both road and rail. Here the British had an advantage over the Americans because a "bridging school" had been established in the interwar period, where a key engineering development was the Bailey bridge, which proved vital to the Allies' success in the conflict.

After the First World War, the British understood that their success had come by virtue of various technological developments during the war, such as aircraft and tanks, but also, notably, bridging. As such, a committee was formed to continue research into this field during peacetime. The Experimental Bridging Establishment, which was based at Christchurch near Bournemouth on the south coast, was largely staffed by civilians who were in turn managed by army officers. The Bridging Establishment developed several bridge designs in the 1920s, but then, in line with appeasement sentiments, the initiative was wound down to such an extent that it was almost shuttered completely. Only one qualified civilian civil engineer remained in post, Donald Bailey—a man whose surname would become synonymous with military bridging. Such was the lack of interest in developing technology for the army that even he faced dismissal, with a Treasury memo asking, "Is Mr. Bailey really necessary?" As it happened, he was, and his continued involvement was the result of a late intervention by the army leadership. As the historian of military railway bridging recounts: "Luckily good sense prevailed and Bailey remained in post, building up the experience that led to the development of the bridge named after him in the early stages of the war that was to come... the course of the war would have been very different without the vast quantities of mass-producible Bailey Bridge that was made available to the Allied Forces."[14]

Bailey was a typical British inventor, a kind of professional amateur, who tentatively put forward ideas that seemed to have been worked out on the back of an envelope but that were, in fact, highly developed professional and revolutionary designs. He was a modest and unassuming man who had worked on the railways after graduating in engineering from the University of Sheffield. After joining the staff of the Experimental Bridging Establishment, he developed various models of military bridges that could be built in haste and with limited supplies.

After the start of the war, the UK government devoted considerable resources to the development of what quickly became known as the Bailey bridge. The initial goal was to produce a bridge strong enough to support a tank and yet light enough to enable the structure's component parts to be carried easily across great distances. The key to the bridge's success was its modular design, making it in effect a giant Lego set with parts that fit together in flexible ways. In the first months of the war, the Bridging Establishment had focused on a design by Charles Inglis, a Cambridge University professor; Inglis's bridge enjoyed moderate success until tests carried out at the end of 1940 resulted in one of the girders buckling under the weight of a tank. After an emergency conference in January 1941, Inglis's design was scrapped and the Bridging Establishment turned to the Bailey bridge. The crucial aspect of Bailey's design was the lightness of the girders, which were 10 feet long but could be linked together easily, with only a steel pin required for each joint. The number of parts was minimal, and the bridge could be assembled easily by semiskilled engineers after a short instruction course. Even the heaviest section could be handled by just six men.

The gradual acceptance of the need for such a bridge led to a massive construction program involving 650 manufacturers and other businesses across the UK, from major engineering firms to small garages but also including confectioners and bookmakers brought in to help the war effort. The speed of the project was remarkable. It was a crash program in the design, manufacture, and testing of the concept over a period of months rather than the years such a development would normally take. After design work on Bailey's bridge started in December 1940, testing began as quickly as May 1941, followed by production just two months later and the first delivery in December that year. The program's scale, too, was enormous. Over the next three years, half a million tons of steel were used to produce a potential 240 miles of bridge involving 700,000 Bailey sections. Various adaptations of the Bailey bridge were produced for particular needs, such as spans for wider rivers or canals, divided highways, and even suspension models.

Significantly, the Bailey bridge was also adopted by the US Army. The Americans built 20 miles of bridge based on the same design because it was a considerable improvement on their own military bridges, which were far heavier and less well engineered. The School of Military Engineering at Ripon, Yorkshire, held courses over the space of a few weeks in which US Army engineers were instructed precisely in how to construct the Bailey bridge. Other GIs were sent to a bridging school near Exeter, between the Yeo and the Exe Rivers, which, according to a contemporary report, was "little more than a cow pasture through which winds a small river." Soldiers learned how to rig derricks, and then to qualify, they had to "undertake the complete assembly and erection of a 185ft multiple span, deck-plate girder bridge over an actual water course, deep enough to require submerged piers, pontoon and other bridge erecting equipment."[15] The teaching was effective because the Americans became adept at building bridges quickly. General Montgomery, the British officer in charge of ground forces on D-Day, would later stress the importance of this innovation: "As far as my own operations were concerned, with the Eighth Army in Italy and with the 21st Army Group in North West Europe, I could never have maintained the speed and tempo of forward movement without large supplies of Bailey Bridging."[16]

Although Bailey bridges were also used for roads, their primary purpose was to enable the rapid reinstatement of railway lines. A second type of bridge, used to cross wider stretches of water, was devised at a bridge research center in Derby by a specialized team led by Lieutenant Colonel William T. Everall, another of those brilliant British amateur inventors. Everall had first worked in India, where he developed a new design based on trusses for use in the wilds of the North-West Frontier (now in Pakistan). In India, a bridge strong enough to support a tank with components light enough to be carried on the backs of camels was required. Even though teams of men and trucks would carry the components in World War II, this requirement was the basis of Everall's modular design for a bridge that could span longer distances than the Bailey bridge in the sweep across Europe. Everall's design proved particularly useful in the later stages of the invasion and helped troops cross the wide, navigable rivers of Holland and Germany. Crucially, Everall ensured that US equipment and UK equipment were interchangeable, despite the differences between UK and US measurements, a necessity given the difficulties of sourcing material during the conflict. Right after Pearl Harbor, he traveled to the United States to advise the Americans on rapid military bridge construction.

The other critical aspect of guaranteeing the rapid reinstatement of railways on the Continent was ensuring a plentiful supply of rolling stock. Even before the war, the French locomotive fleet was relatively small and in poor condition, and stocks were further depleted by Allied bombing or sabotage and by the Nazis redeploying the best ones for use in Germany. Allied strategists quickly realized that bringing large numbers of locomotives and freight cars across the Channel would be essential to their success.

Rather conveniently, a sizable number of American locomotives had been sent over to Britain even before Pearl Harbor. The first batch of US locomotives arrived in conditions of strict secrecy under the Lend-Lease program as early as 1941, according to railway photographer Kenneth Oldham, who had fortuitously spotted one. In June of that year, Oldham took two photographs of one of the engines, which was hauling trains between Glasgow and Fife; he wanted to publish them right away, but the censor prevented his magazine, *Railways*, from releasing them until three years later. Oldham wrote that "people had noted 'a new sounding whistle,'" the distinctive warning sound made by US locomotives, but the censor allowed the magazine to reveal only scant details.[17]

The number of US engines on the British rail network quickly rose to 400, all of which were put to use transporting the extra loads caused by the arrival of American troops and supplies. The design of these American locomotives was based on a simple and basic British model dubbed Austerity. The principal consideration was ease of construction and operation but also the ruggedness to withstand combat conditions on the Continent. Unfortunately, the trains were flawed: the boilers could fail, with devastating consequences for the crew and any unfortunate bystanders. As the railway writer John Westwood later commented rather blandly, "The design appears to have been prepared by committee and...it was not a great success, its lubrication system being primitive and its boiler having a tendency to explode."[18] Such incidents, however, were kept secret to avoid arousing concern.

In the months following D-Day, around 2,000 locomotives were transported across the Channel, including 840 US Austerity engines and a further 935 similar engines built in Britain; the latter crossed the Channel after D-Day, when the pressure on the British rail network abated. Also, an estimated 181 smaller steam engines, along with 65 diesels, were sent over to France for use in railway yards. Moreover, a total of 20,000 basic freight cars were sent from the United States to the UK for onward dispatch to France after D-Day.

Although the role of the railways was crucial in the preparation for Operation Overlord, even this massive effort would be overshadowed by events after D-Day. Transporting this matériel across the Channel was only the start of a far more complex logistical exercise that was made considerably more difficult by a controversial policy of bombing and sabotage that intensified as D-Day approached.

2

DESTRUCTION

By D-Day, the French rail system was no longer a network but a patchwork of short disconnected lines separated by collapsed bridges and pockmarked with bomb craters, many of which were flooded. The map of the railways for June 6, 1944, reveals that almost all major towns and cities were no longer connected to each other or, crucially, to the wider network. This complete breakdown of the rail system resulted from a two-pronged assault by Allied bombers and a semiofficial army of French Resistance saboteurs. In early 1944, when Allied Headquarters decided to target the French rail network with a massive and deadly bombing campaign, it was only building on the destruction the Resistance had already wreaked.

The activists' campaign to undermine the railway system through sabotage had started almost as soon as the Germans invaded. The invasion raised fundamental questions about how a population should react to such an occupation, and every household and workplace debated the issue intently. These fierce discussions were colored by the presence of a substantial group of Nazi sympathizers within the French ranks. Although it would be comforting to expect that every French citizen had been active in the Resistance, the harsher reality was soon exposed by the many arrests and executions of those careless enough to express their feelings about the invaders too widely. Not only were there active supporters of the Germans, but also many French people viewed the armistice of June 22, 1940, with relief. They recalled the wretched four-year-long stalemate of the Western Front in the First World War that had cost the lives of millions of young men and were hopeful it would not be repeated. Others, too, were initially impressed that the Germans were treating the local people of this newly conquered nation relatively well.

The question of how to respond to the German invasion was particularly pertinent for the *cheminots*, the French railworkers who were fiercely proud of the role they played in the state-owned Société Nationale des Chemins de Fer Français (SNCF). After the Germans took over both the country and its railways in 1940, many *cheminots* balked at having to cooperate with their new masters and, especially, the 2,000 German railworkers imposed on them to ensure the network remained operational. Indeed, many *cheminots* itched to go further, to sabotage the system to make it unworkable for the enemy, but they were reluctant to do so because it would result in food shortages and further deprivation for their own people, who were already suffering the psychological and practical effects of occupation. Because the railways were a lifeline for the French people, every act of sabotage was a form of self-sacrifice. Bernard Le Chatelier, who joined the railway in 1938 and survived deportation to a concentration camp, recalled decades later his mixed feelings over the fate of the railway: "The bombing by the Allies and the attacks by certain organisations of the Résistance were part of the struggle against the enemy...but they did make our work difficult. Making sure the trains could run resulted in a dilemma: a large proportion of the traffic was for the benefit of the Germans, supported their economy and contributed to their military activity...yet, the French had to eat and live, so the trains ran."[1] Indeed, the whole economy of the country depended on the railways carrying food and other goods.

The pressure on the *cheminots* was all the greater because they were in a unique position, and even those who were reluctant to do so were expected to join the cause. They had the ability to travel, a freedom unavailable to other citizens, which opened all sorts of possibilities for subversive activity. They could gather information and carry messages across the country, just as they could turn a blind eye to passengers who did not have the right papers or travel documents. Many actions carried out by the Resistance would have been impossible without the cooperation of railway workers; it is therefore unsurprising and perfectly accurate that every film with a Resistance theme highlights the essential role of these patriots.

———————

The accounts about the French railway workers produced in the aftermath of the war invariably reported only their heroism and unequivocal opposition to the German occupation, but the accounts of individual *cheminots* highlight the quandary they were in. Jean-Claude Huckendubler, who was based at Badan near Lyon, sympathized completely with the Resistance but did not join in any organized group. He noted: "I thought, if I entered the Résistance, it would end badly. I saw too many people who had confided in their chums only to find that they were not of like mind and ended up being arrested and deported. I was discreet. When I was on my own in the countryside and I saw a German phone line, I would cut it. I did little things like that." Huckendubler guessed only a small proportion of railworkers were prepared to take action: "The *cheminots* were like the rest of the French, which means, I would guess, there were 10 per cent collaborators, 10 per cent committed résistants and 80 per cent who just want to survive the war."[2] As he points out, railway workers, especially train drivers, took great pride in their equipment and in their ability to secure the safety of their passengers. Acts of sabotage might have been seen as going against the very ethos of why they joined the railway: "The *cheminots* were in a dilemma: as they were real railway workers and consequently they hated their equipment being tampered with. But on the other hand, they could not do otherwise, they knew it was necessary."[3]

Moreover, no one ever knew who could be trusted. Marcel Péroche, a train driver who served throughout the war, remembered how he particularly disliked one of the inspectors, an expert in braking systems, who was a fastidious rule follower and enforcer to the extreme. Péroche recalled an incident in which he found a connecting hose had been slashed and the inspector remarked, "That's the work of idiots, it's not worth doing." It was only after the war that Péroche discovered that the inspector was actually head of the local Resistance group in the railways.

Small acts of mischief were often ignored by the Germans but still posed a risk to those perpetrating them. When he was far from his base, Péroche wrote that it was, at times, hard to find food. Occasionally, on long trips he would drop off his fireman at a passing farm and then pick him up with a load of food on his return, tossing lumps of coal into the ditch as payment: "All the crews did this as it was the only way to get food." He also recalled how "a crew from my depot exchanged an entire pig for a tender of coal." Unfortunately, the journey was delayed and the coal had to be shoveled back into the tender. "The police got on to it and arrested the two railmen... but they were released on orders from the Germans following the extenuating circumstances... these men had no canteen and so they had to make out as best as they could."[4]

These acts of resistance added to the difficulties of running the railway, which was already in a poor state because of the state's underinvestment and lack of maintenance before the war.

The Blitzkrieg in May 1940, which spearheaded the invasion, had caused further damage to the network in northern France, and much of that—including to buildings and other structures deemed unimportant—was left unrepaired in the subsequent four years of occupation.

In the immediate aftermath of the occupation, the rail system managed to keep operating at near prewar levels despite the loss of thousands of locomotives and freight cars, which had been confiscated for use on the German network, and the forced removal of experienced railworkers to Germany. Putting further pressure on the weakened network, usage rose from prewar levels, with a third more passenger-miles traveled in 1943 than in 1938 and an increase in freight because of the lack of an alternative transport method given the fuel shortages. "The Allied air attacks hit a weakened system in which physical and economic circumstances made men, machines, and materials work under heavy stress and strain."[5]

The resilience of the French rail network was further hampered by German management, which ran it as the western region of a Continental rail network centered on Berlin. To make matters worse, the system was pared back with the closure of minor lines, and this reduced the dispatchers' ability to find alternative routes when blockages occurred. German efforts to run the French system were further hindered by the fact that French coal was inferior to coal mined in Germany and Belgium and was not suitable for railway use. Railway managers constantly struggled to maintain coal stock levels.

After Hitler's attack on Russia in the summer of 1941, the service deteriorated badly after a clampdown on employees suspected of Communist leanings, who were hounded out and imprisoned. To make up for the deficit in personnel, the Germans increased normal working hours for the majority of the workforce from 48 to 60 hours per week, which only added to the sense of disgruntlement among the remaining *cheminots*. Therefore, even before railworkers began in earnest to commit concerted acts of sabotage in the middle of 1943, the railways were in a parlous state.

————————

Canny saboteurs, especially the *cheminots*, with their intimate knowledge of railway operations, could disrupt the operation of crucial military convoys and railroads in numerous ways. Locomotives could be run directly into the pit of a turntable, for example, or they could be allowed to run out of steam or coal could be dumped on the tracks instead of in the furnace. One of the least risky but most effective techniques was to alter the proportions of lead and antimony in the alloy used in the engine's pistons, which affected their antifriction qualities. Cracks would then develop in the lining, and though the pump would appear to be working normally, it would lose pressure and impair the performance of the locomotive. Such subtle acts were almost undetectable and yet had serious consequences.

The most pervasive and often the most effective form of action was *le travail au ralenti*, effectively, passive resistance, or what British trade unionists used to call "work to rule." This tactic is well summed up in a leaflet produced by workers in a Parisian railway workshop in November 1942, which stresses, "*Le devoir de Français, de patriote des cheminots c'est: sabotage par tous les moyens*" (The duty of the French, of the patriotic railworkers: Sabotage by every means). The leaflet explains in detail how to disable a locomotive by, for example, unscrewing a valve or inserting sand in an oil cylinder ("*une poignée de sable vaut une bombe*"; a handful of sand is as good as a bomb), causing "hot boxes" (overheated axle bearings) on freight cars by draining oil, or causing derailments by tinkering with switches. The language of the leaflet is an incitement to radical action, a call to arms, with little reference to the dangers those taking action would face. The pamphlet implies, all too optimistically, that the war was close to an end: "At the time when the Hitlerian hordes are mounting their ultimate attack against the valiant Red Army, at the time when the Nazi bosses, sensing the coming catastrophe, it's the urgent duty for all of the French people to deliver blows on the German army to precipitate its defeat."[6]

As the reference to the Red Army suggests, such an unequivocal call to arms was mostly the work of the Communist Party, whose members became the key movers in many Resistance groups. Although initially compromised by the Molotov–Ribbentrop Pact, after Hitler's attack on Russia in June 1941, many Communists joined the fight against the Germans. These well-organized Communists were behind most of the big set-piece attacks at the other end of the scale from "*le travail au ralenti*": acts of war that resulted in multiple German deaths and considerable damage but also, inevitably, reprisals against those who had nothing to do with the attacks themselves.

Between the summers of 1941 and 1942, there were two phases of increased sabotage activity, both of which were met with heavy reprisals. As hopes of liberation rose — prematurely in the autumn of 1943 — the attacks stepped up, both in number and in intensity. Not only did the scent of possible liberation spur on these raids, but so did the Nazis' decision to forcibly deport a large portion of the French workforce to be used as slave labor in German factories. Many of those who escaped the roundup fled to the Maquis, the French underground that operated from the countryside, which resulted in a rise in armed attacks on the German occupiers.

The most staggering attacks involved explosives and the destruction of ammunition trains, but the railways were most vulnerable where trains ran fast on longer stretches of open track, which were difficult to police. Derailments there caused spectacular disasters. The bloodiest example was at Airan in Calvados, where twice within a month in the spring of 1942, a group of Communist Resistance members disconnected a section of rail to derail trains carrying German soldiers on leave from Cherbourg to Maastricht. Technically, causing a derailment was easy, but it required inside knowledge, such as how to ensure the electrical connection—known as the track circuit—was not broken, which would immediately turn the signals to red. Therefore, typically local railway personnel were involved in these actions. Forty Germans were killed in the two incidents, which led to severe reprisals. Dozens of political prisoners were shot and 130 "communist and Jewish" hostages were arrested in Caen and subsequently deported to Auschwitz while 14 of the perpetrators were eventually tracked down and executed.

During the course of 1943 and into 1944, the scale of sabotage increased exponentially. More than 300 locomotives were blown up in January 1944 alone, and there were 423 derailments in the five months preceding D-Day. One clever form of attack was to destroy the rescue cranes needed to repair lines, with 50 being destroyed by the railway saboteurs. All this destruction was having a devastating effect on the railways. According to the US Army account of the liberation of France, "Rundstedt [Field Marshal Gerd von Rundstedt, the commander of the German forces in the West] in October 1943 noted with alarm the 'rapid increase' in rail sabotage which he attributed to the heavy supply of arms and explosives that the British had parachuted to Resistance groups. He reported that in September 1943 there were 534 acts of sabotage against railroads as compared to a monthly average of 130 during the first half of the year."[7] Rundstedt's response was to bring in 20,000 German railway workers to oversee the work of the *cheminots* and to prevent sabotage.

Although the sabotage campaign was undoubtedly successful, the toll on workers and other civilians was heavy because the Germans acted in response to attacks. According to Cécile Hochardin in her book on the Resistance in the railways: "In the years 1940 to 1944, 1,106 railworkers died after being deported, 502 were shot and 39 died on French soil after being arrested."[8] To put this in perspective, when the Germans invaded France in 1940 there were more than 400,000 *cheminots* spread over a network of more than 24,000 miles.

The moral dilemmas, however, remained. Every act of sabotage entailed risk and an assessment of the potential reaction. If the tracks were cut, the subsequent derailment would quite possibly kill as many French people as Germans. Causing damage in a depot or workshop could be attributed to a single person or group of workers, who would then face punishment. Even that favorite trick of messing with the paperwork to ensure freight was sent to the wrong place could put people in danger because the clerk or conductor might be held responsible. Every incident that the Germans discovered to have been deliberately caused led to reprisals, with ordinary citizens being shot as examples.

In the days just before D-Day, the activities of this secret army of *cheminots* really came to the fore and had a significant impact on the conflict.

With the help of agents and supplies parachuted in by the British, the Resistance became incorporated into a wider scheme to undermine the Germans' transportation system in the run-up to the Normandy landings. In preparation for Operation Overlord, the program of attacks on the railway was given the code name Le Plan Vert. The origins of the idea went back as far as March 1942, when the Free French troops in London started organizing clandestine activities in their home country under the rather confusingly named Le Bureau Central de Renseignements et d'Action, the principal goal being to unite and organize the disparate Resistance groups operating in France. One of the bureau's earliest tasks was to submit a plan for how to destroy the French railway network to the Special Operations Executive, which managed the underground war that undermined the German occupation. At the core of the plan was the creation of a secret army—L'Armée secrète—which, in the days before D-Day, it was hoped would effectively neutralize the French railway network.

The most important yet underrated responsibilities of the Résistance Fer—the section of the Resistance dedicated to the railways—was to gather information in anticipation of the invasion. The British at the headquarters of Operation Overlord were particularly desperate for any scrap of knowledge about the French railway network, so much so that authorities put out a request via the BBC for the public to send in old postcards from France, which helped British intelligence piece together detailed information about the towns, cities, and countryside they planned to invade. Resistance agents provided further information in regular briefings, including detailed updates and studies of bomb damage, network capacity, state of track maintenance, location of depots, number and size of bridges, and even the kind of water and coal facilities needed to operate the railways. Using this intel, the US military produced a detailed map, 40 feet in length, which "was so accurate that not once during the movement of the vast amount of supplies to the front did a question of available rail facilities arise."[9]

Le Plan Vert was a comprehensive scheme describing how the dozen regional military groups established by the French and British forces in London would cripple the railway system through widespread acts of sabotage. Claude Serreulles, an aide-de-camp to de Gaulle's Free France in London, informed a group of senior Resistance figures of the plan and then parachuted into France on June 16, 1943, to work with Jean Moulin, the leader of the Resistance—who, unfortunately, was arrested five days later and executed. Nevertheless, the plan was distributed throughout the Resistance and was updated by coded announcements from the BBC. Le Plan Vert was one of four operations to be carried out by the Resistance, along with Plan Violet, which focused on neutralizing German communications, notably the wire network of the PTT, or Postes, Télégraphes et Téléphones; Plan Bleu, which focused on disrupting the electricity supply; and Plan Bibendum, which aimed to disrupt the road network and blow up bridges and junctions.

This detailed organization served twin purposes. De Gaulle wanted not only to harness the potential of the Resistance but also to control it. The growing strength of the Resistance, with its strong Communist affiliation, was not always welcomed by the more moderate elements of the fight against the Germans, especially not by de Gaulle's Free France headquarters in London. He was concerned that allowing too much freelance activity by this well-organized group of determined people strongly influenced by the Communists could lead to a postwar revolution, as had happened in Germany after World War I.

Le Plan Vert was the most ambitious and most detailed of the four plans, largely because an extensive network of railway workers already involved in sabotage activity existed. Whereas 30 planned attacks were aimed at the roads (only 11 of which were carried out), there were 571 rail targets. The hope was that, together with strikes and the "*travail au ralenti*" by the *cheminots*, the rail network in Normandy would be paralyzed for at least 8 to 10 days, limiting the enemy's access to supplies in a crucial period of the war.

Instructions to begin these acts of sabotage were sent out through the BBC in a series of coded messages tailored to the 12 regional groupings of the Resistance. Each region was led by a Délégué Militaire Régional who had been dispatched from London to coordinate activities and interpret the meaning of the messages. To limit the number of times that radio operators had to be on alert, the initial messages were sent out only on the first, second, fifteenth, or sixteenth of each month. Consequently, the messages triggering the start of the sabotage activities coinciding with D-Day on June 6 were transmitted on June 1 and 2. After that, operators were required to check in every day to listen for further information, knowing the invasion was at most two weeks away.

The most famous codes were a series of lines taken from a well-known poem by Paul Verlaine called "Chanson d'Automne." "*Les sanglots longs / des violons de l'automne*" (The long wail / of the violins of autumn) — this line alerted operators to be ready to receive precise instructions on their specific targets within the next few days. On the night of June 5, a second series of coded messages was sent out with precise instructions about the actions that should be taken immediately. All messages referred to something green — *Nous nous roulons sur le gazon* (We are rolling about on the lawn) — or contained the sound "ver," such as *Véronèse etait un peintre* (Veronese was a painter). Originally, the actions were supposed to be spread out over a few days, but this was deemed impractical because the Germans would be on full alert, so the actions were coordinated to take place over the course of a single night.

The intricacy and detail of the plan were quite extraordinary, representing the fruits of two years of work by a team of French and British railway experts. As an example, Annex No. II focused on targets around Amiens specified precisely: "It was essential that the derailments, to be effective, had to be arranged in such a way as to ensure both tracks were blocked."[10] The annex then goes on to list five places where the saboteurs were expected to target around Amiens, which was a crucial junction town north of Paris, even citing the specific best locations for attack. Organized down to the most minute detail, the annex listed each site to be attacked and the exact amount of explosive required at each location.

There were hundreds of successful raids that night. One of the most effective was carried out by a group led by Guillaume Mercader, who had been a champion cyclist before the war. Blessed with amazing charm and chutzpah, Mercader used his prewar fame to convince the Germans to allow him free movement around the coastal parts of Normandy, where, disguised in his cycling gear and riding his sponsored La Perle bike, he gathered vast amounts of information about the location of the invaders' defenses over the space of three years. According to Giles Milton, the author of a study of D-Day, "Within a day or two of Guillaume Mercader cycling along the coastal road of Normandy, the architects of Operation Overlord were in possession of the very latest news of the German beach defences."[11] This wasn't at all easy for the cyclist; Mercader had a number of close shaves and was stopped frequently on the heavily patrolled roads. Had the maps he'd tucked into his cycling shorts ever been discovered, he would have been summarily shot.

At the beginning of June 1944, after a hard day's training on his bike, he came back to his home near Bayeux to receive the BBC message *"Il fait chaud à Suez"* (It is hot in Suez) and the rather obvious

"Les dés sont jetés" (The dice have been thrown). A few days later followed *"Le champ du laboureur dans le matin brumeux"* (The field of
the plowman in the morning mist), and he knew that in the evening,
he was to go to a prepared rendezvous with his fellow resistants.

After picking up his friend, André Héricy, a young carpenter who
later related how he had been waiting for this moment since 1940,
the two met up with the rest of the dozen or so in their clandestine
group and its leader, "Captain" Jean Renaud-Dandicolle, who had
parachuted in with his radio a few weeks earlier after serving with de
Gaulle in London. The captain then gave out the instructions — and
the explosives. The mission was simple but vital: blow up the line
running north from Laval to Caen, a crucial supply line for Normandy's second-largest town, which was to play a crucial role in the
forthcoming battle.

Héricy later elaborated on his preparations: "I was given a pistol,
a rucksack full of explosives, detonators and an American jacket."[12]
That last item was critical because the Germans were all too prepared
to take villagers hostage and interrogate them until they gave away
the names of the local resistants. Héricy added, "We had to make
the Germans believe it was the work of American commandos rather
than the French Resistance." The group of five chosen to carry out
the attack then cycled the back roads to the village of Grimbosq, 18
miles south of Caen and the site of a bridge and a junction.

Héricy watched as his comrades attached plastic explosive to
all the rails and connected the charges with wiring. Having set the
five-minute detonators, they waited behind a woodpile until they
witnessed the massive explosion: "The rails were sent more than five
metres up in the air. There was no ballast for 50 metres. The track was
totally unusable. We were drunk with happiness and we shot bullets
into the nearby apple orchard. We felt like kings." Quickly, the reality of the situation set in, forcing them to flee into the bush to retrieve

their bikes and head home in the dark, accompanied by the faint growl of the early D-Day bombers. What Héricy did not know at the time was that, throughout the operation, they were being watched by a second group, whose task was to ensure that the line was blown up should the first attempt fail.

There was inevitably a price to pay. The team managed to escape capture that night, but later some of them were caught by the Gestapo. A local farmer, Georges Grosclaude, who helped in the attack, was arrested and tortured. Still, he did not give away the names of his fellow Maquisards, despite having all his nails pulled out while he was attached to the wheel of a cart. Grosclaude's body and that of his wife, Eugénie, who had been taken by the Germans at the same time, were never found. Owing in part to Grosclaude's bravery, Mercader and Héricy survived the war. Alas, Renaud-Dandicolle, their leader, was captured three months later and shot.

There is no doubt that all this activity and coordination paid off handsomely. According to Major Charles Benda, a British officer who was later asked by the Supreme Headquarters Allied Expeditionary Force to assess the damage done by the saboteurs: "At least 50 per cent of the targets of the Plan Vert were successfully destroyed and that harassment by the Résistance led to the [elite SS Panzer] Division Das Reich taking two or three times as much time to cover 650 kilometres."[13] Other assessments suggested an even greater degree of success. According to British Army reports: "In the immediate aftermath of D-Day, in terms of sabotage alone, 1,050 actions were ordered and on the night of the 5/6 June, 957 of these were carried out successfully."[14]

However, Benda was equally supportive of the second method Allies deployed for railway destruction: the huge bombing campaign initiated in the months before D-Day. This was a bigger and

better-coordinated operation that involved a considerable allocation of scarce resources and proved to be far more controversial. The
Allied military leadership did not believe that the efforts of a few
brave *cheminots*, even with explosives parachuted in by the Allies,
would be enough to seriously disrupt the whole rail network. The
wider destruction would have to be carried out by Allied bombers,
but this plan was initially met with widespread skepticism and even
opposition. The debate over this air operation raged for several weeks,
bringing in Churchill, Eisenhower, and, finally, Roosevelt.

The bombing campaign originated in the Transportation Plan,
a scheme that, despite its name, was actually about the destruction
of the enemy's transport system. It was conceived in the early days of
the war as part of an assessment of the effectiveness of bombing raids.
The Operation Overlord planners had as their first priority the establishment of air superiority. Without that, essentially very little could
move safely. But, second, they sought to ensure that the enemy's railway system was put out of action to limit the potential movement of
German troops.

The idea of targeted bombing of the railways lay at the heart of
the Transportation Plan. This plan, focused on transport destruction, was the brainchild of a brilliant and charming polymath,
Solly Zuckerman. After the outbreak of war, Zuckerman, a qualified doctor who became a scientific adviser to the military, studied
the effects of bombing, both physical and psychological, on human
beings. Through studies on Hull and Birmingham, he found that
targeting industrial facilities, and in particular railway centers,
was particularly effective and greatly impacted the morale of those
under attack.

Zuckerman's Transportation Plan aimed to paralyze the rail system in France and its neighbors. Zuckerman worked with two officials from the little-known Railway Research Service, which had been created in 1939 by the highly secretive Ministry of Economic Warfare after the UK declared war on Germany. The head of the Railway Research Service was a Captain E. R. Sherrington, who, together with adviser to Bomber Command E. D. Brant, monitored developments on the French and other European railways. Notably, they established contact with the *cheminots* to learn about the state of the rail infrastructure and rolling stock but also to obtain information on troop and freight movements.

At a meeting in January 1944, Zuckerman explained the concept of the Transportation Plan to Sherrington and Brant and proposed that it be implemented three months before a potential D-Day of June 1, 1944. Zuckerman used the human body as a brilliant analogy for his concept, likening red blood corpuscles to the locomotives on a railway network. When a man died of a heart attack, he said, it was not through lack of corpuscles but rather because the arteries were clogged. What counted, therefore, was not the availability of the locomotives but the capacity of the arteries—the rail network—to transport them around the body. And just as a body needed to be kept healthy to stay alive, the operation of a rail network depended on maintenance and repairs carried out in workshops and sheds. He recognized that, even though the whole railway system could not be brought to a halt, it could be widely degraded with a series of attacks on classification yards, maintenance centers, and key junctions. Even though a few destroyed lines could easily be put back into service, damage to key centers would hamper the capacity of the system overall.

The Royal Air Force under the command of Arthur "Bomber" Harris was initially reluctant to support this targeted form of

attack, arguing it was not feasible. Harris favored indiscriminate—
"carpet"—bombing of a whole area, which was deemed feasible.
Despite this opposition, Zuckerman continued to work up details of
the Transportation Plan, confident that it would one day be effective—even though he was, as he later admitted, naive about the constant controversies and debates that occurred between US and UK
senior military personnel in wartime.

Not only Harris and his team queried the value of Zuckerman's
Transportation Plan. Others' concerns about what today would be
called collateral damage mounted throughout the spring, eventually
reaching Churchill, who was worried that the deaths of large numbers of French citizens would undermine the Allies' cause.

While the controversy about the plan raged, a limited number of test runs were launched in March 1944. The first was on
the town of Trappes, 15 miles west of Paris, the most important
gateway for connections between the capital and eastern France.
Compared with the previous year's raids on factories in France, targeting was much more accurate thanks to the new Pathfinder system. Previously, the planes would drop flares to highlight targets
and then return to base. With Pathfinder, four Mosquito planes
remained—perilously—above the target during bomb runs,
dropping markers of different colors to highlight additional targets. Raids were also used to assess the weight of bombs needed
to destroy a particular facility. A total of 1,388 tons of munitions
were dropped that night and, miraculously, none of the 267 planes
was lost.

Over the next three weeks, half a dozen other railway facilities,
including Amiens and Le Mans twice, were bombed. Remarkably,
of the 1,500 sorties made, only seven planes were downed, which
greatly reassured the leaders of Bomber Command who had been
concerned about the toll of this type of raid. The railways were clearly

less well defended by German antiaircraft guns than were German factories, which had been the focus of Bomber Command's earlier attacks in 1944 where Harris's squadrons had lost up to 12 percent of their planes in a single raid.

And it was not only the low casualty rates that suggested raids on railway facilities might be a more successful initiative in the long run than carpet bombing. The stations and yards at Trappes, where 1,500 freight cars had been processed daily, were rendered unusable, not least because the Pathfinder system proved impressively effective. More widely, 600 military trains were delayed by at least a half day, a third of which had been headed to Normandy.

Although these raids resulted in fewer civilian deaths than carpet-bombing attacks, there were still significant numbers of casualties. The raids no doubt sowed terror among the local populations. Years later, the son of a survivor of the raid on Trappes, where more than a hundred people were killed, relayed his mother's vivid description:

The [first wave of] bombs fell with a terrifying noise, but not on the centre of Trappes but on La Boissière two or three kilometres away.... We all rushed to secure help for the people there... but they had hardly started out when a second wave of bombs delivered its rain of steel, trapping many people on the Rue Jean Jaurès which runs parallel to the station. Marcelle [the narrator's mother] hid in the entrance of a basement next to a café. The bombs whistled and exploded everywhere. The windows disintegrated and the bottles in the bar clattered to the floor. The terrible windstorm created by the bombs was appalling. A bomb destroyed the market square and the resulting gust was poisonous, making everyone cough. Then, at last, the hell stopped.[15]

Inevitably, each attack resulted in the deaths of civilians: for example, 36 in Amiens and 79 in Le Mans. What's worse, much of the effort was wasted. Half the planes returned having failed to dispatch their bombs for technical or navigational reasons. About a quarter of bombs dropped missed the target. The inaccuracy of bombing was hardly surprising; bombs could never be perfectly targeted. A typical bomber traveled at around 5 miles per minute, or 300 miles per hour; consequently, a two-second mistake would result in an error of 60 yards.

But precisely how much collateral damage rendered the initiative too costly for the local populations to bear was a subject of fierce debate in London. Despite agreeing to the initial attacks, Harris wavered on whether to give the Transportation Plan his full support. Matters came to a head when Zuckerman was called to speak with the Defence Committee on April 5, 1944. Winston Churchill headed the meeting attended by various senior politicians, including the deputy prime minister Clement Attlee and several military leaders. Churchill had expressed concerns about civilian casualties in the bombing of rail facilities that were situated in town centers, where adjoining properties were likely to be hit or to catch fire. He had been briefed that up to 160,000 people could be killed in the raids.

These concerns prompted Churchill to write to Eisenhower, warning him: "The argument for concentration on these particular targets is very nicely balanced on military grounds.... The advantages to enemy propaganda seem to be very great, especially as this would not be in the heat of battle but a long time before."[16] Eisenhower's response was unequivocal: both he and his military advisers had "become convinced that the bombing of these centers will increase our chances for success in the critical battle, and unless this could be proved to be an erroneous conclusion, I do not see how we can fail to proceed with this program.... The French people are now slaves. Only a successful Overlord can free them." He concluded: "I think it would be sheer folly to abstain from doing anything that can increase in any measure our chances for success in Overlord."[17] However, Churchill still equivocated.

The Americans were confident that a base—the lodgment—could be established on the beaches because the German Seventh Army, the defenders in Normandy, was reckoned to be weak. But they were worried about the potential of the railways to allow German reinforcements to be deployed. In particular, the worst-case scenario was the rapid arrival of the German Fifteenth Army, which was east of Normandy in Pas-de-Calais, waiting for an attack that never came. The Fifteenth had the potential of not only stopping the invasion but also pushing back the invading forces to the sea, creating a second Dunkirk, as it were. This would have prolonged the war for months, if not years, according to General Walter Bedell-Smith, who later wrote, "Counter attack was what we most feared. The whittling down of the Luftwaffe, the bombing of the French railroads, the blasting of oil targets had all been designed to hamper the Germans in reinforcing their Normandy garrisons."[18]

Given Churchill's doubts and the importance of unity among the Allies on this crucial issue, it was with much trepidation that Zuckerman descended the steps into the Defence Map Room, the small basement bomb-proof room around the back of Downing Street where key meetings were held. Zuckerman later described how "Churchill came in from his nearby bedroom wearing his celebrated siren-suit, with a large tumbler of what looked like whisky and soda in one hand, and a big cigar in the other."[19] Churchill called these late meetings "midnight follies," but despite their informal moniker, they were some of Churchill's favorite assemblies when many crucial decisions were made. Upon Zuckerman's entrance, Churchill inquired in a rather jolly tone, "Where's the prof?" referring to

Lord Cherwell, his chief scientific adviser. Cherwell spoke first and expressed his long-established hostility toward the Transportation Plan, arguing that the French railways had plenty of spare capacity and could therefore be quickly reinstated only a few hours after an attack. Zuckerman retorted that, as a scientist, albeit not a railway expert, "I explained that the AEAF [Allied Expeditionary Air Force] plan was based neither on theory nor speculation, but on an analysis of real events."[20]

Churchill, who according to Zuckerman was quickly becoming bored, remained concerned that the casualties would cause an irreversible breakdown in relations among France, the United States, and the British Empire. He brought up the fact that various contradictory figures for potential casualties had been presented with no clear indication of which was correct. The meeting ended long after midnight, with Churchill still undecided and concerned that "it would damage the prestigious reputation of the Royal Air Force across the world."[21] Zuckerman was instructed to make further assessments of the likely number of casualties, and after consulting both UK and US military leadership, he estimated around 10,000 to 12,000 deaths, provided certain targets with potential high losses were omitted from the plan. This was fewer than a tenth of the previous estimate given to Churchill.

A decision had to be made. The Allies knew there were not enough planes and bombs to launch coordinated attacks on the railway targets and at the same time maintain the raids over Germany.

Despite the urgency of the situation, a month later, with D-Day just weeks away, President Roosevelt finally broke the deadlock. Unlike Churchill, Roosevelt rarely intervened in military matters, which made his pronouncement all the more decisive. He wrote on May 11, "Although civilian losses are regrettable, I will not, from this distance, impose any restrictions of action by our military chiefs which, in their view, could prejudice the success of Overlord or result in additional losses among the invading forces."[22]

In fact, despite Churchill's misgivings and lack of a final endorsement of the plan, the missions to attack railway centers had already resumed with nightly raids. Finally, Zuckerman was allocated some 40,000 tons of bombs out of the total of 100,000 that had been earmarked for the prelanding attacks. Wide-ranging attacks involving hundreds of tons of bombs were made on towns with major railway facilities, and smaller raids focused a few aircraft on unlikely places that happened to be on the railway or that had a tunnel or a bridge. Zuckerman was initially skeptical about destroying bridges, but as the campaign developed, he realized that bridges were both a feasible target, thanks to the greater accuracy of the attacks, and if successful, a very effective one, given the difficulty of rebuilding them.

Zuckerman was keen to focus the destruction on the area close to where the landings would take place because he believed this would most damage the Germans' ability to bring in reinforcements to counter the invading troops. Correspondingly, a list was drawn up of 80 targets, many of which were not in Normandy but farther east in Pas-de-Calais and Belgium. This was, in fact, a rather fortuitous extra advantage of the plan. A key part of Overlord preparations was to fool the Germans into thinking the attack—by Patton's phantom army—would be made through the ports of Calais and Boulogne and their surrounding beaches because they were nearest to the English coast. Concentrating attacks on the railway centers east of Normandy was not only strategically useful but also helped reinforce the ruse that the landings would be focused on the region of Pas-de-Calais.

Zuckerman was particularly pleased that, despite his initial reluctance, Harris got behind the plan. He noted that "its execution...was all that could have been asked for."[23] By the middle of

May, Sir Arthur Tedder, the RAF air chief marshal and Eisenhower's Overlord deputy, was satisfied that the railway network in the North had been so degraded that only military trains were running. This meant civilian passengers no longer had access to the service, further reducing the risk of casualties and enabling attacks to be made on any moving train.

The range of the attacks was broadened to support the upcoming August landings set for the southern coast of France. Nice, Lyon, Grenoble, and Nimes were all attacked, but the bloodiest raid of the whole Allied bombing campaign in France occurred on May 27 in Marseilles. It resulted in 1,700 deaths and 2,800 injuries and the destruction of 10,000 homes and the Saint-Charles central station. In the North, Rouen was the site of the most deadly attack, which had killed 900 just a month earlier. The raid was targeted at railway facilities, but many bombs were dropped on the city center, including seven strikes on Rouen's world-famous cathedral.

In the final month running up to D-Day, Tedder convinced the joint air forces to target locomotives for destruction to reduce the capacity of the enemy's transportation network. With the American military's characteristic joviality, the operation was dubbed Chattanooga Choo Choo after the hit tune by Glenn Miller and his band. It was launched on May 21 with 763 aircraft, including Hawker Typhoons, which could fire air-to-ground rockets. On the first day alone, 67 locomotives were destroyed and a further 91 damaged. However, the operation was not without cost. Flying low, the planes were vulnerable to flak from antiaircraft guns and 60 aircraft were lost, a high toll of 8 percent. Still, these operations effectively allowed fighter pilots to practice attacking ground targets, a skill they would hone after the invasion. Raids on rail networks continued up until two days before D-Day and extended into Belgium, Germany, and even, on one occasion, Poland.

As well as inflicting considerable damage, the Chattanooga Choo Choo operation served a wider propaganda purpose. French train crews deserted in large numbers, especially after fighters began using the murderous tactic of dropping their spare belly fuel tanks on stranded freight trains. The fuel tanks would burst upon impact, spilling fuel that could then be ignited by strafing. This situation caused the Germans to employ their own crews for more hazardous runs. After May 26, the number of railway operations in daylight was sharply reduced, even where lines remained open and unscathed.

After Zuckerman changed his mind about destroying bridges, a plan arose to target specific crossings over the Seine and the Loire that would be crucial in enabling German reinforcements to reach Normandy. However, bridges were still difficult to destroy because they were far smaller than the Transportation Plan's main targets of railway yards and stations. A bomb that missed a bridge even by a few yards would likely fall harmlessly into the river; therefore, proportionately, a far greater tonnage of bombs was required to be effective. In the first attack intentionally aimed at a bridge on May 7, the 200-yard-long railway crossing over the Seine midway between Paris and Rouen was successfully brought down. By chance, Field Marshal Erwin Rommel, who that very day had been instructed by Hitler to handle defensive operations at Normandy, was garrisoned nearby and was forced to watch helplessly as the bombers—with very little interference from the Luftwaffe—took apart the bridge with a mere handful of well-directed 2,000-pound bombs. It was a lesson in air superiority that Rommel did not need to learn. Ever since his "Desert Fox" days, he had been pressing Hitler to strengthen the German air force, but to no avail.

Raids three weeks later on other Seine bridges ensured that all those linking the western environs of Paris with the sea were impassable for rail traffic. According to the postbattle analysis: "Interdiction in the Seine section, where the rail routes were perhaps the most vital to the enemy, was completely successful. Despite the fact that the two bridges were re-established, no traffic crossed the Seine from the north into the tactical area during the entire campaign with the single exception of one train which crossed the re-established Oissel bridge in early August."[24]

The Loire bridges were not attacked until after D-Day, but by then, thanks to the bombing of nearby rail centers and junctions, traffic levels across the river had been halved from their normal 14 trains per day. When the bridges were targeted immediately after D-Day and the main lines were severed, traffic was further reduced to a train per day via a small diversionary route. Even though the Germans put considerable resources into bringing the main routes back into service, repeated bombing hampered their efforts. They could muster only four or five trains per day across the Loire until liberation in September.

Overall, by D-Day, the Transportation Plan resulted in attacks on 93 railway targets, 15 of which were in southern France and the rest concentrated in a ring around Normandy. And it did not stop there. The post-D-Day plan envisaged "a task of major importance, [which] will be the continuance of air attacks against the enemy's rail communications leading into the lodgement. The primary aim will be to compel the enemy to detrain at a considerable distance and continue by road."[25]

Despite the intentions laid out in the post-D-Day plan, subsequent analysis suggests Allied troops lacked a coherent strategy for railway bombing as they prepared to sweep through France. And controversy over the effectiveness of the Transportation Plan continued long after the war. In his book on the bombing campaign, Jean-Charles Foucrier points out that moving the Fifteenth Army, which was garrisoned in a large swathe of territory between the

Seine and Holland, would have taken a gargantuan effort even in the best of circumstances. He argues that the French railway system had already been degraded by sabotage and overuse by the German authorities, who paid little attention to maintenance. However, even Foucrier, who is critical of the high death toll of the aerial bombing campaign, accepts that "Zuckerman's plan undoubtedly eased the task of the Allied troops. Just as Ultra [the surveillance work of Bletchley Park] possibly shortened the war by two years, the Transportation Plan probably shortened the battle of Normandy by several weeks, which implies a saving of human lives, at least of those of the Allied soldiers."[26]

Apart from continued attacks aimed at crippling enemy air power, the raids on railway facilities were seen as the most important task of the combined air force, accounting for around 30 to 40 percent of sorties in the run-up to D-Day. During the campaign, a total of 121,000 tons of munitions was directed against rail centers—71,000 tons before June 6 and 50,000 tons after. To put this in perspective, just under a third of the tonnage of bombs dropped by the Allies in the whole European Theater of Operations before D-Day and about a sixth between June 6 and August 20 were aimed specifically at railway facilities. By then, Zuckerman's arguments had clearly gained traction because the destruction of the railways became a key aspect of Overlord policy.

Certainly, in the weeks before and after D-Day, the railways were all but interdicted through the combined efforts of the air force and saboteurs. Considerable evidence of the impact of the degraded network accrued. Once news of the D-Day landings reached Germany's military command, the Germans made efforts to send troops to the front. The 10,000 men of the German 275th Infantry Division, stationed in Vannes in Brittany, were ordered to Normandy on a total of 14 trains. The first train left a day late, on June 8, because of bombed-out track, and it was further delayed by a rail break carried out by saboteurs. Worse, the same train was then held up on open track, where Allied planes attacked it and inflicted casualties. After further delays, which ended with a route march, the troops reached their new area of operations at Saint-Lô between June 11 and 13, having taken nearly a week to cover just 150 miles. Two other Brittany-based divisions, the 266th and the 353rd, mostly consisting of experienced veterans of the Russia campaign, were dispatched on June 10 and 14, respectively, and had to march most of the way. As Jonathan Trigg recalls in his account of German preparations for D-Day, "With the railways out of action and the jabos [Allied fighter bombers] overhead, both units were forced to travel on foot, and then only at night. It took more than a fortnight to get to Normandy, having advanced to the sound of the guns at a pace slower than a typical American Civil War march eighty years earlier. By contrast, a UK-based Allied infantry division could reach the Normandy front in less than two days."[27]

Normally, German divisions moved up to 75 miles by road but used the railway for longer journeys, and for panzer divisions, the cutoff point was 200 miles. Of the 15 divisions stationed east of Paris that were ordered to move westward, the lack of available tracks meant that only one division could travel by rail. The others were forced to make alternative arrangements. The Grenadier regiment resorted to making a 75-mile trip in three days on bicycles. As a result, it took between 3 and 10 days for these divisions to reach the front line, far longer than if the network had been running normally.

In the weeks before D-Day, the Transportation Plan's targets had widened to include not only railway facilities but also 25 airfields within a 125-mile range of Caen and a series of radar stations dotted along the coast. This was to reinforce the air superiority the Allies had established. The Luftwaffe was already in a bad state even before the Allied attacks, and subsequent raids prevented it from becoming a viable force after the landings. As it happened, the German air force was particularly ill prepared to counter the massive Allied air campaign.

The Luftwaffe had only about 1,800 aircraft throughout western Europe, many based at airfields far away from the front. A mere quarter of the total were fighters or ground-attack aircraft that could be used immediately in combat with Allied air forces. The rest were either the wrong type of aircraft or grounded for maintenance. The Allies, however, could muster six times that number. Moreover, the attacks on the radar stations had damaged the Germans' remaining planes' ability to react quickly. The Germans were simply not in any position to regain aerial domination.

Complete Allied aerial domination had been Zuckerman's first goal when he created the Transportation Plan, and it was the only objective he perceived as more important than the destruction of the rail network. The targeting of airfields in the latter stages of the Transportation Plan's rollout delivered the coup de grâce to the already-weakened Luftwaffe. Not only did those attacks damage the airfields and destroy many planes on the ground, but also, as a result, the Luftwaffe pulled most of its aircraft back to Germany by D-Day.

According to historian Jonathan Trigg, "By D-Day, the imbalance between the two opposing sides had become absurd. Against [Luftflotte 3's leader Hugo] Sperrle's 170 combat ready fighters, the Allied could field 4,029, with Luftflotte 3's 100 sorties on landing day met by 14,674 Allied ones."[28] The domination was so complete that within hours of the first beach landings, the hydrogen-filled barrage balloons anchored over the beaches to protect Allied planes were left to fly away. That suggests the famous shot in the film *The Longest Day* taken from a German plane overflying and attacking the invading forces was an out-of-context exception.

Although aerial dominance was a lost cause for the Germans, it did not stop Hermann Goering, who was in charge of the Luftwaffe, from belatedly trying to keep a commitment to channel all available aircraft into resisting the Normandy invasion. Thus, aircraft from both the Italian and Eastern fronts, as well as the Reich's home bases, were transferred to France in a vain attempt to disrupt the Allies' air attacks. Many of the redeployed pilots were elite aviators of the Luftwaffe, known as Experten, who had downed dozens, if not hundreds, of Allied planes. But the majority of pilots who were shot down in this initiative were novices, those who had received only a few weeks of training and were no match for the superior flying skills of the Allies' pilots, let alone their number. By the end of August, the Luftflotte 3 had lost a staggering 2,127 aircraft in combat, more than double the number that had been available on D-Day.

If the targeting of the railways and the establishment of air dominance were successes, the attempt to disrupt road traffic failed miserably. Plan Tortue mirrored Plan Vert in many ways but on a much smaller scale, with bombings intended to destroy road junctions. The problem was that not only were these junctions tiny targets but they also were invariably sited in small towns and villages, which increased the risk of numerous fatalities. In the run-up to D-Day, this plan generated considerable controversy for this very reason. Zuckerman warned that targeting roads was impractical and that, even if successful, the attacks would only cause minor delays; however, Eisenhower considered these raids to be a key part of the Overlord strategy. Montgomery and the head of the combined air force, Trafford Leigh-Mallory, also argued strongly in favor of the raids. A list of 26 targets for "road blocks" was drawn up, but concern about civilian deaths reduced this number to 11.

On the morning of June 6, the Allies carried out these attacks, but despite using the most up-to-date targeting methods, the results were disastrous. By the end of the day, some 500 civilians had been killed and the military impact was minimal. Several planes returned to base with their bombs because they could not find their intended targets. Even where the attacks destroyed targets, it was all too easy for road traffic to bypass the affected areas using fields or country lanes. According to the historian Jean Quellien, "In total the aerial bombing of the 6th and the night of the 6th and 7th was responsible for 3,000 deaths of Bas-Normands inhabitants."[29] After a couple more nights, the plan to create "choke-points" was officially abandoned.

Fortunately, lack of fuel and limited availability of road vehicles meant that train travel was the key component of German logistics for moving soldiers and supplies, and there was no doubt about the impact of the attacks on the rail network. The only question was whether the main credit for the rail system breakdown should go to the French saboteurs or the Allied bombers.

Zuckerman of course had no doubt the railway bombings as set out in his Transportation Plan were the crucial measure, but he was, to say the least, parti pris. In fact, any objective analysis would show that both aspects were essential. The saboteurs' attacks resulted in very few civilian deaths and were highly effective. A US Army analysis concluded: "Damage done by saboteurs compared favorably with that inflicted from the air. In the first three months of 1944 the underground sabotaged 808 locomotives as compared to 387 damaged by air attack."[30] At first, only the saboteurs were involved, and the number of sabotage incidents rose markedly through 1943 into 1944, when the aerial bombing campaign started in earnest. It was only when, in April and May, air attacks were stepped up that they accounted for more damage than the Resistance fighters, putting 1,437 locomotives out of commission compared to only 292 by saboteurs.

The combined effect of air and ground attacks smoothed the way for the sweep of the Allied invaders and, crucially, saved many lives—on both sides—in the process. At the outbreak of the war, there were 15,000 usable locomotives, a number that movements to Germany and lack of maintenance had cut nearly in half by early 1944. According to a postwar analysis, "By 20 May, when intensive strafing operations against trains began, the number of utilizable locomotives had fallen to 7,600...and by mid-July, there were 5,900"—half of these further losses were attributed to strafing.[31] Even Churchill was impressed. He later wrote that the delayed arrival of reinforcements in Normandy was the greatest contribution of the bombing campaign in support of Overlord. De Gaulle, on the other hand, was less fulsome in his praise; in his autobiography, he cited the estimated 30,000 killed in these raids, but did not overtly criticize the policy.

The postwar analysis by the military authorities was unequivocal about the overall effectiveness of the attacks on the rail network:

> In the case of rail transport, air attacks had by D-Day caused both general military and total traffic to decline more than 60 percent. It is obvious that a rail system which has been subjected to reductions of this magnitude has lost most of its normal excess capacity. If the system had been functioning as it was before attack and if the Germans had not been in doubt regarding the possibility of a second invasion, there is every reason to believe that the German forces would have been both committed and moved to the battle area far more rapidly.[32]

The paralysis of the rail network brought with it two consequential advantages. First, it ensured that the enemy's precious resources of fuel would be used up when trucks replaced trains. In fact, remarkably, the German army still depended on horses and carts for transport, and they further clogged up the already-overcrowded roads. Second, these road convoys and marches became sitting ducks for Allied air attacks.

Probably the most balanced assessment came from Major Charles Benda, the British officer charged with evaluating the impact of the damage done. His report found that the attacks on the railways "resulted in long delays... forced the enemy to disperse and to waste its personnel, and affected the morale of the troops."[33] He also made a distinction between the bombardment that cut off the main lines in the North and the South and the damage to secondary routes carried out by the Resistance. With some exceptions, the bombardment in the North was so intensive that the work of the Resistance may have been superfluous, with some significant exceptions (such as the destruction of a viaduct at Chérisy in the Pas-de-Calais, which was attacked unsuccessfully 15 times until it was blown up by saboteurs).

By D-Day, the rail network was all but at a standstill, yet there was more destruction to come, both through bombing and the activity of the ever-growing Resistance. Once the invasion began, communications with London were difficult to maintain and the Resistance fighters began to choose their own targets, many of which were intended to disable German transport facilities.

Indeed, after the war, Resistance members recalled that the initial landings led to an increase in acts of sabotage; according to Gilbert Guédon, "We felt that, at last, something was happening, it really helped us... we could imagine the liberation of Paris and of the whole region." Guédon also related that soon after D-Day, on the orders of Résistance Fer, he was involved in a major operation in Seine-et-Marne, a big department east of Paris. Thanks to this endeavor, "14 trains were stopped, 7 ended up in the sand as it were [derailed], and seven others were stuck behind...2 locomotives and 20 wagons were put out of use and 300 metres of track ripped up."[34]

For many railway workers, however, it was a particularly difficult time. They wanted to do everything they could to hinder the progress of the German military trains, but the soldiers supervising and guarding them had become ever more alert and trigger happy. It was risky, too, because the increased activity of the resistants put the lives of the railway workers in danger.

Marcel Péroche recalled an especially perilous trip that he faced just two days after D-Day. On the evening of June 8, he was summoned to the depot at Saint-Médard-de-Guizières, about 12 miles east of Bordeaux, to work on a troop train heading for Normandy. He tried to get out of this duty, arguing that it was his day off, but it was made clear that he would be shot by the guards if he refused. Péroche was at the controls of the second of the two locomotives hauling the train when it started picking up speed down a steep grade. The driver of the first locomotive noticed a small red lantern in the distance and applied the brakes. This was fortunate because the resistants had blown up a bridge on the Bordeaux–Saintes line. Had the train, with several hundred German troops aboard, not stopped, it would have hurtled into a ravine. Péroche was amazed that the first driver had spotted the lantern: "His reflex was all the more remarkable since there was nothing else to warn us of the danger," and then Péroche reflected philosophically on how the Maquisards had realized their own men would be killed: "For them it was a case for conscience: sacrifice five railwaymen to accomplish a blow for France....our wives would have become widows and we would have become heroes....It's not that the Résistance was wrong, but on that day Providence was against them."[35]

Péroche survived several more scrapes over the coming weeks, notably having to disable his own locomotive in full view of German soldiers, who were increasingly wary of sabotage attempts. Péroche also recounted that soon after the landings, "the Americans, not worrying about details, executed a group of German railwaymen on the spot. The international rules of war deemed that anyone not wearing a uniform could be judged as a sniper and so could be executed without trial."[36] As a result, the German High Command mandated that the railwaymen wear uniforms, but as Péroche wryly notes, "The change of clothes did nothing to bolster the German railwaymen's morale."[37] Such incidents would continue well into the summer as the Germans desperately made use of the railways that remained in operation in the territory they occupied.

The early days after D-Day were confusing. While the Allies set about repairing sections of railway in territory they controlled, in German-held areas the resistants were still wrecking sections of line, and Allied air attacks continued. The reconstruction in Allied territory, however, started immediately and rapidly gathered pace.

3

FIRST TRACKS

After D-Day, the British headquarters, the 21 Army Group, was responsible for a huge and unprecedented logistical exercise. Despite all the detailed planning of Overlord, the invasion essentially was a stab in the dark; every inch forward was fraught with difficulty. Moreover, the railway had to *always* be available just behind the lines to provide the logistical support needed to maintain the advance. As soon as territory was gained, the local railway tracks had to be taken over, made safe, rebuilt, and then utilized with an intensity many of these lines were not designed for. And always, in the advance guard just behind the front line were the men of ADSEC, the Advance Section of the Communications Zone, whose role was to work out how to reestablish the railways and plan the logistics of the next move forward.

In January 1944, Colonel Emerson Itschner, an ADSEC engineer, was appointed chief of transportation and given responsibility for the reconstruction of bridges, ports, and highways in France. His duty would involve not only laying track but also reconstructing road culverts, bridges, and watering and coaling facilities. Much to their surprise, Itschner's engineers found far less damage to the *Routes Nationales*, the main road network, than expected, which allowed several general service regiments that had been earmarked for work on roads to be transferred to railways, the new priority following D-Day.

A clear three-phase process of how to use the newly reclaimed railways was set out. First, the lines would be patched as quickly as possible to enable military personnel to operate them. At this stage of the war, the railway was, in effect, part of the front line, and military strategists acknowledged that maintaining the track and operating the services in such proximity to the enemy was too dangerous to put civilian lives at risk; it would have to be undertaken by the military. As the front line moved farther away, the second stage envisaged passing the responsibility of operating the railway to local civilian authorities under military direction. And finally, in the third phase, the lines would be returned to the French government-owned railway company, the Société Nationale des Chemins de Fer Français (SNCF), although routes that were main lines of communication would be retained by the military.

The logistics to support Operation Overlord were unprecedented. The sheer numbers involved were daunting but also explain why the railways were fundamental to the whole process of shifting supplies from the ports to the front. The 21 Army Group's transportation service, largely staffed by enlisted men but occasionally supported by civilians, "discharged 5,487,600 tons of military cargo...with an average daily lift of 18,000 tons, reaching a maximum of 40,000 tons."[1] Numbers can be dull and impossible to understand, so to help break down these figures, consider that the best army trucks at the time could carry 6 tons—and most managed just 3. To move 40,000 tons daily by road over an average distance of 100 miles would have required around 13,000 three-ton trucks, each with a driver, and an extensive support network encompassing a large maintenance, spares, and repair organization. This was quite simply logistically impossible. That is why, from the first days of the landings, special railway troops, both British and American, were given the task of re-creating and ramping up the broken rail network.

Even the best-laid plans risk being inadequate when they face the complexity of the real world. Overlord was, indeed, an excellent and astonishingly detailed plan more than two years in preparation. Even though its implementation was crucial to the Allies' war effort, large sections of the plan were, in practice, ditched, and conversely, the plan failed to envisage many actual outcomes of the conflict. Overlord had a 90-day timetable, and inevitably, working out in advance the likely progression of the war over such a long period involved considerable informed guesswork based on tenuous assumptions. In particular, the timetable needed to be precise about the progress of the front line, but given the complex nature of warfare, it was impossible to predict. Overlord was never going to be perfect. As the assessment by the US Army reported afterward: "Overlord represented the fruits of two years of strategic thought, argument, experiment, and improvisation and included compromises reflecting American and British aims."[2] The assumptions, some accurate, some wildly wrong, were inevitably based on speculation.

Overlord was all about logistics, and from the beginning transport issues were at the heart of its military strategy. From the scale of the assault on the beaches to the choice of lodgment area, selection of immediate targets, and assessment of the maximum speed of progress, logistics took top priority. Initially, the logistics focused on shipping and port availability, but as the troops advanced into France, the ability of roads and railways to facilitate the lines of communication became crucial.

Once the beachhead—the lodgment, as it came to be known—was established, Caen was to be the first major town taken, largely because of its importance as a transport hub that also included a major road junction and two key waterways, the Orne River and the Caen Canal. Whereas Caen was expected to fall almost immediately, planning envisaged that capturing Cherbourg, at the northern tip of the Cotentin Peninsula, would take a couple of weeks longer. Cherbourg was listed as an early target precisely because of its value as the main port through which men and goods could be brought in; it was hoped its seizure would end use of the beaches as part of the Allies' supply chain.

The timetable for Operation Overlord encompassed three phases. About 20 days after D-Day, it was expected that the advance section would be able to move inland off the beaches to a headquarters where the communications would be organized. After a further 20 days, a second army would be introduced, and then after another 50 days, the overall command of the operation would move to France. After the capture of Cherbourg, the key Normandy port, the Overlord plan was for Allied forces to head southwest to cut off the Brittany peninsula and pave the way for opening its ports. The area west of the Seine was to be cleared, but Overlord planners did not expect the river to be crossed until well after the end of the operation's 90-day timetable. To build up the transport lines of communication and ensure that the forward army could continue to be supplied, there was then to be a pause before the advance westward to take Paris and proceed to the Rhine.

Inevitably, the pattern of the invasion and, as a result, the logistics supporting it ended up being very different from what had initially been envisaged. Because Caen was not seized until August, taking two months longer than expected, the beaches continued to be used until the autumn and dealt with much greater quantities of supplies than anticipated, as did the minor ports, which were originally intended to be stopgap measures until the capacity of major harbors could be

developed. The Brittany ports, which had been intended to play a significant role, were little used because they were captured later than
planned and were deemed to be too far from the front line. Conversely,
Cherbourg was under Allied control by early July, and despite its distance from the front line, it played a key role in the supply chain, at least
until Antwerp, the largest port in northwest Europe, became available
in late November.

The railway troops who were to play such a vital part in establishing and maintaining the lines of communication in the Overlord plan started arriving within days of the first landings. There
were, in fact, two separate groups of railway troops, the British and the American. Although some American soldiers had
attended training schools for bridging and other railway functions
in England, little attempt was made, with the odd exception such
as at Antwerp, to meld these two countries' forces together. The
troops' experience, military traditions, and even methods of working railways were different. For the British, many aspects of the
French railways were the same as in their home country—notably,
they were even driven on the left—but the Americans had to adapt
to a completely different style of railway. Even though the gauge
(the distance between the two rails) was the same 4 feet 8½ inches,
US locomotives were much heavier and stronger, and the freight
cars wider. American soldiers were used to long stretches of open
and mostly straight track in contrast to the winding French railways with their frequent stations, numerous grade crossings, and
old-fashioned labor-intensive working practices. Rather quaintly, as
a military analysis put it, "each [French] level crossing has a small
house for the gate keeper, generally a man, his wife and children
who rush out and wave as the train passes."[3] It was a description
of a prewar bucolic idyll that was not wholly inaccurate but that
would never be fully regained.

Another uncertainty was the condition of the railways left behind in enemy territory. In Italy, where the railways had also played a key role in the Allies' advance northward from Sicily, the Germans deployed a flat railcar hauled by a locomotive that systematically tore sleepers from the roadbed and at regular intervals dropped a charge that shattered the rails. Surmising that they would use this same technique in France, the Overlord planners estimated that 75 percent of the track would need replacing, although some sections of line might be salvaged. This implied that huge quantities of ties and rails would need to be brought over and that, therefore, it would take months rather than weeks to make the railways fully operational.

These assumptions about the condition of the railways proved to be overly pessimistic. In many cases, there was less damage than expected because the rapidity of the Germans' retreat left them no time to destroy the railway facilities. The "wrecking machine" had not been deployed on the railways in Normandy.

———————

That is not to say the railways were in anything like working order. Parts of the network, especially around Cherbourg, and later farther east, had been systematically destroyed by the combination of Allied bombing and French sabotage. There were instances of German sabotage, too. Overall, parts of the railway system would require weeks of intensive work to repair. Although a track could be patched quickly so that a few low-speed trains could pass, bringing the railway up to full working standard would be a much more protracted affair.

The assumption that all the bridges had been brought down and would need replacing also proved to be overly pessimistic. Bridge work was undoubtedly the most challenging aspect of rebuilding the railways, but several bridges in the immediate vicinity of the landings were intact despite Allied bombing. Still, others—to the east and south—needed to be rebuilt rapidly. Allied bombing had destroyed all the bridges over the Seine, and as they retreated, the Germans wreaked further damage on those that had been temporarily repaired. Farther east, where the Germans had time to carry out their scorched-earth strategy, the Rhine bridges and virtually every bridge in Holland and western Germany, however big or small, needed to be reconstructed. One strange outcome of the railways being less damaged than expected was that thousands of tons of railway equipment that had been carried across the Channel went unused and were left to molder on the beaches long after the war ended.

The Overlord plan for initial work on the railways was rather unambitious. Even though the importance of the railways in the longer term was recognized, because of the assumption about their state of repair the railways were given little role to play after the initial landings. The Allies planned to rely on motor transport, which greatly limited the amount of supplies that could be imported. Thereafter, restoration of the railways and ports would be the priority because "important as motor transportation was to be in operation Overlord, it was not expected to sustain the mounting volume of supply movements after the first few weeks. From the beginning the Allies counted on the railways—a far more economical carrier over long distances—eventually to bear the larger portion of the transportation burden." The Overlord planners concluded, "Restoration of the French rail lines took on added importance in view of the anticipated shortage of truck transport."[4] Overlord determined that British engineers would be responsible for two sets of lines around Caen, while the Americans would work on the main line from Cherbourg down the Cotentin Peninsula to Avranches and south to Rennes, as well as on the route eastward to Lison junction, 44 miles from the port.

The Overlord planners had assumed that even after six weeks, they would only be able to complete rail restoration from Cherbourg to the Lison junction. Even three months after D-Day, it was expected that only 245 miles of railway, consisting principally of the main line between Cherbourg and Rennes, would be in operation. Progress was indeed slow. The line between the port of Cherbourg at the top of the Cotentin Peninsula and Carentan at its base was first on the list for reconstruction, but the route could only be repaired once the Allies had taken the whole peninsula. Farther south the Allies ran into a major barrier: after clearing out the Cotentin in July, the advancing forces found that the line from Avranches, a town on the southwestern coast of the peninsula, south to Rennes had been so extensively damaged that an alternate route to Le Mans and ultimately Paris needed to be hastily rebuilt.

On June 10, American railway equipment began to arrive on Utah Beach by Landing Ship, Tank (LST), which was the main method of carrying men and matériel onto the beaches. The first American railway personnel landed around the same time, led by the chief of Itschner's Railroad Section, Lieutenant Colonel A. D. Harvey. Housed in an ADSEC camp at Isigny close to an airfield that was bombed every night, the men in his reconnaissance party immediately found themselves on the front line. The idea was to have railways functioning as close to the Allied front line as possible to avoid using trucks for hauling long distances. Their initial task was to assess the condition of any surviving railway facilities, calculate the supply requirements needed to bring the line back into use, and plan the initial services on the railway. This work of necessity brought these first arrivals close to the enemy. Their primary area to survey was the section of the Carentan–Caen line that paralleled the coast. Lison, 44 miles southeast of Cherbourg, was a key junction where a branch went to Isigny, a small port used in the initial phase of the invasion. It became the boundary between the British section, working eastward toward Caen, and the Americans, working westward and responsible for all lines on the Cotentin Peninsula and the main line south to Rennes.

The American reconnaissance team, which numbered just 10 officers and men, traveled in a special jeep whose tires could be removed to reveal flanged wheels for driving directly on railway tracks. On several occasions, the jeep was targeted by snipers. The invasion's first railway casualty took place on June 28, when a shell burst nearby, injuring an officer, Major J. B. Stone, in the neck. A subsequent army report acknowledges numerous other near misses: "Every man in the party was subjected to bombing, shelling and strafing, and they were frequently shot at by snipers."[5]

The reconnaissance team also had to watch out for mines and booby traps. Although the jeep proved itself useful for some tasks, for the most part, Harvey and his colleagues walked the track to ensure it was safe to use. The formal, unemotional military language of Harvey's daily diary entries masks the reality of the dangers these railwaymen faced working so close to enemy-occupied lines. There is, nevertheless, a sense of urgency in every word he writes as he was under constant pressure from his superiors to open the railway as quickly as possible.

Harvey, in his twenties and with movie-star looks, cut a rather dashing figure. Like many of his fellow American officers, he was in a hurry to get things done. Not entirely enamored with his British officer colleagues, in a postwar speech to a Rotary Club in Medford, Oregon, he called them "slow and conservative" (mostly the result of their experience at Dunkirk).[6] Even so, he did begrudgingly accept that the British "were fully cooperative and made important contributions to the success of the landings."

Harvey arrived in France just four days after D-Day, and by June 13, accompanied by a single technician named Williams, he had walked most of the seven-mile branch line from Isigny to Lison, stopping only a half mile short of the junction when he got too close to enemy lines. Shells from his own artillery flew overhead, battering the nearby German positions.

Harvey reported to Itschner that the track on the branch line from Isigny to Lison junction was ready to use, with the only major damage being three shell holes in the yard at Isigny. He also reported that the main line through to Carentan, the town at the eastern foot of the Cotentin Peninsula that the Americans captured on June 14, also appeared to be in good condition, but he needed to ascertain the condition of the bridges. The following day, he flew low over a long section at an altitude of no more than 600 feet in a tiny two-seater—an act of real courage with the enemy in the vicinity because the little Piper Cub offered its occupants no protection. He discovered, much to his surprise, that the track was intact but for one key bridge that supported a 150-foot double-track line over the river Vire that had been downed by Allied bombing.

Harvey reckoned that because only one section was lying in the river, the bridge could be repaired in 10 days. A smaller crossing over a canal needed to be completely replaced, but fortunately, it was short enough that a Bailey bridge could be used. His subsequent recommendations in the report were remarkably detailed, given this was only nine days after D-Day and he had flown just once over the line: "Distance covered by report is 27 miles. Rail ties and fillings at rate of 222 tons per mile have been ordered for repair of this section, totalling 4,000 tons."[7] He requested that the 332nd Engineer General Service Regiment get to work immediately, but unfortunately, unbeknownst to him, the men had not yet arrived in France and would not even cross the Channel until June 28, two weeks later than scheduled. Harvey went to the Vire bridge two days later in a borrowed weapons carrier to take detailed measurements and noted coolly in his diary: "German shell landed approximately 300 yards from car after it was parked...returned to 342nd HQ. Had tooth pulled." He fails to explain why or by whom this little bit of dentistry was carried out in the midst of his vital reconnaissance work for which he had little support.

After his flight, Harvey headed to Carentan. Although the Germans had abandoned the town, the line was still well within artillery range of the enemy. One of the town's two railway yards had been left intact, but the other had been all but destroyed by Allied bombings. Two wrecked freight trains and one passenger train needed to be cleared, and about a quarter mile of track that had been ripped up needed to be rebuilt. Amazingly, Harvey noted that "there is enough material in the yard to do this," and the very next day, he organized a team of 90 men to work in two shifts of 10 hours to complete the cleanup quickly. Harvey also allowed the commanding officer of the 1055th, a port and construction unit that was carrying out the work, to hire local French labor, the first use in what would become common practice in rebuilding the railroads. A day later, 80 local men signed up and began working in the yard.

Despite the rapid progress, the risks the railway workers faced were all too apparent. Harvey, cool as ever, mentions in his diary, in parentheses no less, "(while we were there [at Carentan] 4 German shells landed within 400 yards, 2 duds and 2 live ones)." There were further dangers, too, resting in the yard. Eight unexploded American bombs were a reminder of the frighteningly high failure rate of the Transportation Plan attacks, while the three freight cars with unexploded ammunition, which required a special ordnance team to clear up, were a mark of the haste with which the Germans had retreated. Harvey expected work in the Carentan yard to be completed by

June 22, but he acknowledged the haphazard nature of the process during his desperate attempts to obtain specialized railway material: "Looked over Class IV dump [supply depot] at Utah [Beach]. Found a supply of railway tools and some bridge tools, such as 20 ton jacks, 5 and 10 ton track jacks, lining bars, bridge wrenches, picks, shovels, ballast forks and spike maul. Also found rail and a few ties (about 250). There are some frogs [crossings] for turning but no points, bridle rods, slide plates, guard rails or swith [sic; switch] stands." There was no bridge material "except some heavy timber which may be useful," but he "felt encouraged about the shipments that are liable to arrive later." This vast array of equipment, which had been brought over in the very early days of the landings, emphasizes the priority railway reconstruction had been accorded.

By then, Harvey was eager to open the line through to Carentan, but he was still waiting for the 332nd to arrive. The most important remaining task was the repair of the Vire bridge, which he noted "was the key to the reopening of the line." After visiting the site, he spent a night developing two possible ways of fording the river: they could either jack or lift the spans from the river, or if this proved impossible or time-consuming, they could abandon the original structure and replace it with a wooden trestle. In the absence of the 332nd, he commissioned the 1055th Port Construction and Repair Group to work on the bridge, but in his diary he expressed skepticism about their ability to carry out a job beyond their expertise. Harvey then spent two days going up and down the line, chivying the work teams. At Lison junction, he found 59 civilians working on track and locomotives but complained "work is proceeding very slowly." All things considered, his complaints seem rather unfair. The bomb disposal team was indeed at work and the master mechanic, a Frenchman, reported that two locomotives were still in working order and could run on the following day. Even so, Harvey was exasperated by the absence of the 332nd, which remained in England: "I cannot be too explicit in asking that the 332nd Eng Gen Sv Reg [Engineer General Service Regiment] be hurried up. We need the men and tools if this work is to be done." He returned to Carentan the following day and found that the work there and at four other worksites was going well.

By June 21, work was proceeding on the main line, but that didn't stop a train from successfully running along the branch line between Lison and Isigny, with Colonel Oeschle, the commanding officer of the 1055th, aboard. Two days later, on June 23, Harvey reported that he was able to carry out a detailed inspection of the Vire bridge because the enemy was far enough away and the tide was low. He expressed concern, saying it was "heavy and our equipment will not handle it without a set of long and hard preparation." Itschner had instructed him to "block up an upstream span," but Harvey was worried this was unsafe and, remarkably, spent the next day "working on design for reconstructing the bridge." On June 25, with no locals available to work because it was Sunday, the 1055th rigged up the span until enemy shellfire halted their progress. The following day, the span was raised and construction of the trestle support began, which took another 10 days. Throughout that period, there was occasional shelling by the enemy, but fortunately none of the missiles landed near the bridge. Much to Harvey's delight, on June 26, he learned that the 332nd had arrived and he eagerly went to find them, only to discover that a mere three enlisted men and a truck had landed so far. He ordered them to wait for the rest of the advance party and then to head to Cherbourg, which the Allies had taken that day.

Farther up the Cotentin, the advanced areas that had only recently been vacated by the Germans required scouting. Sergeant Merritt C. Becker, who was just 19 when he left his job working on steamships to join the Union Pacific Railroad's 723rd Railway Operating Battalion, was the leader of one advance party of railroad troops who suddenly found themselves on the front line. His platoon was dispatched to work under cover of darkness very close to the German lines and had to check for booby traps, some of which had been laid by the Resistance. In his papers, left to the University of New Orleans for an unpublished memoir, Becker describes how "the whole area had been blown to pieces with dynamite leaving twisted metal and rails bent at impossible angles. We had to replace every wooden tie and rail anchor."[8] The immediate task of his team of eight former civilian railroaders was to restore a damaged section of rail in order to reach a locomotive that had been derailed and partly blown up. Initially, they had to load all their equipment on a trolley car, which they then pushed down the surviving section of track: "We had all our heavy jacks with hand crowbars and gear loaded on a push trolley car and we oiled the axles to ensure they made as little noise as possible so as not to alert any German troops. We knew that at any moment we could be shot."

When his platoon finally reached the worksite, "the plan was to go out with a small military force circling the boundary with their rifles to root out the German snipers... all the tools had to be muffled while we crawled on our hands and knees under the locomotive with water and soot with oil dripping down on us." While they were scrabbling about under the locomotive, a second group of engineers restored the track. Becker said the most hazardous moment was when it came time to heave the damaged locomotive back onto the rails in preparation for hauling it away: "The squeals from the locomotive's driving gear attracted sniper fire from the Germans as we progressed slowly and I heard the whine and ricochet from a bullet, thinking it was lucky there was no scream from anyone." He found out later that the escorting infantrymen had rooted out and killed the German sniper hiding in the bushes. Becker, incidentally, later became a committed rail enthusiast and a renowned train and ship modeler. He donated his remarkable collection, which he had mostly built himself, to his local University of New Orleans a few years before his death in 2014, and it was valued at more than $1 million.

As Harvey found, some equipment was brought over in the early days, but nothing like enough and often the wrong type. The immediate need was for major shipments of railway equipment, and it was an American innovation that proved to be revolutionary in bringing supplies to France efficiently. Even when Cherbourg came into use, the port was overstretched, which was why the beaches were used for far longer than originally expected, some until autumn. The Allies realized they needed a method to haul all this material off the beaches and quickly onto the rail network. Or the alternative was to take it straight onto railway tracks. This remarkable solution was developed by Colonel H. Bingham, a longtime railwayman who became the head of the New York subway after the war. Bingham arrived in Britain in 1942 and supervised the arrival of the huge amount of rolling stock brought across the Atlantic. He then stayed in the UK to lend his expertise to Overlord planning, where he supported Zuckerman's idea of focusing Allied bombing attacks on railway facilities. A serial inventor, he also put his design skills to use in producing the armored train in which Eisenhower traveled.

Bingham's priority was ensuring that sufficient quantities of railway equipment could be brought across the Channel rapidly. The two conventional ways, both cumbersome and slow, were by train ferry or by craning locomotives and railcars onto the deck of a large ship. Instead, Bingham developed a way of bringing the vehicles right onto the beach using a series of 54 specially converted LSTs whose decks were fitted with rails. The big advantage of using LSTs was their flat bottoms, which enabled material to be brought right onto the beach when the tide receded. Preventing the heavy freight cars and locomotives from sinking into the sand meant they had to remain on rails all the time. Bingham's solution, which he had developed in London, was neat and effective: the engineers installed "breathing bridges" on the sand that consisted of railroad tracks set in quick-drying concrete (there were just 90 minutes in every 12 hours when the tide receded far enough for the concrete to cure before the water came in again).

On the LSTs, one end of a section of track was laid on the lip of the deck, and the other end was mounted on wheels that connected with the rails on the beach. Despite the strong tides, this ingenuous system enabled the Allies to bring considerable stock across the water in the first few weeks of the invasion before the port of Cherbourg was available, and even after that, they continued to use this impressively efficient system. Initially, they used smaller LSTs, which could carry just four railcars and a locomotive, but large vessels were soon deployed and carried 22 railcars fully loaded with equipment that could be hauled straight to the supply dumps. Essentially, the LSTs were converted into roll-on roll-off ferries, which were already in use on the Channel then. The Allies kept this revolutionary method secret so that the Germans were unaware of how much equipment was brought over so speedily, lest they try to disrupt the operation.

In a speech after the war, Bingham explained how this innovation made a tremendous difference to the whole logistics chain. "Colonel Bingham pointed out that never before in history had railroad rolling stock thus been landed in an enemy country. If ordinary train services had been relied upon, it would have taken 3½ years to have landed the volume of rolling stock which the invading forces took with them."[9] Hitler, a keen advocate of roads who had little understanding of railways, had expected that the Allied invaders would be stymied by a slow buildup of supplies. Bingham's brilliant concept proved to be a game changer that his enemies never saw coming.

This was by no means Bingham's only invention. He was an extraordinary visionary whose range of innovations stretched from automatic air traffic control to monorails for Disneyland. Earlier in the conflict, he had devised and built in a matter of weeks a super jeep, a kind of huge tow truck that could carry all the tools and equipment needed to repair a railway. It was a beast of a vehicle, a precursor of the monstrous SUVs of the twenty-first century, weighing 57 tons and capable of traveling over the roughest country to reach remote railway lines. It had 10 wheels and could carry a full team of seven engineers. The truck included a simple but clever innovation: a silhouette painted on the side showing where every tool was supposed to be stored, which meant that after use, each tool would be replaced in the right spot, ensuring no time was wasted rooting for equipment. The first super jeeps were built in the London Underground workshops and deployed in the North African theater; subsequently, 60 were sent to France after the initial Normandy landings. And after the success of that idea, Bingham became heavily involved in the design of hospital trains, which became the principal method of evacuating soldiers, with nearly 50 put into service in France.

While the Americans were progressing westward on the 44-mile main line between Lison and Cherbourg, the British were responsible for the 35-mile stretch from the Lison junction to Caen. And, with a typical bit of British one-upmanship, they managed to beat the Americans in providing the first military train service in France.

———————

The first British railwaymen to arrive in Normandy were two officers who landed on the beach at Arromanches on June 10 and were followed a couple of days later by an advance group of 60 men from the 181st Railway Operating Company. The latter had been split into three groups for the crossing to ensure that, if one platoon failed to arrive through delay or sinking, all the relevant trades required to rebuild a railway line would still be represented. Luckily, they all arrived safely and set up a temporary camp at Luc-sur-Mer.

Neither the officers nor the men had been given any information on what they were expected to do upon arrival, and only when they arrived were they charged with rebuilding the line between Lison and Caen. However, the delay of several weeks in capturing the town hampered their work, which meant that the crucial main line connecting Cherbourg and the whole Cotentin with Caen remained in enemy hands. Instead, the railway troops started repairing a parallel route along the coast linking Courseulles and Luc-sur-Mer. Despite war damage, the line was relatively easy to bring into operation earlier than the Overlord plan called for, and the troops set about the task urgently so that the huge amounts of supplies stacking up on the beaches could be offloaded. To provide the traction, on June 11 two small diesel locomotives, the first engines to reach France, were shipped across the Channel overnight.

Their crossing was far from easy; the two ships carrying the locomotives were machine-gunned by an E-boat, a small but fast German attack craft, which was eventually chased away by the escorting ship. Upon arrival at the beach, the locomotives were hauled to the nearby rail line on a tank transporter fitted with tracks rather than wheels. The locomotives were then maneuvered onto the rails by a system of jacks and were immediately put to use, the first engines to be deployed by the Allies on French tracks.

The initial test train, which consisted of a couple of railcars hitched to one of the newly arrived diesels, set out on June 14 to check whether any mines or other booby traps had been left on the tracks. It was not until three weeks later, after the men had repaired the line and the enemy had retreated sufficiently far away, that a useful freight service between Courseulles and the transportation stores depot at Luc-sur-Mer could be established.

The inaugural run of a diesel locomotive hauling a handful of freight cars set out on July 4, just 30 days after D-Day. At the time, it may have seemed like a modest affair on a ramshackle line, but it was the first service to run on what would become the largest military railway network the world had ever seen. Services were soon operating regularly on this stretch—albeit at slow speed, given the poor condition and sharp curvature of a previously little-used coastal line. It was also confined to freight.

Fortunately, the ever-growing number of railwaymen arriving from the beaches became adept at using jacks to rerail coaches and even locomotives after the frequent derailments. Back in late June, the British railway contingent had become 200 strong, but the failure to capture Caen stymied their efforts to reopen the line, which had been expected to have been operational shortly after the initial landings.

Nevertheless, the rapid establishment of this short service was welcomed as good news because it suggested that the condition of the railways, at least in Normandy, was not as bad as expected. Several dumps (a rather misleading military term for supply storage depots) were established along the line as supplies were brought in from the beaches and small ports. Even though Caen was still in enemy hands, by the end of June the coastal line was working through to Ouistreham on the mouth of the Orne River, just eight miles north of the city. Caen was finally liberated on July 9, but only after one of the bloodiest battles of the Normandy invasion and what was ultimately viewed as "excessive" bombing by the Allies had reduced most of the town to rubble and killed hundreds of its citizens. In response, the Germans committed a notorious war crime by executing 80 suspected members of the Resistance who had been held in the town prison.

The railwaymen waited just three days after the departure of the Germans before they moved into the town. On July 12, a party of 2 officers and 50 men—a full complement of experienced railway workers, including engine crew, fitters, welders, and boilermakers— entered the north end of the city to set up camp in a set of abandoned boxcars. This was the first use of railway rolling stock as billets, a practice that both US and British personnel would adopt widely. In addition to occasional sniper fire, the advance party's reconnaissance trips encountered strafing attacks by the Luftwaffe, though fortunately the bombs fell in a field nearby. As the railwaymen inched into the town, where snipers were still operating, they found a scene of utter devastation, caused mostly by Allied bombing but also by Resistance sabotage. All the bridges were down and the station and depot had been flattened, as had the coal hopper used for filling tenders. Furthermore, the French saboteurs had disrupted the Germans' ability to depart quickly by running a large main-line locomotive into the pit below the turntable, rendering it ineffective. As a result, the Germans had left behind a handful of locomotives. Fortunately for the Allies, these abandoned locomotives, although damaged, were easily brought back into use with spare parts from engines destined for the scrap heap. The rails in the yards were completely destroyed, but those in the immediate vicinity were mostly intact.

It was here, at Caen, that the British were at last able to deploy the skills in bridge building they had developed in Blighty. The first railway bridge completed by the Royal Engineers was a 300-foot-long structure over the river Orne at Caen. The Germans had cut the lattice girders, plunging a section of the bridge into the river, and these were replaced by four sections of Bailey decks rolled into place over the existing pier and abutments. This was the first of three

similar structures over the Orne River that was completed by the end
of August, the first of more than 1,200 Bailey bridges — mostly for
railways — that the Allies would eventually complete as they swept
through France, Belgium, Holland, and Germany. By August 9,
a single line into Caen was reopened, but because of the extensive
damage farther east, it was not until the end of the month that trains
could travel beyond the town and toward the Seine, which was the
next major obstacle.

Meanwhile, farther west, the British established a permanent
headquarters at Bayeux, which had been surrendered without a fight
24 hours after D-Day. The Germans' rapid departure left the city,
including the station, undamaged, and the railway troops' first task
was to guard the sizable coal stocks that had been abandoned to prevent the desperate locals from helping themselves. Although the city
and station remained more or less in good shape, the rail facilities in
the freight yard and depot had been severely damaged. On July 13,
the soldiers started to repair them by relaying seven miles of track
and 53 switches. The plan was to transform Bayeux into a vast and
crucial transfer point between road and rail. Already, many of the
local SNCF staff had returned to the railway, and the British were
quicker than the Americans to allow them to take on responsibility, such as driving some of their former locomotives that had been
patched up and put in steam. Within days, Bayeux became a hive of
activity from which several trains were dispatched daily, at first to the
east and later toward Cherbourg.

———————

The fall of Caen and Cherbourg marked the start of the major reconstruction work for the teams of railroad men who were now arriving in large numbers. Though both armies allocated substantial

manpower from the outset, the labor force expanded rapidly as the Allies advanced and the need to get the railways running became ever more urgent. The Operation Overlord planners expected 15 British railway companies, including 2 bridging companies, would be sent over in the initial weeks, backed by the same number of pioneer companies—a total of 30 companies, around 200 officers and 7,000 men. Similarly, the Americans earmarked 12,000 men for railroad construction and operation to arrive in the first 12 weeks.

The fierce and prolonged battles to capture Caen and Cherbourg meant that Allied shells and bombing, combined with sabotage by the retreating Germans, left these key cities devastated. Taking Cherbourg proved especially difficult because Hitler, conscious of the importance of the Channel ports, ordered his generals there to fight to the end. The German army initially formed a line across the bottom of the Cotentin, and though it was soon breached, the tactic gained the Germans time to wreak havoc.

The advance party that reached the port on June 27 while fighting still raged were shocked by what they saw. Of the two main docks, the Quai de Normandie had been blown up and the rubble had scattered over the remains of six cranes that had been toppled and pushed into the sea. The modern Quai de France, where ocean liners crossing the Atlantic used to dock in peacetime, had also been systematically but not quite as effectively destroyed, leaving only 5 percent of the quay space available for landing large ships. It could have been worse: the Germans had planned to drive a series of locomotives straight into the sea, expecting the boilers to explode, but the attempt was foiled when the tracks on the quay were put out of action by Allied bombers.

Sorting out the railway in and around Cherbourg provided the Allies with a crash course in how to repair and operate a railway in difficult wartime conditions. The first priority was rehabilitating the port at Cherbourg, the responsibility of Lieutenant Colonel W. T. Elmes; until the port could be brought into use, all supplies had to be landed on the beaches and at a couple small fishing ports, which had very limited capacity. Once Cherbourg was liberated and the port repaired, it would become the key entry point for locomotives and rolling stock.

Immediately after the capture of Cherbourg, newly arrived railway reinforcements set to work. Elmes, who was head of the Engineering Division of the Second Military Railway Service, landed at Utah Beach on June 24, smarting that he had missed arriving on his birthday by a single day. In one of the jeeps converted to run on rail tracks, Elmes spent a day scouting the area around Lison, where his colleague Major Morgan had nearly been killed when he wandered into no-man's-land between the two warring armies. On June 28, the day after the Americans captured Cherbourg, Elmes and his colleagues walked the entire 10-mile branch line between Valognes, the junction with the main line, and Saint-Vaast on the eastern coast of the Cotentin. Elmes reported later that "pockets of resistance were still found in this isolated section...the party was shot at on several occasions."[10] Accordingly, though the men initially walked single file between railroad crossings, they later decided it was safer to walk in pairs, sticking close to the tracks out of fear of booby traps. One particularly dangerous type of device was discovered: "a potato masher was stuck under a rail, with a wire strung across the track and anchored on the other side. Any pressure on the wire would explode the line."[11]

Colonel Alvin G. Viney, who prepared the original plan for port rehabilitation, later recalled: "The demolition of the port of Cherbourg is a masterful job, beyond a doubt the most complete, intensive, and best planned demolition in history."[12] Various types of mines were strewn across the harbor entrance. All the basins in the

port were blocked with sunken ships, and the left breakwater for the
inner harbor was cratered so that the sea poured through. Hitler even
rewarded Admiral Hennecke, who had been in charge of the demolition, for what the Führer described as "a feat unprecedented in the
annals of coastal defence."

Antoine Vosluisant, the deputy manager of the Cherbourg port
at the time of its liberation, described the scene that met the Americans as they took over the city: "Scuttled boats blocked the access to
the ports. The gare maritime had collapsed...and lines of wagons
lay in the remains of the main hall," and then he outlined the state
of the railway yard: "Most of the workshops had collapsed or been
burnt out, machine tools had been sabotaged. There was no water
(the pumps had been destroyed); there was no electricity, no working turntable (although the central table itself had survived). The
coal stocks had been burnt out, 12 locomotives completely wrecked
and the others damaged. The route to Paris was blocked by 1,500
cubic metres of debris as the Germans had blown up the tunnel on
the route of Martinvast. Everything needed to be rebuilt."[13] And
the Germans were not the only ones to blame for the destruction
because, ironically, some of the worst damage had been caused by an
Allied bombing raid on June 12.

The liberation of Cherbourg, together with the later decision not
to make use of the Brittany ports, emphasized the Allies' need to
upgrade and expand freight-handling facilities beyond their prewar
capabilities. Fortunately, Hitler had been too quick to compliment
Hennecke's efforts; as it happened, the destruction of Cherbourg's
transport infrastructure proved to be less comprehensive than the
Germans had boasted.

This was particularly the case with the railway structures. As
Vosluisant mentioned, the Gare Maritime station had been blown
up by mines contained in two railcars pushed under the roof and

detonated. The control center for the port's electricity supply and the heating plant had been completely destroyed, but other facilities remained intact. The Americans' advance party was particularly pleased to discover that part of the perimeter wall that protected the station from the elements remained unscathed, and although tracks in the yards and port area had been ripped up farther down the line, the rails had been left mostly intact. Even more pleasing, the line running down the Cotentin, which was the key line of communication from the port to the rest of France, was in a far better state than expected. As the reconnaissance team reported: "The main lines along the Cherbourg Peninsula [the Cotentin] were in quite good condition as very little demolition had been carried out by the Germans."[14]

Moreover, the sabotage had not been systematic. Parts of the railway that were easy to repair had been blown up, but other sections, such as junctions and switches, which are far more difficult to replace, had been left untouched. Nevertheless, great care was taken at these sites to inspect for German booby traps. The railway troops were delighted to spot a crane that had been left intact, but on closer examination, they discovered it was booby-trapped to blow up as soon as the engine was set in motion. The troops' training had ensured that they were aware of such devices and able to defuse them safely.

Vosluisant described how the French *cheminots* and other volunteers helped the Americans not only restore the port but also increase its throughput far beyond its historical capacity — and quickly, too. Although all the bridges in the Cherbourg area were down, they were small enough to be rapidly restored, except for one, which was bypassed easily. The tunnel that had been blown up was transformed into an embankment for the sake of expediency. According to Vosluisant, by the end of July, the roundhouse for the engines was

in working order, the water and electricity supplies had been reestab-
lished, and the offices were rebuilt. (In his account, Vosluisant also
noted, with a railwayman's typical obsession for detail, that at the
beginning of August, the first locomotive put back in steam in liberated France was number 141 C 168.) None of this work was without risk, particularly given the presence of mines and the continued
activity of snipers. Casualties were inevitable, notably the death of
Ernest Pruvost, the French colonel who had coordinated the railways
in liberated areas alongside the American and British military. He
was killed by a sniper on August 9.

The overarching goal was to enable the port to handle 20,000
tons or more of material daily. The planners knew that the existing
yard, once reconstructed, would be capable of handling only around
750 freight cars per day, whereas they needed the ability to handle
6,000 railcars. Running this many trains in and out of the city not
only would require intensive use of the tracks well beyond prewar
capability but also the construction of a vast new classification yard
where the railcars could be stored and sorted.

In the event, these targets were exceeded. It was this rapid expansion of the port facilities, which was effectively a 25-fold increase
from prewar levels, that most impressed Vosluisant. By the winter
of 1944, the 20,000-ton daily target had been reached, with almost
half this material being forwarded by rail. Cherbourg, according
to Vosluisant, "became the Allies' most important supply body on
the globe and handled more than half American goods despatched
around the world."[15]

———————

However, for the first few weeks, before the Allies broke out of the
initial lodgment, only a few miles of track were under their control,

and as a result, the use of the railway was necessarily limited. As the repair teams worked toward Carentan at the foot of the peninsula, they discovered extensive damage to virtually all railway buildings, yards, and offices. All along the line, the stations had been reduced to rubble, not least because the Germans had used these sturdy and solid buildings as their last desperate holdouts. Fortunately, not all the rail facilities had been wrecked; the platforms had fared much better and, for the most part, remained usable.

The destruction was not confined to buildings. Just 10 miles north of the key junction of Pontaubault, Folligny lay in ruins, a scene of devastation and death, a grim reminder of the horrors of war. As a key German storage dump, the yard at Folligny had been the subject of repeated attacks by Allied bombers. The first US soldiers to arrive found "an indescribable mass of burned cars, twisted steel and bomb craters. The craters were so numerous in the yard proper they overlapped each other."[16] Like most of the adjacent town, all the railway buildings were down, and the cleanup started with a gruesome task for the newly arrived soldiers: "The engineers, while working in the yard, would unavoidably scoop up bodies and parts of bodies that had been buried there after each bombing. Evidently, the cadavers had been buried with no regard to location and no attempt had been made to mark the graves... corpses had been dumped into craters and the soil scooped back and in some cases the line rebuilt over the graves."[17]

To ensure the rapid reconstruction of the lines in and out of Cherbourg, French civilians were hired and, within a few days, more than 150 were working with the Allied troops. The surviving French railway workers mostly retained their existing jobs, and several senior personnel even enlisted in the French Army, which meant they could then be attached to the Military Railway Service. As well as being the main port through which supplies were passed, Cherbourg became the key railway workshop in liberated France. There, the joint US and French teams could handle the locomotives arriving from the UK, either on the beach or through the port, and quickly put them into operation. By mid-September, nearly 500 steam and diesel locomotives were repaired and operating in Allied-controlled areas of France. Moreover, the engineers of both nations worked in concert. A training school for diesel drivers was established in the Cherbourg depot, and the engines were fitted with instructions in French so that locals could drive them.

Despite generally working well together, some disagreements between teams inevitably crept in, given their very different ways of working. One seemingly trivial example was the French train engineers' desire to drive the new American diesel locomotives, which were just arriving, rather than only being allowed to handle their own engines. The US Army report on the retaking of Cherbourg describes, in a somewhat patronizing tone, how "the whole situation took on the flavor of one child with a big new toy and another child wanting to play with it. This was finally settled by allowing the French to make runs with the G.I. engineers, where it is assumed, they were allowed, occasionally to play with the levers and controls in the cab."[18] In fact, the French drivers' knowledge of the local area was very helpful in ensuring the safety of the operation. Also, there was a shortage of suitably trained Americans. Many of the heavy freight trains leaving Cherbourg were doubled-headed (hauled by two locomotives); typically, the French crews would drive the second locomotive, but then over time, they took over the controls of both. In effect, according to Vosluisant, the local drivers adapted to working under challenging military conditions: "They sleep in their engines, they eat K rations, and after a shift of four to five days they return by road or by special train." One French crew even volunteered for a special task at the request of an American colonel who could not find any of his soldiers to do the job, and then spent 113 continuous hours without rest at the controls of their engine.

Given the lack of a common language, the occasional misunderstandings could quickly flare into arguments: "It was not unusual to find a G.I. trainman and a wildly gesticulating Frenchman trying to clear up some point in the operation, the air blue with English and French railway phrases."[19] The ideal solution was to find an Italian or Mexican GI whose language skills in a Latin-based tongue usually proved sufficient to broker some sort of truce and resolve the issue.

Despite their technological know-how, the American railroad managers were not immune from mistakes. When the first trains were put into operation, the Americans insisted that they should operate on the right-hand track even though French custom was that trains passed each other on the left, as was the case in the UK. As it turned out, right-hand working would never have been feasible over the existing double-tracked lines because of the way they were designed. Rather sheepishly, the postwar report on the military rail operation around Cherbourg concedes: "As the traffic increased, this [running on the right] was found to be unsatisfactory because on the French Railroads the signaling and switching system are designed to run on the left side principle."[20] It was somewhat of a "doh!" moment, given the obvious difficulty of operating trains on the wrong side of a massive rail network, but the change to left-hand driving was delayed until August 9, after a train derailed as a result of attempting to drive through switches from the wrong direction.

The rolling stock left behind by the Germans was immediately put to good use. A quick inventory revealed that, along with a large stock of rail, there were 50 locomotives, 1,384 freight cars, and 11 luxury streamlined coaches available. Most of the locomotives dated from the First World War, including a dozen that had been sent over by the United States, though according to the railroad engineers inspecting them, they had barely been maintained since. There were also real museum pieces, including a handful of Austrian engines dating from 1865. Although this find was useful, most of the engines, once fired up, were only good for switching in yards because they were so antiquated. On the other hand, the railcars—originating mostly from Belgium and Germany, and some from France—were nearly all in perfect working condition, though every one still needed to be examined carefully for booby traps before being used.

The streamlined coaches were another unexpected boon, enabling the soldiers to initiate a first-class service through to Carentan as soon as the line was opened. On the morning of July 11, precisely five weeks after D-Day, the inaugural train service operated by the US Army on a main line in France ran from Cherbourg to Carentan, part of the route between the Cotentin and Paris. It was a modest affair, headed by a small French shunting steam engine pulling a freight car directly behind the tender based on the idea that if the locomotive hit a mine, the delay built into the detonating system would ensure the boxcar took the full force of the explosion rather than the coaches farther back. Fortunately, this ill-conceived idea, which relied on an accurate assessment of the delay built into a mine's mechanism that was impossible to make, was not put to the test, and the first run passed off uneventfully.

Rather incongruously, behind the freight car were two of the elegantly streamlined coaches found in Cherbourg, which carried an assortment of senior military staff, including Brigadier General Clarence L. Burpee, the head of the Second Military Railway Service (but not, incidentally, the inventor of the dreaded "burpee" deployed by fitness trainers across the world). The military VIPs could savor their triumph in a luxurious carriage adorned with an assortment of posters left by the Germans extolling the unique charms of the Côte d'Azur and signs forbidding anyone other than Wehrmacht officers to enter.

The inaugural train took precisely 1 hour and 45 minutes to cover the 31 miles between Cherbourg and Carentan via Valognes because the track was in no condition for fast running. Despite the slow speed, it was a significant moment and Burpee himself was so excited that he took over driving the engine on the return journey.

Within three days of that first trip, the line was being used to transport people for the Bastille Day celebrations in Cherbourg, the key annual French holiday marking the 1789 revolution, which were being held in liberated parts of the mainland for the first time since the German invasion. Acknowledging the importance of the event, the US Army suspended military work for the day, and the soldiers were allowed to join in the fun, despite the urgency of the task to bring the port and railways into operation.

Even more significant in reestablishing a sense of normalcy for the local population, a regular train service down the Cotentin was launched, despite the proximity of the Germans. Railwaymen love nothing more than a timetable, and within days, a schedule of four trains per day, starting at 0600 hours from Cherbourg and with the last return from Carentan at 1800 hours, was established. The details were proudly published in a timetable booklet typical of the day, the sort produced by any self-regarding railroad company, with a cover that read:

US Military Railroad, Cherbourg Peninsula Division, Timetable Number 1, comes into force 00 01, 17th July 1944, for the information and government of Military Personnel, C.L. Burpee, Brigadier General, General Manager, 2nd Military Railway Service

The booklet contained the precise timing of arrivals at each station, along with mileage charts. Publishing this little leaflet was testimony to the fact that these soldiers were, at their core, railwaymen, and ones who took immense care and pride in providing reliable train service under extraordinary circumstances. Indeed, they ran what they called a "first-class service" given the excellent rolling stock that had been left behind for both military personnel and local people, who flocked to use the line. Right from the start, fares were charged to the locals, who needed permission from the army's Civil Affairs to travel on the railway. Military personnel, however, could use the service for free just by showing their uniform, and the instructions noted that "the MRS [Military Railroad Service] is not concerned if a soldier is AWOL [absent without leave]," presumably to avoid provoking disputes mid-travel. Unfortunately, by the end of the first week, however, services were temporarily reduced to two trips per day due to the shortage of locomotives.

As soon as the line to Carentan was open, the soldier-railwaymen went to work expanding the railway, both on the main line and along the branches—a further 9 miles on July 15, 10 miles the following day, and another 16 miles by the eighteenth. By July 22, the line running along the west side of the Cherbourg Peninsula, and the gateway to the crucial town of Avranches at the foot of the Cotentin, reached Folligny, although work in the devastated yards continued apace. The rebuilding of the railways by the British and American forces was an incremental process with dramatic impact. Two hundred fifty-nine miles were operational by August 10, many more than Overlord had envisaged by that date.

These reopened lines, however, were by no means entirely safe. On the day General Burpee took Lieutenant General Lee, commander of the General Communication Zone of the European Theater of Operations, United States Army (ETOUSA), for a rail trip to Carentan, the town was shelled, resulting in several casualties. Burpee spoke to a company of troops hard at work on reinforcing a bridge, and they told him they had faced intermittent fire ever since they started on the project after the capture of Cherbourg. And it was not just the workers; the safety of rail passengers could not be guaranteed either. For the first two weeks of services running from Cherbourg, the tracks to Carentan paralleled the German front line and "every time an engine steamed along it, the Germans opened up on it with their eight-eights."[21] These "eight-eights" were highly effective guns originally used for antiaircraft fire but that had been adapted for use against tanks and, now, train cars.

Even after Cherbourg was liberated and trains started operating out of the port, the railroad workers were unable to forget they were in a war zone. Freight trains, mainly carrying cement for reconstructing the port, started arriving in Cherbourg on July 13, and troop trains began operating out of the city a few days later, even though the railway was not secure. An article in *Railway Age* describes these first days of operations: "Combat forces were still in town; so were the snipers. Everyone wore his steel helmet and arms. Nobody wandered about at night."[22] The article, written just a few months after D-Day, recounts how early railroaders had to operate trains in conditions that would have tested far more experienced men: "The initial operation was accomplished entirely with captured power and rolling stock operated over hastily reconstructed track by young G.I. engine crews who in many cases had less than a year behind them in a cab of an American locomotive."[23] If that wasn't hard enough, the crews drove mostly at night, and although the Allies dominated the air, there were "still daily visits from Jerry," the Luftwaffe. The author evocatively describes: "Imagine yourself climbing pulling back the throttle moving over some very bad track that you know disappears beyond the next hill to an indefinite place they call 'Carentan,' you will have a picture of the courage and initiative shown by the G.I. cheminots."[24]

The men's lack of experience and working on a strange, foreign railway meant that basic operational errors compounded the difficulties caused by the ever-present "Jerries." Although a few experienced *cheminots* with knowledge of the local tracks had come forward, many of the young GIs faced unprecedented situations without any help from the locals. For example, most of the early trains consisted of 50 freight cars, weighing a total of 1,000 tons, and required double-heading to ensure there was enough power to climb grades. However, a lack of communication between the two crews resulted in frequent stalls, and sorting out a service that had been stopped halfway up an incline relied on clear instructions but was made terribly difficult because communication with dispatchers was impossible in the absence of a telegraph system. Instead, the crews had to muddle through as best as they could—with drastic results. On one occasion, no fewer than six drawbars to which the railcars are attached were broken before the train was able to proceed.

If one train broke down, the solution often was to break it into two to lighten the load and run half the train into a sidetrack to allow other services through. But coordinating such an effort was extremely haphazard, and at times, trains, which for safety reasons were dispatched at half-hourly intervals, were backed up for several miles, presenting an easy target had the Luftwaffe been more active. Finding water for trains in this situation was another cause of delay, and it was not unknown for crews to simply rig up a flow from a nearby pond or river.

As a result of these myriad issues, crews frequently worked for 72 hours straight, living off the ubiquitous K rations and never knowing what faced them down the tracks. They were dispatched with no idea of how long it would take to reach their destination or what to do once they got there, as all too often no path (slot) could be found to enable a return working. Engineers and their military commanders occasionally argued over which trains should be prioritized and which left in sidetracks. The postwar report on these early services around Cherbourg is clear about what should have been done: "Much of this could have been avoided if an officer had been put in charge of say, each group of six trains to untangle such problems and make spot decisions."[25] Alas, this often did not happen.

Despite the challenges, much effort was put into trying to make the system more efficient. The trains, which each carried only one type of freight, were dispatched in a set order—ammunition, gasoline, and medical supplies—to facilitate off-loading at the railhead. At railheads, specialist battalions then transferred supplies to trucks for delivery to the dumps, which were mostly open-air warehouses. The fundamental problem was that, despite all the preparations, no one had worked out the precise way these military railways would operate. Though the Military Railroad Service was staffed with experienced railway personnel, it was, in effect, merely the supplier of services that worked for the Movements Division and, consequently, had little say in deciding priorities. Many delays were caused by overloading freight cars, which was a result of lack of knowledge by Movements Division officers, who were not railwaymen and did not understand technicalities and limitations regarding loading and weight. This mirrored similar mistakes made in past wars; putting inexperienced people in charge of any complicated system, such as a railway, frequently led to preventable mistakes.[26]

Gradually, the overloading issue was resolved as the Military Railway Service was given more information about what needed to be carried and the crews became more knowledgeable about local conditions. Their long shifts, too, were reduced as different battalions took responsibility for shorter stretches of track, enabling the drivers and firemen to be replaced by a fresh crew at the end of a section rather than having to continue all the way to the train's destination. A communications and signaling system was implemented, greatly improving the service's efficiency, with every railway battalion including a company of 24 men responsible for these two crucial functions.

Invariably, however, numerous complications plagued the service. Communications were down frequently when bombs dropped near lines or departing Germans engaged in sabotage. The telegraph lines that accompanied every railway carrying messages between stations were frequently out of commission, requiring the signaling and telecommunications men to rig up temporary solutions. Salvaging existing sections often proved to be more time-consuming than simply creating a new communications system. The key was to run at least one wire alongside the track, but this required considerable ingenuity because often the telegraph poles had collapsed or been removed by retreating Germans. As a solution, lines were strung across trees and hedges or attached loosely across roads using whatever poles or newly felled trees were available. Unsurprisingly, hastily created systems were vulnerable and could easily be severed by German sympathizers or stragglers and consequently required frequent repairs. To carry out the work, a jeep had to be dispatched across the section of line with orders scrawled on any available scrap of paper. At times, the recipients of these orders were bemused to find that they had been written on sheets from abandoned notebooks of German dispatch orders adorned with Nazi insignia and headed with titles in elegant Gothic font.

Establishing a signaling system was a more difficult process. To avoid the possibility of deadly head-on crashes, two-way traffic was prohibited on single lines, which greatly impeded the return of empty stock that was so essential for continuing operations. The only way stock could be returned, then, was to halt all the trains heading toward the front and channel them into sidetracks before any trains were allowed to run in the opposite direction. Inevitably, there was much improvisation. Sometimes the signaling system consisted solely of "blockmen" standing by the track every mile or so holding up boards indicating whether the trains should proceed or stop. This was dangerous work. Signalmen often stood in isolated locations, without the protection of escorts, and thus were highly vulnerable to attack by groups of enemy soldiers displaced by the fighting. At night, according to the army report on railway operation, "in the absence of a signal system, for example, flagging of trains during darkness was at first accomplished largely with flashlights, cigarette lighters, and even lighted cigarettes."[27] Trains often had to run significant distances with these primitive signaling systems, resulting in frequent, though mostly low-speed collisions and derailments.

In effect, these signalers were the vanguard because they often worked nearest the enemy lines. The report on the capture of Cherbourg explained that "at this point many of the signalmen erecting these lines were often on the tail of the retreating German Army. They were subject to shellfire, and were working at the utmost speed with a minimum of tools and equipment. The plan was to string [a] temporary line for use until more permanent facilities could be established."[28] At times, the train drivers were simply at the mercy of the dispatchers, who might have had little idea of what was happening on the tracks a couple of miles down the line. As such, trains could be held up for long periods. According to the military report: "The story of the first group of trains which ran east from the Cherbourg Peninsula is highlighted by many wild dashes across the country by couriers in jeeps, while loaded trains stood waiting all along the line, tied up because of the lack of orders."[29]

Henry Mettze, a 25-year-old brakeman who served with the US 732nd Railway Operating Battalion, worked on these early trains and reflected on the chaos of his working environment: "Everything was in a blackout. We had no headlights and it was surprising there were not more wrecks."[30] As the brakeman, whenever the locomotive came to a halt, he would have to "walk to the back of the train and down the track to light flares so other trains would know we were stopped—nothing worked, there was no timing—we just had orders." His team also had to contend with the effects of sabotage: "Tracks and bridges had been blown up and we had to deal with that," which involved quickly patching breaks in the track with rails brought from other lines and using wood from fallen trees for the sleepers. He, like all his men, carried a pistol, but there were no guns onboard to protect the trains, which, when the engines were fired up, could be easily detected by the enemy: "When you ran the engine, huge plumes of black and gray smoke spew up in the air, immediately announcing your position to the German air force. Yet, you ran the train and moved the troops where they were needed."

The dependence on stock the Germans had left behind was reduced somewhat by the liberation of Cherbourg because the arrival of Allied rolling stock sped up. The ubiquitous Colonel Bingham, who was now in charge of bringing over vast numbers of locomotives and freight cars, became a cross-Channel commuter in order to supervise the loading and unloading of stock. In addition to the landing craft, three British train ferries—*Hampton*, *Twickenham*, and the rather incongruously named *Royal Daffodil*, all owned by the Southern Railway—were redeployed. The first ferry arrived at the port on July 29.

Starting in early August, the Americans used two "sea trains," the *Lakehurst* and the *Texas*, vessels designed specifically to carry loaded freight cars that obviated the need to load and unload supplies at the dockside. Much bigger than the train ferries, they were significantly more cumbersome, too, because the stock had to be loaded and unloaded by crane, whereas the train ferries had a roll-on roll-off system. Sea trains were deployed to the fullest extent from the start: the *Lakehurst*'s inaugural trip brought 16 diesel locomotives and 56 railcars of various types, such as tankers, flat cars, and cabooses; the *Texas* carried a similar number and 20 of the first steam-powered locomotives to land. In the operation's early stages, Montgomery had banned their use because of concern that the puffs of steam sent high into the air — the phenomenon much beloved by rail enthusiasts — would act as a target indicator for enemy artillery.

The first trip, however, was not without mishaps. As it was being unloaded and hauled beyond the deck, a steam locomotive from the *Texas* plunged to the bottom of Cherbourg harbor, as the result of a winch failure. The subsequent investigation found that the winches were not strong enough to hold the 72-ton locomotive but also revealed that the two winchmen had been on duty continuously for 36 hours, and consequently their tiredness may have been a contributing factor. Amazingly, the engine was rescued and, after repairs, was used in the war effort alongside its fellow locomotives. As a measure of the enduring importance of Cherbourg, 19,383 freight cars and 1,521 locomotives were to pass through the port by the end of 1944.

The buildup of the railway teams was equally rapid. After arriving on June 28, Burpee quickly set up the headquarters of the Second Military Railroad Service in an office building in the center of Cherbourg. (The first service operated in North Africa and Italy and would support the Allied forces in southern France after the Mediterranean landings in August 1944.) At the time, there were just 12 officers and 52 men of the MRS in Normandy, but by the end of July, this number had risen to a total of 161 officers and 3,324 men. The MRS was effectively a railway business in military clothing that worked through operating battalions such as the 728th (which ran trains in Cherbourg) and the 729th (which operated the line down the Cotentin Peninsula). The men operating, maintaining, and controlling the railways were mostly experienced railroaders. For example, the 728th had recruited from the Louisville and Nashville Railroad, while men of the 729th were from the New York, New Haven and Hartford Railroad. These operating battalions were also given responsibility for the maintenance of the track, whereas shop battalions were in charge of yards and depots, as well as supplying parts and equipment.

Initially, these battalions were under the control of the 707th Grand Division, which was effectively a regimental headquarters, the equivalent of the general manager's office in railway parlance. In other words, the Grand Division was responsible for strategic decisions on timetabling, maintenance schedules, rolling stock deployment, and operations. Like the operating battalions, the 707th Grand Division was sponsored by a railway company, the Southern Railway (the American railroad, not the British company of the same name). This organizational structure would be replicated across France and the rest of the European theater. Unlike in Italy, where US and British forces joined to create a single organization, the Military Railway Service was strictly a US operation. Each battalion, which, apart from the occasional exception, was sponsored by a US railway company, consisted of around 800 men and two dozen officers and generally had four companies that dealt, respectively, with headquarters and signals, train dispatching and communications, maintenance and structures, and train operations.

Eventually, about 10 Grand Divisions were overseeing 52 operating battalions and a half dozen shop battalions. By the end of the war, 44,000 men were serving in railway units, the vast majority in northern Europe. The Second Military Railway Service had become the busiest railway operator in continental Europe. The British railway operating companies remained separate, running trains in the French territory to the northeast of the American units and eventually encompassing parts of Belgium, Germany, and Holland.

In the first 10 days after services started in and out of Cherbourg, the Second Military Railroad Service was operating an average of 30 trains per day, and already some 60,000 tons of supplies had been carried. Cherbourg became a bustling port once again, and its citizens had to cope with what they found to be a surprising phenomenon: more than half the troops working on the reconstruction were from what were then called "negro" regiments. In fact, the author of the army report seemed rather surprised to find that "there was little trouble between Negro and white soldiers, but both were the subject of complaints filed by citizens."[31]

The buildup in the lodgment area was impressively fast. With ships able to cross the Channel safely and the Luftwaffe effectively powerless, huge quantities of supplies were landing alongside whole divisions of men. The sheer numbers were staggering. While on D-Day, 59,900 personnel, 8,900 vehicles, and 1,900 tons of stores were landed, that number grew exponentially over the next 50 days. By July 25, there were as many as 631,000 personnel, 153,000 vehicles, and 689,000 tons of stores in France. All those men and supplies were stuck in the tiny, crowded lodgment area, which had expanded far more slowly than anticipated. It was time to break out.

And that was the idea. On August 1, General George Patton, whose brilliance as a tactician was at times masked by his impulsive and hotheaded manner, took over the Third Army and immediately set about disrupting all the strategists' carefully laid plans. He had bided his time for two months in England as events in France unfolded, and now, at last, his chance to make a difference had arrived. First, his army was to head west and recapture Brittany before advancing steadily back toward Paris. But before this could happen, he had to wait for the First Army to break out of the lodgment at Saint-Lô. Backed by Montgomery, Patton argued that after the breakout, capturing the Seine ports of Le Havre and Rouen should be the next objective, followed by a rush to Paris rather than a detour to Brittany.

With this huge buildup behind them, the sweep through France could begin. The logistics, however, would prove problematic.

4

THE GREATEST CHALLENGE

The US Army's official account of the Normandy landings suggests that "until the breakout at St. Lô on 26 July, railroad reconstruction other than that on the Cotentin peninsula received relatively low priority."[1] Although that is *technically* correct, the large-scale reconstruction of the French rail network was always central to the Allies' invasion plans—and preparations were now in full swing. As we have observed, railroad troops started arriving as soon as the lodgment was established and got to work with alacrity right behind the front line, bringing the railway back into use as soon as possible. With Allied troops confined to a small section of the coast and the Cotentin Peninsula, the use of railways at this stage was limited because the distances were short, making rail transportation inefficient and uneconomic. Apart from a few loads, such as the cement taken to Cherbourg, no freight of any significance was hauled by rail during these early weeks—but this was about to change radically.

The Overlord planners envisioned that railroad reconstruction would intensify and expand rapidly following the breakout. In the first 50 days after D-Day, the invading troops and their supplies were confined to the small lodgment, but in the next 50 days, the armies moved forward at an average of 10 miles per day, taking over much of the territory of France and Belgium. Inevitably, this strained the whole logistics operation of the invading troops. As the subsequent analysis on the functioning of the Transportation Corps put it, "This movement far outstripped anything that had been considered in the original plan. It was during this stage that railroad reconstruction became a primary, rather than a secondary, ADSEC engineering mission."[2]

The need to extend the territory under Allied control became an urgent priority. Not only was the transport system in the lodgment paralyzed by the buildup of men arriving on the beaches and in the port, but also the front line was approximately 40 days behind the schedule set out in Overlord's plan. The breakout from the lodgment, originally planned for early July, was twice delayed—first by the Germans' stronger-than-expected resistance, then by bad weather. Operation Cobra, as the offensive to break through the German defenses was code-named, was eventually launched from Saint-Lô on July 25 but started in the worst possible way, with two of the most deadly friendly-fire incidents of the entire Allied European operation. The plan, devised by General Omar Bradley, commander of the US First Army, was to soften German resistance with a massive bombing campaign of more than 2,500 planes before breaking through around the village of Saint-Lô. To Bradley's east, British forces led by Montgomery were still unexpectedly tied up around Caen. Bradley reasoned that attacking Saint-Lô would put pressure on the Germans' western flank, both providing relief for the British and allowing Allied forces to finally break out of the peninsula.

The bombers' initial sorties were supposed to target a four-mile-long column of German forces on the main Cotentin road, with the idea that a large concentration of bomber aircraft would directly support units on the ground. The very proximity of the Allied troops, however, led to a tragic series of errors. In preliminary bombing the day before the ground attack was launched, several bomber aircraft approached the target from the wrong direction, attacking the line in an east–west direction instead of parallel to the road. The targets were supposed to be highlighted with colored smoke, but the wind, coming from an unexpected direction, pushed it toward the Allied forces. Several bombers dropped their bombs on the US troops, killing 25. Worse, the next day, the error was repeated, with an additional 111 Allied deaths, including that of General Lesley McNair, the highest-ranking US soldier to lose his life in the war. Although largely kept secret, this episode cast a pall over the subsequent progress of the Allied troops.

Despite these terrible setbacks, it was the beginning of the endgame for the Battle of Normandy, and Allied progress was swift. Within three days, Coutances, on the main road along the western side of the Cotentin Peninsula, was taken, and its capture was quickly followed by the fall of Avranches, the town at the foot of the peninsula through which the armies had to pass to reach the rest of France. Its capture on August 1 coincided with the official establishment of the Third Army led by General Patton and provided him with the perfect opportunity to demonstrate his emphasis on the need for armies to be mobile and to move forward as quickly as possible.

Avranches lies alongside the Sée, the northern of two rivers about four miles apart that flow westward to the bay of Mont Saint-Michel. Once traffic crossed the bridge over the Sée, there was only a single route leading to a second bridge over the Sélune just north of Pontaubault, where the highway split into roads accessing the East, South, and West. In other words, Avranches and its two rivers were the perfect bottleneck—a military strategist's nightmare. If traffic got stuck there, it would present an easy target for the remnants of the Luftwaffe.

Patton demonstrated that his reputation for speed was well deserved by threading his army of 200,000 men and 40,000 vehicles through this gap in the space of three days. To do so, he disobeyed all the conventions of army movement, according to the military author Geoffrey Perret: "Every manual on road movement was ground into the dust. He and his staff did what the whole world knew couldn't be done: it was flat impossible to put a whole army out on a narrow two-lane road and move it at high speed."[3] But Patton did precisely that. When, unsurprisingly, the traffic became snarled in Avranches, it was Patton himself who leaped into an empty police box in the town center and, for the next hour and a half, acted as a traffic cop to untangle the mess.

And he succeeded. The convoys started moving smoothly, even though few of the drivers could have realized that it was their commander, a three-star general, waving his arms furiously to direct them. According to one of his biographers, "Patton felt fear but never showed it. When he catapulted two corps through the narrow gap at Avranches, he had plenty of secret misgivings. A slight mishap or a traffic jam might have precipitated a total disaster. But throughout the operation, he was the essence of complete confidence and optimism."[4] That is, except when he was shouting at the jeep drivers to speed up.

Patton was both the most famous general of the Second World War and the most controversial. He cut his own path, judging, often correctly, that he knew better than his superior officers. In his book on Patton, historian Robert Allen accurately pinpoints the general's ambiguous character: "Patton always led his men. He did not rule them. Throughout his life, he completely dominated every unit he commanded. But in dominating, he did not domineer" — other than over his own superiors.[5] Patton clearly wanted to reach Paris as quickly as possible, and he was not going to be stopped by high command. As Allen explains, "Very few of his superiors liked him.... But all respected him professionally. Most of them feared him and were jealous of him."[6] As a result, "Patton fought two wars in the ETO [European Theater of Operations]—one against the Germans, the other against higher authorities for permission to fight the enemy."[7]

Patton's achievement in mobilizing the army so quickly was all the more impressive because the various units were intermingled, something that should never happen according to conventional military practice, and yet, they came out the other end as ordered divisions prepared to fight. The army was finally ready and the rest of France beckoned. Initially, Patton's idea had been that Brittany, to the west, should be the initial target, but on August 3, Patton received revised orders. It was decided that the Third Army should split in two, and the main thrust would be made east toward Le Mans and Paris rather than westward. This entailed the capture and retention of a huge swathe of territory stretching south to the right bank of the Loire. To the east, he was to take over a 60-mile stretch of the river Mayenne, which ran on a north–south axis. Although he had no specific orders for any action beyond the Mayenne, Patton's ambitions looked further forward. As the army report on the breakout suggests, Patton "was thinking of an eventual Third Army advance forty-five miles beyond Laval to Le Mans—to the east. When, by which unit, and how this was to be done, he did not say."[8] It was typical Patton, ever eager to drive onward, beyond what his commanders expected but not always having planned precisely how.

Progress in Brittany, from which the Germans had removed all their mobile units, was remarkably rapid. With the help of a very active French Resistance, which was morphing into an official fighting force, the Allied forces captured Quiberon Bay in the south of Brittany by August 5 and started attacking Saint-Malo, 40 miles west of Avranches. Brittany became something of an irrelevance because its ports were too far from the main theaters of war to be the principal line of communication, an obvious fact that the planners had strangely overlooked.

The main thrust, therefore, was eastward, and progress was swift here, too. Possibly too swift. After weeks of being stuck in the hedgerows, where every yard was fought for, the troops were now advancing at a rapid 20 miles per hour through territory that the enemy had mostly abandoned. It was tempting—but a mistake—to think they could continue at this pace all the way through France.

The movement toward Le Mans and ultimately Paris was led by the Ninetieth Infantry Division, which first headed toward the town of Mayenne, halfway between Avranches and Le Mans, with the intention of reaching it before the key road bridge over the eponymous river was destroyed. They met with little resistance, as the bulk of the German Seventh Army was to the north. Thanks to a rapid attack by the Ninetieth, the bridge at Mayenne was captured intact on August 5, thus opening the route to Le Mans just 45 miles away, a town Patton immediately obtained permission to try to capture. This was part of a wider new plan based on the rapid advances that Patton had achieved. Eager to deliver a decisive blow to German forces west of the Seine, Patton ordered the Third Army to continue its eastward drive to secure crossings over the Sarthe River, just west of Le Mans, in preparation for an advance to occupy the Chartres plain and close the Paris–Orléans gap between the Seine and the Loire. Accordingly, the US forces pushed beyond Mayenne, and on August 7, they advanced to within 12 miles of Le Mans, which had been the headquarters of the German Seventh Army but was now being hastily abandoned. Though the US troops met some opposition, an armored division bypassed Le Mans to the south, then swung around back toward the eastern outskirts of the city, forcing the remaining Germans to escape to the north. By midnight of August 8, Le Mans was surrounded, with all exits closed off, and infantrymen starting to clear the streets of stragglers and the few remaining holdouts.

This was extraordinary progress by any standard. In four days, the Third Army's XV Corps, led by General Wade H. Haislip, had progressed about 75 miles, from the Saint-Hilaire–Fougères line just south of the Cotentin all the way to Le Mans, at very little cost of men or machinery. Moreover, the speed of the advance had frustrated German plans to organize strong defensive campaigns at Laval and Le Mans and also opened the way to progress both to the east and to the north, where the German Seventh Army was still located.

The Allies' confidence was boosted by the failure of a German counterattack at Mortain, which could have breached the supply line between Cherbourg and the Third Army. But Bradley had been prepared for it, and the First Army saw off the attack with some fierce fighting. Thankfully, the whole of the Cotentin had been made safe.

This was perfect preparation for crossing the Seine, once its bridges were rebuilt, and proceeding farther east. But there was a problem. Rather than lagging behind the timetable set out in Overlord, Patton's haste meant that the Allied forces were well ahead of schedule, which raised concerns among the logistical planners that the supply line would not be able to sustain the advance.

At long last, the railways came into their own. From being a marginal part of the logistics, they were now at its heart. The Overlord strategists knew there could never be enough truck capacity to catch up with the expected rate of advance. And the unexpected speed of the advance only exacerbated the potential supply difficulties. To reach the Seine by the end of August, "the planners estimated there would be a shortage of 127 truck companies which could be compensated for only by additional rail reconstruction."[9] Long-distance truck transport depended on having a series of intermediate depots, and the speed of advance meant it was impossible to establish these dumps; additionally, no spare truck companies were available to take on this role. Railways were the only option, as the report on the Transportation Corps later explained: "It was only after July 30th, when our railway lines began their expansion eastward toward Le Mans and southward into Britainny [*sic*], that freight operations were possible on a large scale."[10] Moreover, the speed of progress made it more important for the railways to be brought quickly into use: "The first important demand for deliveries by rail resulted directly from the Third Army's forward lunge at the beginning of August. Rail transportation suddenly became economical and essential, for the long hauls to the army area immediately placed a heavy strain on motor transport."[11]

This was the reason rehabilitation of the railways in newly occupied territory began almost as soon as territory was taken. Nearly overnight, the railway companies that had been pouring into Cherbourg over the previous month went from being relatively idle to having their hands full. Top of the agenda was the reconstruction of the yards at Saint-Lô that had been almost entirely destroyed by Allied bombing and that were now needed to help bring supplies farther into France. So complete was the destruction of the yards that engineers had to ask for plans from the SNCF before they could work out how to re-lay the track.

On August 4, two companies of the 347th General Service Regiment began work at Saint-Lô. However, as a general regiment, they did not have sufficient access to specialized equipment and were forced to recycle existing material or use supplies hauled from beach dumps in trucks. They discovered that the track at Saint-Lô station was buried under "a mass of rubble and steel including many damaged railway cars [that] was piled many feet above the original track grade."[12] Simultaneously, two other general service engineer regiments began working on the main Saint-Lô to Rennes–Le Mans line, though a later discovery of a large bridge blown up by the Resistance

at Laval meant that this route to Le Mans would not become available until late August at the earliest.

As an illustration of the type of work involved in these hasty
reconstructions, on an eight-mile length of line between Saint-Lô
and Torigny, "1,575 feet of track was destroyed, 10 craters needed
filling, 15 rails needed replacement at scattered places and one turn-
out was destroyed. In addition a concrete overpass two miles west of
Torigny had collapsed on the rail line, destroying 75 feet of track."[13]
Repairing this damage, together with sorting out the destruction farther down the line caused by four blown-up ammunition railcars,
became the responsibility of Company A of the 347th.

Other companies of the 347th began rebuilding the double-track
masonry-arch railway bridge over the Vire River on the Lison–
Saint-Lô line. One of the three spans had collapsed into the river,
and a second was severely damaged. Even though the engineers had
not yet received any training in military bridging, they were able to
replace the central span with a timber-trestle section and repair the
damaged span with stone and concrete. Simultaneously, the engineers rehabilitated two single-track lines, one south of Saint-Lô and
the other to the west. The track running to Vire, about 20 miles
southeast of Saint-Lô, would provide an alternate route to the main
line down the west side of the Cotentin, which ran from La Haye-du-
Puits to Coutances and Avranches.

The official history of the 347th, published right after the war,
describes an "interesting incident" in the unemotional language of
military reports that in reality was a quite astonishing act of courage.
While investigating a small collapsed railway bridge near Coutances,
the company sergeant, John N. Bertrand, spotted an antipersonnel
mine protruding from the ground. As he walked toward it, he heard a
telltale click under his foot. He stopped instantly, keeping his foot on
the device, and, expecting it was his last moment on earth, shouted

to his colleagues to flee. To his good fortune, there was no explosion, only a seeping of mustard gas that burned his legs. According to the official account, "This was the only incident in which an American soldier had walked on one of these mines without receiving serious wounds."[14] Not surprisingly, Bertrand received the Purple Heart given to all wounded service personnel.

In the event, just 10 days after the breakout, an unprecedented and unexpected order was issued by Third Army headquarters that forced the 347th to stop much of this work immediately. As the report into this crucial incident would later explain, "On August 12th, it became apparent that unless rail construction could be pushed more rapidly, the Third Army would be halted for lack of supplies."[15] Patton, however, was not a man who paid much heed to details. If troops had to be somewhere, and somewhere fast, then they would be. If supplies were needed, and needed immediately, then they would arrive. As a cavalryman, it was not his business to sort these things out — that was the job of the engineers, the logistics people, and the transportation units. Decisions about the feasibility of maintaining a line of communication to a forward position were not within his purview — or concern.

However, in this instance, things were different. Patton's impatience served a greater purpose. Speed was of the essence to ensure the Third Army's progress toward Paris. The French capital was his goal. Marching his troops down the Champs-Élysées had always been his aim, ever since he was appointed to head the Third Army. The risk of leaving his advance troops without supplies, crucially gasoline, threatened to stymie this prospect. To stall now, to waste time while supplies arrived, was unthinkable. It could delay the end of the conflict or, even worse, affect its outcome since at this time the ultimate result still remained uncertain.

This, at least in part, explains why the order given to Colonel Itschner was so specific and comprehensive. Of course, army orders never brook argument or dissent, but this one was exceptional in its all-encompassing nature and extremely demanding timetable. First issued on the morning of August 12, 1944, the order involved a complete reallocation of resources and objectives:

> *General Patton has broken through and is striking rapidly for Paris. He says his men can get along without food, but his tanks and trucks won't run without gas. Therefore the railroad must be constructed to Le Mans by Tuesday midnight.*[16]

Specifically, the order required the following:

> *The construction of a line to Mayenne by Tuesday noon August 15 and to Le Mans by the same time.... [The completion of these lines is] so important that the success of the current and impending operations is clearly dependent upon it.*

Patton's breakthrough and unexpectedly swift progress had demonstrated the extent to which such a daring approach could reap dividends. His strategy was predicated on momentum and aggression, and he relied on advance scouting parties to determine the enemy's strength and positions. However, this tactic resulted in an ever-lengthening supply route, which was a constant concern to the strategists behind the lines. Patton's sweep through France was later described as unprecedented. Historian Robert Allen, himself a veteran of the war, concluded that the Third Army "had advanced farther and faster than any army in all history. It had conquered more territory than any other army in a comparable time. Now it was closing in for a great kill."[17] Such a move would have trapped the German Seventh Army between the English Channel and the Allied forces, which had advanced south and east of the enemy's position in northern Normandy.

However, in one of the most controversial decisions made by the high command in the post-D-Day battles, this did not happen. Patton was stopped—not by the Germans but by his own superiors—from launching an all-out assault on the German Seventh Army, which Patton was convinced would have brought an early end to the war.

Later, this episode was considered to be a great missed opportunity. The Seventh Army was almost encircled at the time, meaning that a quick closure of the only possible escape route—the Falaise Gap—could have entirely defeated it. However, on August 13, Bradley ordered Patton to halt the advance over fears that he did not have sufficient resources to maintain an encirclement, and consequently, an estimated 20,000 to 40,000 German soldiers managed to pass through before the gap was eventually closed a week later. Bradley's many critics saw allowing those soldiers to escape as a mistake, but in fact the Germans still suffered great losses in the battle—10,000 dead and 50,000 prisoners, as well as leaving behind much of their equipment.

Stymied by his superiors, Patton's new focus after reaching Le Mans was therefore to push as quickly as possible to the Seine and then, if the river could be successfully crossed, achieve his goal of reaching Paris ahead of the Overlord schedule. But, again, overrunning his supply line threatened to stall his advance, and as we have seen, Patton hated static armies. He was now too far from Cherbourg to rely on trucks to deliver the fuel he needed to continue the advance, and the pipeline from the ports that was designed to supply the frontline troops ran only as far as Saint-Lô, nearly 150 miles from Le Mans.

There was only one way to keep fueling his army: by rail. In fact, the enormous fuel requirements of the fast-moving Third Army had been anticipated almost as soon as the force officially came into being at the beginning of August. The 728th Railroad Operating Battalion, sponsored by the Louisville and Nashville Railroad Company and one of the first railway regiments to land in Normandy, was given the task of repairing the fuel tank cars that had been recovered in and around Cherbourg.

At an urgent 3:00 a.m. meeting on August 1, an order was given to Carl Love, the commander of the 728th, to prioritize the transport of gasoline. According to a history of the 728th: "The reason given for the priority was that Patton needed the gasoline and other matriel [sic] for the completion of his St. Lô campaign, which would complete the breakout from the Normandy peninsula. From this point onward, members of the 728th worked 12, 14, 16, and even 24-hour days to expedite the movement of supplies to the front."[18] Indeed, by August 12, there were already five general engineering service units working on restoring lines in the Cotentin to run trains through to Avranches.

In short, Patton issued the order to rebuild and put into operation more than 100 miles of railway track in just over three days. Itschner's first move was to fly over the railroad from the line's starting point at Folligny all the way to Le Mans to select the route that could be repaired in the shortest time. The most direct course would have led from Folligny down the Cotentin via Avranches to Pontaubault, then south to Vitré directly west of Rennes, where it would turn east using the main line via Laval to Le Mans. Unfortunately, Itschner had to rule out this route because the spans and piers on two bridges had been brought down and there was no chance they could be reconstructed in time. One was a 40-foot-high bridge over the short Sélune, a river through the town of Pontaubault just south of Avranches; the other, a 90-foot-high bridge over the Mayenne at Laval, blown up earlier by the Resistance.

Instead, following information gleaned from his flight and the aerial photography taken by Roosevelt Junior's team, Itschner settled on a cross-country route over obscure minor railway tracks that were never intended to be used as a vital war supply route. Just before Pontaubault, the route turned east through Saint-Hilaire-du-Harcouët, then veered south to Fougères before turning east again to the town of Mayenne. There, another rural line headed south, where, at last, the main line beyond the collapsed bridge at Laval could be rejoined through to Le Mans. The whole route was 135 miles long, adding some 30 miles to the usual journey on the main line between Folligny and Le Mans but with the benefit of using tracks that had suffered far less war damage. The subsequent Transportation Corps report outlined the task: "Very briefly, here is what this job entailed. It meant the rebuilding of seven railway bridges; the repair and laying out of new main lines in three railway yards; the laying of many miles of new lines approaching the yards and the bridges and which had lain in the target area; and the provision of facilities, such as watering points for locomotives where watering towers had been damaged."[19] All this involved bringing the railway up to standard in 75 hours, a job that in normal circumstances would have taken weeks if not months and that "seemed impossible," according to the report.

Moreover, the work was not merely a matter of repairing the line, as the route also had to be upgraded and improved. The line running through this sparsely populated rural department normally carried only modest two-carriage passenger trains that, in peacetime, would have trundled gently between the numerous villages and small towns of southern Normandy carrying a few local farmers and their produce. These single-track lines had been built during the French railway boom of the 1870s, when a new national government was intent on connecting every small settlement across the nation. In the effort to link the deepest rural parts of what is known as France profonde, the government provided generous funding to the local authorities to carry out this work. However, in the interwar period these minor railways struggled in the face of competition from road vehicles, and little money was available from the local authorities to maintain them. Indeed, it was precisely small rural lines like these that had suffered most from the overall neglect of the French rail network in the years before World War II. Their parlous state made the task of bringing them up to standard all the more difficult.

Even before Patton's order had been transmitted, work had started on establishing the line down the Cotentin between Cherbourg and Avranches, which would ultimately form part of the supply route through to Le Mans. On August 10, Company A of the 347th, which had been reconstructing the line between Saint-Lô and Vire, was moved farther down to work on the line around Folligny, and Company E was deployed on the section between Folligny and Montviron, halfway to Avranches. The following day, Company C began work on repairing the bridge at Pontaubault and reconstructing the line east to Saint-Hilaire, where another crucial bridge was down, while Company B was allocated the 18 miles between Villedieu and Vire.

Meanwhile, at Coutances, D Company of the 347th rapidly repaired a damaged viaduct railroad bridge, a very typical design found across France. One of the six spans of the single-track masonry-arch bridge, whose tracks ran high over the Soulle River, needed replacing. American engineers used the British Bailey bridge system, which involved pushing a "launching nose" across to span the gap. This initial section was then supported by timber struts. The viaduct was the first of many such railway bridges to be replaced in this way. As the subsequent report explained, rebuilding a bridge that was just 18 feet wide but 80 feet above the river was a complex task because of the lack of space in which to maneuver equipment. Nevertheless, work started on August 6; the men used a massive 250 cubic yards of concrete (as a measure, a wheelbarrow can typically carry around a tenth of a cubic yard) to support the embankment and completed the job on August 12. The engineers demonstrated their complete confidence in the stability of the construction by inviting Major General Cecil R. Moore, the chief engineer of ETOUSA, to ride on the first train across the bridge, which according to the history of the 347th was carried out "without mishap." His very presence emphasized the importance with which such work was regarded by the top echelons of the military, and he complimented the men on their "splendid achievement."

The project set out in Patton's instructions was doubly challenging given the time available and the need not just to reinstate the railway but also to make these winding, rural tracks suitable for carrying the heavy freight of military traffic. Therefore, eight new passing points were to be added to increase the capacity of the line. Moreover, considering that the local railway services had long been shut down because of war damage and the staff had disappeared, the incoming troops had to create a safe railway out of lines abandoned by the SNCF as well as ensuring the trains were protected from attack by German soldiers operating in the area. However, there was no alternative plan. The order sent out by Itschner after his flight over the railway made this clear: "Every stretch of demolished railway must be worked on simultaneously. If additional strength is required to do this, information to that effect must be sent to the temporary OP [observation post] of this HQ at Fougères railway station."[20]

Itschner, as it happens, possessed precisely the right skills for the job, even though he had become a military man by accident. In school at the tender age of 15, he had joined an Illinois militia that had formed during the First World War to patrol the streets during the 1918 race riots in Chicago. His calm demeanor under pressure was spotted by his superior officer, who recommended him to West Point, where he graduated in 1924. After earning a degree from Cornell University, Itschner worked on road construction for army projects in Alaska and Mississippi. In the early part of World War II, he was given responsibility for the construction of military airfields across the United States, an urgent task that, like the Avranches–Le Mans railway project, involved huge numbers of men.

By 1943, Itschner arrived in London to work on the planning of engineering projects that would be needed to support the invasion of continental Europe. In an unpublished interview, he recounted how he was involved in drawing a map of Cherbourg and its harbor from aerial photographs and how this proved to be invaluable when he later crossed the Channel as a chief engineer. There was no doubt he was the right person to be in charge of the railway project. According to an analysis of ADSEC's effectiveness written in 1945: "Colonel Itschner has a rich administrative ability and a rare faculty for conveying to subordinates a feeling of complete fairness and detachment in all decisions, yet a real concern for their personal welfare [which] accounts to a large degree for the day and night devotion to their jobs that ADSEC engineers have displayed since D-Day."[21]

Itschner responded to Patton's instructions by issuing Order No. 7, which was sent immediately to every railway regiment and service unit that could be mustered to help rebuild the line. The order included this statement: "Work on all other railway lines will cease at once, even at the cost of efficiency in order to concentrate on the line given above."[22] Specifically, Order No. 7 countermanded previous instructions sent out only a day or so earlier, suggesting that behind the scenes Patton had won the argument for speeding up his progress toward Paris, something that, in all likelihood, he had always intended.

Patton expected the line to be ready before the deadline, so the urgency of the matter was emphasized in Itschner's order: "If possible, the date should be beaten—hours count." The manpower requirements were unprecedented: "Use one man per foot if necessary." Around 2,000 men were in situ, but another 8,000 scattered around the lodgment would be called in for the task. It is likely that no other single engineering task in the whole of World War II required the immediate attention of 10,000 men.

All this haste came about because Patton had specifically emphasized that, although his men could get along without food, his tanks and trucks could not run without gas. His desperation for fuel was based on a calculation that the sweep through France could only continue if 31 trains were delivered to Le Mans, and the first train needed to set out by midnight on August 15. How he arrived at this precise figure of 31 (subsequently reported as a range of numbers between 30 and 36) is something of a mystery, although it seems to have been based on an estimate that each train could haul 1,000 tons and that the advance to Paris would require 25,000 tons of POL (petrol, oil, and lubricants) along with other supplies, principally ammunition.

The report on the line's rebuilding provides more detail of the work needed: "Despite the fact that the enemy had had little time for thorough destruction of the rail system in the headlong retreat into which he had been thrown, the damage of this area due to artillery fire, bombings, wrecked trains, completely demolished rail yards and a demolition of major bridges by German sappers posed a traffic problem in meeting this stringent deadline."[23] That was something of an understatement. Just to make matters even more challenging, there were no telecommunications between the various work parties on the line. Instead, contact between units — such as messages about the need for extra personnel or equipment — had to be carried out by jeep messengers, who raced perilously close to enemy lines on minor roads, many of which were in poor condition.

Despite the large number of men already deployed on the various lines across the Cotentin Peninsula, when Order No. 7 went out, the line between Cherbourg and Avranches was nowhere near complete and reconstruction of this section had to be accelerated simultaneously with the start of work on the route farther south. The order was very specific about how the reopening of the line could be achieved by reallocating resources and setting out the precise role for each available regiment. Every part of the line, as well as every task, was assigned to a specific unit, and several newly arrived regiments were "attached" to existing units, increasing the number of men available on particularly challenging sections of track.

Initially, 11 engineering general service regiments were allocated sections of the line to repair because most of the railway battalions were not yet available. For example, the 390th was given responsibility for the repair of the Folligny yard, the key railhead on the Cotentin south of Cherbourg. As the report puts it (with no hint of irony), "The yards at Folligny had been particularly well bombed."[24] Two days after D-Day, the bombers had completely destroyed a large German troop train, causing hundreds of casualties. According to the report, "Work which had been proceeding at a normal pace was accelerated when the Third U.S. Army demands became known, and with additional equipment rushed in, a single line through the yard with additional trackage to take care of traffic problems was completed by August 13th."[25]

A single line used by all trains heading for Le Mans was similarly squeezed through the wreckage of Avranches station, which had also suffered extensive damage from the Allied air attacks. To avoid the major collapsed bridge at Pontaubault, one of the two adjudged too wrecked to be repaired quickly, the line just south of Avranches diverted 15 miles east to Saint-Hilaire-du-Harcouët. This required the repair of five smaller bridges, but it was the one near Saint-Hilaire that proved challenging. Indeed, of all the tasks of reconstructing the line, that bridge's repair was the most difficult undertaking and posed the greatest risk of failure in meeting Patton's deadline. Here, too, the 347th was in charge, but given the difficulty of the task, they were supplemented by men from the 341st Engineer General Service Regiment.

A French observer, Robert Lerouvillois, who arrived on August 12 when the bridge reconstruction began, was aghast at the chaotic process, particularly given the proximity of the enemy: "It was a human ant hill at the north east end of the town around the bridge over the Sélune. Lorries, cranes, bulldozers, compressors. The most extraordinary aspect is that apparently this demented activity had, despite the sound of distant explosions, no relation to the fierce battle taking place, a mere 14 kilometres away"[26]—a reference to the Germans' counterattack at Mortain, which fortunately fizzled out the following day. Rather more comfortingly, the Allied army was also close by, as reported by the *Military Engineer*: "Even as the General Service Regiment constructing the railway was at work on the railroad right of way, combat engineers from the Third Army, less than 25 yards distant on the highway, were strengthening a Bailey bridge over which troops were passing."[27]

The anonymous author in the *Military Engineer*, writing in late 1944, just a few months after witnessing the event, waxed lyrical:

*For me, there was something symbolic in that meeting of combat
and SOS Engineers at Ste. Hilaire; in one sweeping glance, you
could see men who, night and day, and night after night, and
day after day, pressed hard upon the Nazi soldiers' heels. And
you could see, too, these men who, night and day for months on
end made it possible for the fighting forces constantly to blow
hard upon the retreating Nazis' necks by keeping supplies rolling to the front. Here, at a glance, you could see the supply lines
meet the battle lines and I think the meeting was good for all
concerned.*[28]

This was a seminal moment for the engineers toiling away on the
bridge. The fact that the soldiers heading for the front, the very men
who would ultimately use the supplies the railway would transport,
were in full sight of those repairing the bridge gave the engineers an
added sense of urgency in rebuilding it. There was, as Lerouvillois
observed, no shortage of men available, but there was still a fierce
debate over how to repair the bridge itself, which jeopardized the
engineers' ability to meet their deadline. The bridge was about 100
feet long, and a bomb had demolished a support, resulting in one end
dropping about 15 feet to the riverbank.

When Itschner arrived on the scene, the commander of the
347th, Colonel Harry Hulen, suggested that the bridge simply be
repaired and jacked up to its original position. However, his officers
were both doubtful that the work could be carried out in time and
concerned that it involved too much risk. Instead, they suggested,
earth should be dumped in the river to create a bypass and the flowing water routed through culverts underneath the dam. Hulen was
opposed to the idea, saying that the culverts, which would have to
be five feet in diameter each, would not be available in time. Itschner

initially favored the culverts plan and promised that the equipment would be available, but Hulen managed to persuade him that they should rebuild the bridge. And Hulen was proved right. With men working in shifts to cover 24 hours a day, the structure was ready to be raised on the morning of August 14, the deadline set by Itschner. As the regimental report then explains, "The delicate task of jacking and cribbing [using interwoven logs as a temporary support] was started and continued through the day and night."[29]

Rather astonishingly, the description of the crucial bridge repair in the 347th's history is interrupted by an account of the regimental band entertaining 200 residents of La Haye-Pesnel a couple miles safely behind the lines with a series of musical numbers ending with a rendition of "La Marseillaise." This brilliant piece of PR was timed to mark Assumption Day, August 15, a public holiday in France, and clearly was warmly received, as the regimental history movingly reported: "The playing of La Marseillaise brought the now familiar sight of people who could no longer control the deep emotions they felt as they realized the significance of the stirring strains of their national anthem. As the band prepared to march back to camp, many people came forward and presented flowers to the men."[30] Possibly the oddest aspect of this story is not that this busy regiment had time to do this but that all the band members had recently crossed the Channel and had somehow brought their instruments with them.

However, Hulen and his fellow officers were too busy to attend the concert; in fact, they did not sleep for the duration of the bridge work. On the morning of the fifteenth, the collapsed part of the bridge was brought back into alignment, and by midday it was connected to the undamaged sections. That afternoon, at 1800 hours, Major General Cecil Moore, chief engineer of the European theater, flew over the site with Itschner and saw next to the bridge the proud engineers had marked out in white cement the message WILL FINISH

AT 2000 . Indeed, the work was complete precisely at that time. There is a hint of "we knew better" in the official account of this episode, which could be interpreted as a veiled attack on Itschner. The report writer wrote: "The successful completion of the scheme was a tribute to all the men upon whom Colonel Hulen had placed so much confidence. The manner in which they performed the work proved that the Colonel's plan was both practical and sound."[31]

In fact, Itschner's promised culverts did arrive on time—except that, because of a clerical error, the diameter of the pipes was five inches rather than five feet, rendering them unfit for use and consequently Itschner's plan would have led to failure. But Itschner, gracious as ever, and possibly conscious of his rare mistake in suggesting the wrong type of repair, later wrote to Hulen commending the performance of his unit. Recalling the urgency of the project, he mentioned that the bridge at Saint-Hilaire had "dropped into the river and presented a most difficult engineering problem. . . . While the task was almost impossible to execute in the time available, your regiment, by working at the highest rate of speed, drove the last spike on the rail over the bridge four hours before the time set for completion." Itschner had learned that "at least one of your officers did not sleep during this entire period of emergency" and "as a result of your work, supplies reached the Third Army by rail and the advance to the Seine was possible."[32] It was, from all accounts, typical Itschner, a man who succeeded by recognizing the importance of bringing people on side.

The Saint-Hilaire bridge might have been the most difficult task carried out by the various units working on Patton's railway, but it was not the only potential showstopper. Across the length of the railway, all the available heavy earthmoving equipment, most of which was stored in or around Cherbourg, was commandeered and allocated for the reconstruction of the line. This caused immense traffic jams because this equipment was given priority over other military demands. On August 13 and 14, men from across the lodgment were being trucked to many of the reconstruction sites to ensure the work was done on time, adding to the road usage. Engineers from regiments such as the 392nd, 390th, and 95th arrived piecemeal but were put to work immediately and without break, increasing the eventual workforce to Patton's called-for number of 10,000.

The urgency of the project is further illustrated by the speed with which units were rushed to their worksites. The 332nd, for example, received orders at 3:00 a.m. on August 13 to proceed from its camp at Cherbourg to the newly captured Mayenne. The men boarded the 7:00 a.m. train to Carentan, where they were then trucked the 90 miles south to Mayenne and set to work right away on a 20-mile section on either side of town. From a technical point of view, the parts of the line closest to Le Mans were the easiest to repair because they were relatively undamaged (having been less subjected to bombing), but they presented the greatest risk to the engineers because of their proximity to the enemy. Consequently, each unit was given short stretches of line; the rebuilding of the line from La Chapelle to Sillé-le-Guillaume was the responsibility of the 389th, supported by the 375th, while the 368th, supported by the 377th, was responsible for the final section through to Le Mans.

In 1945, the US House of Representatives received an account of this hasty reconstruction, which included an excellent summary of the last stages of the task: "Three additional regiments were rushed into the area. All the heavy equipment that could possibly be spared from other equally pressing jobs was rushed to the bridge and yard sites by day and night. Highways leading from Cherbourg and the beaches were jammed with trucks immediately dispatched for essential material. Even while the bulldozers were clearing the debris — a 48 hour job in itself — engineer officers in hastily thrown-up drafting tents were designing new bridges for the jobs."[33]

Building the line itself, however, was only one part of the equation — a great achievement, but useless without any trains running on it. Now it was up to the operational teams to get the trains moving. And they were working in circumstances with which no railroad engineer had ever expected to contend. Back in Cherbourg, the trains had been prepared in the huge newly created yard at Équeurdreville, on the western side of the city. According to Lerouvillois, it was "an unimaginable sight, the awesome atmosphere of a great departure. Wagons and locomotives stretching as far as the eye could see accompanied by the noise of hammers being used to check the wheels and the scraping of coal being tossed into the ever hungry fireboxes.... To which unknown destination was all this for?"[34] He further describes the loading of shells in boxes marked HANDLE WITH CARE, as well as rockets, grenades, and mortar rounds. Trucks filled to the brim were disgorging vast quantities of supplies onto the railway cars, but most numerous were the tank cars marked POL.

Lerouvillois accurately concluded that all the work at Cherbourg had come together to fulfill its true purpose: "One can see now that over the past few weeks, all the movements of the cranes, all the transfers to the port from heavily loaded barges, all the trips by the amphibious trucks, were all destined to end at this point here." As soon as Order No. 7 had gone out, a test train had begun its journey carrying supplies for the worksites on the route as well as testing the safety of the newly laid tracks. It took five days to complete the near 200-mile journey through Itschner's roundabout route. Now, the huge trains carrying vital supplies were leaving at half-hour intervals. They were driven by men the majority of whom were newly arrived in France and for whom this was genuinely a trip into the unknown.

5

ALL ABOARD TO PARIS

The men of the 740th Railway Operating Battalion were in a state of confusion as they waded ashore on Utah Beach early on the morning of August 15. Sponsored by the Chesapeake and Ohio Railway, these men were mostly experienced railroaders supplemented by a few raw recruits with no practical experience of running trains. After weeks of kicking their heels at a camp in Cardiff after being told they would be operating trains in the UK for the rest of the war, they were suddenly ordered to the English coast. Within a day, they found themselves on board an old Dutch ferry heading overnight across the Channel. They transferred to a landing craft and arrived on the beach — still a seemingly random mess of unquantifiable amounts of equipment and supplies — just as dawn was breaking. As they trudged across the sand in the Normandy drizzle, weather familiar to them from their time in Wales, these men had no idea of the role they were about to play in the conflict. The gray weather did not let up as the men were led off Utah Beach and quickly taken by truck to Mayenne, where they arrived after nightfall. Unable to locate the town mayor, who was responsible for allocating accommodations, they had to camp overnight in a field. The following day, they found a billet in an old military building, Caserne Mayran, which the Germans had used as their headquarters until their hasty departure just 10 days earlier.

The building was littered with German bureaucracy of war, including countless pictures of the Führer, which an earlier group of GIs had used to line receptacles for human waste. The GIs delighted in ripping down posters still up on the walls and doors indicating in German the purpose of each room.

The Germans had mounted fierce resistance in the Caserne and not a single window remained intact, but the soldiers of the 740th were grateful to be sleeping under cover. The rest of their unit, who had been trucked to Mayenne after marching six miles to a transit camp, joined them that evening. Just before their departure, this group had finally been given their orders, which were to operate the section of the railroad around Mayenne.

Upon their arrival in the gloom of a wet night, Lieutenant W. E. Mason, the commander and trainmaster of Company C of the 740th, went to assess the state of the railway yard that the men of the 332nd had repaired and was surprised to find himself accosted by Brigadier General Ewart G. Plank, who was no less than the commanding officer of the Advance Section of the Communications Zone (ADSEC). The very presence of such a senior military figure demonstrated the importance of the situation. Plank dispensed with formalities and informed Mason of the task ahead: "There are 31 trains of ammunition, rations and gasoline coming through that General Patton needs in fourteen days to take Paris. When can your crews get to work?" Mason realized this was not a request but an order. According to the account in the history of the 740th, "Although the men had no work clothes or equipment, Mason answered 'Right now,'" even though privately he doubted it could be done.[1]

While the men of the 740th headed down to Mayenne, the initial trains had already started their slow ride trundling down the tracks. At 1900 hours on August 15, the inaugural train with a load of gasoline ran over the tracks past the barracks at La Hay-Pesnel, north of Avranches, where it was met with cheers and waves from the engineers of the 347th. The train reached the bridge at Saint-Hilaire, a mere 25 miles farther down the track, at 1730 hours the next day, demonstrating the slow progress on the reconstructed route. The fear of rail breaks was ever present, and the engineers, new to the route, did not know what was around the next bend. Frequently, extra precautions were taken: "At night and even during the day in stretches where the view was clear, it was necessary to send a flagman ahead to relay to the engineers the news on track condition."[2] These men were constantly on the lookout for booby traps, evidence of sabotage, or damaged embankments that might not support the weight of the train. No wonder progress was little faster than walking pace.

Nevertheless, by the time the 740th started work at Mayenne late on August 16, three trains had already passed through without any help from staff on the ground. However, from that moment on, the 740th was charged with bringing some order into the running of this recently refurbished railway. It was certainly needed. With no telecommunications or signaling systems, men holding boards or sometimes torches or cigarette lighters were the only "shore-to-ship" form of communication, a signaling method that was dangerous and caused delays.

The following day, the test pilot train reached Le Mans without mishap. The French writer Robert Lerouvillois, who was there to witness this momentous occasion, described how the arrival of that train on the afternoon of the seventeenth took the French stationmaster by surprise.[3] Lerouvillois reported that the stationmaster was not expecting any trains to arrive on the main line from the direction of Rennes because he was aware that the bridge at Laval was out of commission. Therefore, imagine his astonishment when, suddenly, a train — hauled by a strange locomotive with three axles—appeared in the distance. The stationmaster watched in awe, apparently unable to speak, as the engine approached slowly, belching smoke and constantly whistling to warn of its arrival. The stationmaster saw "inscribed, in great white letters on the boiler…the words 'U.S. Army Transportation Corps.'" Open-mouthed, the poor fellow was rendered "immobile, glued to the same spot in astonishment," and a confused conversation ensued. He told the American engineer, whose face was covered in sweat and coal dust, "I can't believe that you have come from Rennes." Fortunately, the engineer, a colonel, William H. Roberts, spoke French, albeit somewhat haltingly, and explained: "Not Rennes, we have come from Cherbourg, it's taken us five days by travelling night and day." Roberts then explained about the lines that had been reopened on Patton's orders and how the train had taken a circuitous route via Lison, Coutances, and Avranches. He managed to recount how the train had used the newly reopened route via Saint-Hilaire instead of the main line toward Rennes, and at Mayenne turned south on a single-track to regain the main line just beyond the collapsed bridge at Laval.

Lerouvillois noted that "the French railwayman looked at them as if they were magicians" and failed to understand the next piece of news when the American urged: "Can you hurry up and clear the track as we need the space? We are the pilot train. There are 32 convoys that will follow behind us."[4] The Frenchman, still bemused, protested that papers had to be filled out before the train could move on, but the colonel swiftly brushed aside his complaints. Giving up, the stationmaster resumed his post in a signalbox that had somehow survived the bombing and sat at the window watching the arrival of the succession of trains.

Back at Mayenne, the men of the 740th set about their task right away. Mayenne was a key junction and shunting area, but the yard had only been partially repaired and there was insufficient coal available. The soldiers, still without equipment except for a few borrowed tools from a group of French trackworkers who had emerged out of the forest when news of the liberation of the town reached them, managed to open three additional tracks in the yard. Within a few days, the telecommunications team, equipped with little more than their GI knives, managed to establish a link to Fougères, but once the trains headed south toward Le Mans, the engineers were essentially incommunicado. Without any telecommunications, regular jeep courier services were established between headquarters and the numerous key stations and yards. According to the history of the Second Military Railway Service, the drivers had to "run through territory just passed—or just by-passed—which abounded with snipers. The story of the first large group of trains which ran east from the Cherbourg peninsula is highlighted by many wild dashes across the country by couriers in jeeps while loaded trains stood waiting all along the line, tied up because of lack of orders."[5]

Even though Mayenne had been captured by the Allies a week previously and the 332nd had endeavored to make the town safe, the surrounding area was still vulnerable to attack because the front line was just six miles away. A small group of German troops missed by the American forces remained active. After the wires were restored during the day, the Germans crept out at night to cut them and use their remaining ammunition to take potshots at passing engines or the men working on the tracks. It was not until August 21 that the railway troops managed to detain the four German soldiers responsible for these attacks as they were about to blow up a bridge. However, a few enemy soldiers remained at large, firing shots at the troops near their billet in Caserne Mayran and later at a passing engine. When the attacks ceased, it was assumed these soldiers had melted into the forest, but a few days later they were tracked down and captured by a unit of US Rangers. Those incidents, however, created an atmosphere of fear among the newly arrived GI railroaders. When a half dozen men checked out a possible billet and were surprised by unusual sounds, they assumed it was another group of German stragglers hiding in the house and scuttled out in a panic. They found their sergeant, who was more of a country boy and fortunately recognized the sound. A flock of chickens found wandering in the streets had been caught, bound, and shut in a closet to await their fate as a welcome addition to K rations.

At Mayenne, the engineers of the 740th took over the controls of all the trains running down to Le Mans, relieving the drivers of the 720th and 729th, who had spent up to three days driving the trains down from Cherbourg. This was not always a simple handover because of the varied types of locomotive in operation and the fact that they were all coal-fired, whereas the American railroaders had been trained on oil-fired steam locomotives on the Santa Fe. The biggest difference was that coal-fired engines—both French and American—required a fireman to ensure that the furnace constantly maintained the necessary high temperature. The non-railroaders of the 740th were invariably given the arduous task of shoveling coal, but keeping the blaze going steadily to produce enough steam is a skilled job—and, as one of their officers put it, "there was no time for on the job training."[6]

The orders given to these inexperienced engineers were plain, if somewhat daunting, given that many had never driven these types of locomotives, and, to add to the difficulties, the French ones were designed for left-hand drive: "Your destination is a place called Le Mans. Get going and keep going until someone stops you, then get down and raise hell until you find out whether you are at the right place."[7] However, the soldier engineers had no idea of the route, the location of intermediate stations, or, more dangerously, the condition of the track. None of them had ever driven on this particular line, and as it happened, some had only been in the country for 48 hours by that point. It was only when the rails sagged under the weight of the locomotive that they learned the location of soft spots—poorly supported parts of the track where a bomb crater had rapidly been filled in—sections that could easily result in a rail break or a collapsed embankment.

There is no doubt that corners were cut in the haste to get the trains running, which meant the railway was not up to the standard to which the more experienced local railroaders were accustomed. There was a gung-ho element in the way the Americans were prepared to operate the trains, which may have been understandable but rather shocked the local railway workers. As the author of a book on the American railway operations in Europe puts it, whereas the French railwaymen wanted to ensure every part of the track had been brought up to normal standards, "the Americans emphasized speed and insisted that the first thing essential was to get the track down so that the trains, or most of them, could get through. The refinements would come later."[8]

Fortunately, the experienced railroaders ensured that the limitations of the track were well understood by the engineers and that, despite the urgency of the need for supplies, there was still a great emphasis on operating safely. Hastily remade bridges had to be crossed slowly, at just 3 miles per hour in one case, because it was still unclear whether the wooden cribbing supporting them was sufficient. Moreover, vision at night was practically nil. Blackout restrictions had been imposed to avoid attacks from the air or nearby artillery, and neither headlamps nor signal lights could be used. In particular, the final stretch of the route just south of Mayenne before rejoining the main line just east of Laval was particularly perilous because it ran along heavily curved tracks in a remote forested area close to enemy lines and consequently was at constant risk from German stragglers and snipers.

There was also the more mundane challenge of meeting the basic needs of railway operation. Running a steam-hauled railway involved copious quantities of both coal and water, so the men of the railway battalions had to be adept at improvisation in order to keep the trains running. Most of the coal other than the contents of the tender was carried in the first railcar behind it because there was no expectation that any extra black gold would be found at intermediate yards. Sufficient water was also a constant problem; it became routine for the engineers to stop in a town or village and refill the engine manually from a local house or garden.

John Livingstone, an officer who served with the 740th battalion during this period and later wrote a history of the unit, outlined some of the men's novel solutions. As the trains trundled down the tracks, gangs of trackworkers hastily repaired sections so that speed restrictions could be removed; other men focused on improving the efficiency of the railway: "An old reciprocating [two-way] pump that had not been used for years was repaired by Company B men for pumping water from the river to the tank; a small open-air engine terminal was established with the aid of a French shop employee who was hanging around . . . a supply of poor coal was delivered which had to be loaded by hand; and an additional water pump was repaired."[9] It was all banal, basic railway work that in normal circumstances would have been routine, but during these extraordinary times, it took considerable invention to keep the trains traveling through to Le Mans.

Furthermore, all the trains from Cherbourg to Le Mans were double-hauled to ensure their 1,000-ton loads could be hauled up the grades. On some occasions, the grades did prove too steep, and the drivers were forced to allow the whole train to roll back down the incline and take a faster running start up, rather like a truck stuck at the bottom of a snowy hill. No wonder it was a slow process with the trains taking up to five days to reach their destination. As a result, crews were routinely on duty nonstop for at least 60 hours and sometimes more.

On August 19, Patton came to inspect the progress at Le Mans, where he met, apparently by chance, Lieutenant Colonel S. H. Pulliam, the commander of the 740th. Patton immediately asked Pulliam, "Are you going to move my materiel up here?" to which Pulliam replied, "Yes, sir, if I have to carry it on my back."[10]

The job of the railway crews was by no means finished with the rapid reopening of the line through to Le Mans. Indeed, quite the opposite: it had only just started and would intensify over the following weeks and months as the lines of communication lengthened, making truck transport less viable. Le Mans was quickly established as the Third Army's main headquarters and became the key railhead for incoming supplies, given its yard's huge potential. Le Mans was also vital as a staging post, and therefore work was soon started on ensuring trains would be able to continue farther east. To enable this, the yards—reduced to rubble by the Allied bombing—had to be restored, because initially only a single, undamaged through track had survived. The shortage of freight facilities at Le Mans was the key capacity constraint of the vital line of communication from Cherbourg, and without a rapid increase in its ability to handle supplies, this bottleneck risked slowing down Patton's advance.

The task of returning the yard and the area around Le Mans to working order was allocated to the 706th Grand Division, which was sponsored by the Pennsylvania Railroad. But neither the 706th nor its associated railway battalions were anywhere near Le Mans when the first trains arrived from the Normandy coast. The unit had only landed on Utah Beach in the late afternoon of August 16 and had been given no further orders about their role.

They were soon to find out. After the same six-mile march to the transit camp as the men of the 740th had made, they pitched their tents on arrival and had just turned in for the night when at 11:00 p.m. they were given orders to pack up and climb aboard the waiting trucks. Clearly, none of this was preplanned but was a knock-on effect of the astonishing Order No. 7, which was to rebuild the line to Le Mans in three days.

The trucks carrying the 706th left before dawn, and traveling slowly without headlights to avoid air attacks, they arrived in Le Mans early on the afternoon of the seventeenth. There was just time before dark for the commander of the 706th, Colonel Louis G. Jamison, and his reconnaissance team to inspect the railway facilities and provide an estimate of the amount of time needed to bring them back fully into use. As they checked out the local railway lines, the railwaymen of the 706th needed no convincing of the town's importance for the railway network. It was obviously a key railway junction, with lines heading in all four cardinal directions, spreading out from a huge elliptical-shaped double-track that encircled the town. At each Y-shaped junction, there were signal boxes, known as *Postes*, to control the traffic on that section of line. All the lines and associated *Postes* needed to be brought back into use in great haste.

The arrival of the 706th had not been anticipated, which meant the men spent that night in a cow pasture several miles outside town. The next day, the unit moved into the remnants of Le Mans station, setting up the mess on the platform and the unit headquarters in the sizable waiting room. Very few of the railway facilities were in a usable state. As the report on the work of the 706th explained, "Le Mans terminal facilities were damaged to such an extent that railhead activity was very limited. The large receiving yard was severely damaged and there were only two tracks that could be used. The engine house layout was almost completely out of service and the classification yard could not be reached and was too badly damaged to be used."[11]

Livingstone, the historian of the 740th, provides a useful insight into the extent of the task at Le Mans, which was typical of the reinstatement work needed in badly bombed depots. It is an amazing catalog of work: "Clearing out yards and repairing track damage; replacing defective rails on the main line; distributing ballast and resurfacing track; making surveys to locate water and coaling stations"; and much more.[12]

Rebuilding and operating the local lines meant far more than merely replacing tracks and firing up locomotives. A railway is a massive interdependent system in which all components must be functioning before any of it can be used. There were prosaic problems, too. Livingstone mentions the issue of feeding crews who were leaving and arriving at all times of the day. Twenty-four-hour kitchens were established at Mayenne and Le Mans, but various "transients," who had been subsisting on K rations for days or weeks and who could smell the food from miles away, also drifted in for their first proper meal in ages, which resulted in "a large overdrawing of normal rations." Although food was an important part of keeping up morale, Livingstone notes that few men complained despite conditions that "in civilian life would quickly lead to labor troubles." Those who "griped," as he put it, were not necessarily those he expected to be moaners; rather, "several of the half dozen men we would have gladly left behind in the States turned out to be excellent workers."[13] He mentioned, too, that not all his stars burned brightly when they faced the rigors of warfare.

Despite all the difficulties and the risk of attack by German stragglers, the trains kept arriving at Le Mans. Patton originally wanted the 31 trains to be delivered to Le Mans within 14 days. Remarkably, with battalions working flat out in the Cotentin to find freight cars, and load and dispatch them, 36 trains—each with around 1,000 tons of fuel, munitions, and supplies—arrived safely in Le Mans within a week. Once the winding little route through southern Normandy had been established, it proved incredibly efficient, not least because trains were limited to traveling in one direction as no return workings were yet allowed. But that went against a key rule of military railway operation—first set out in the Civil War by Herman Haupt, the foremost strategist of railways in warfare: empty railcars must be returned. As a result of the one-way traffic, supplies began to dry up toward the end of this frantic period because the railway battalions around Cherbourg had no more empty cars available to load. Both GI crews and French engineers had parked vast numbers of empty freight cars on one of the main-line tracks that had not been brought back into use to get them out of the way; in total, 1,200 railcars had accumulated in and around Le Mans. The military railway operators should have organized their return earlier, but it was only belatedly, as the last of the 36 trains arrived, that permission was finally given for the flow on the tracks to be reversed. The empties were sent back to Cherbourg in batches of 40 hauled by locomotives driven by GIs who had earned a couple days rest after their arduous journey to Le Mans.

Meanwhile, Le Mans was up and running as a key railhead in just a few days. Initially, trains could be unloaded on the one surviving track, but a second one was quickly brought into use. Improvisation was the name of the game. Medical supplies were routed to the out-of-commission main line to Alençon, where temporary unloading facilities were rustled up.

Crucial to the 706th's ability to get the railway functioning so rapidly was the decision to employ local French workers. Within a couple of days, more than a thousand locals signed up and were deployed not just to clear the tracks and yards but also to operate the small shunting locomotives, abandoned and undamaged by the Germans, and to shift debris and empty railcars. Cannily, in anticipation of liberation, French trackworkers had buried a vast quantity of tools away from the prying eyes of the Germans, and they dug these out to make up for the shortage of equipment, much of which was still back in Cherbourg.

Within four days, more railway troops arrived to support the 706th and oversee the operation of services. By August 22, a week after work had started, a key bridge into Le Mans station was reopened, enabling up to 15 trains per day to be discharged through the main yard. The mechanical section of the unit had set up shop in the old engine house, and within hours of arrival of the 740th, a combined French and American workforce had created a maintenance facility for both steam and diesel power.

Although the majority of trains were steam-hauled, some diesel locomotives had arrived, sometimes causing confusion for the inexperienced men. While the first train loaded for Chartres, 80 miles toward Paris, was waiting for a crew, the officer in charge, Captain Jordan, spotted five men next to the idle diesel engine and ordered them to board and pull the train out. Without comment, they jumped in the cab, but nothing happened for 10 minutes. Jordan returned to investigate, and an engineer named Shogren told him: "Sir, I come off a steam road and have never been on a diesel before, but if you'll start this goddamned thing I'll run it."[14] Jordan did not know how to start it either but fortunately was spared his blushes by the speedy arrival of the real crew.

———————

As impressive as it was, the little line through to Le Mans reconstructed in three days was never going to be sufficient for the vast amount of traffic coming from Cherbourg. Therefore, once Le Mans was reached, the 332nd Engineer General Service Regiment, the first to arrive at Mayenne, was quickly redeployed to rebuild the long bridge over the Sélune River at Pontaubault, the biggest bridge-rebuilding project the US Army had to tackle to date. Itschner's assumption that the damage to the viaduct was too great to be repaired within Patton's deadline proved to be correct. Not only had two spans, each around 70 feet long, collapsed into the river, but also the supporting pier was unrepairable. The surrounding destruction included huge bomb craters that had to be filled in, and the two sections and supporting pier needed to be reinstated. The bridge at Laval, which was simultaneously being reconstructed, had similar damage, and because of its importance work continued through the night using floodlights, despite fears the Luftwaffe could still mount a nighttime attack.

With such rapid progress being made, there was just enough time for a breather to celebrate a happier event. The 347th, having played a crucial role in opening the line to Le Mans, briefly broke from its task of maintaining and patrolling the track to celebrate a wartime shotgun marriage. A lieutenant in Company E, Michael Pochan, had fallen for a nurse, Nancy Brand, who was attached to the battalion, and their union was made official at a ceremony on August 20 in Martinvast, a village a couple of miles south of Cherbourg. The ceremony was performed by none other than a local aristocrat, Le Comte de Portalès, who also happened to be the mayor, while the commander, Colonel Hulan, gave the bride away. But the risks of the GIs' work on the railways remained all too apparent that day as almost simultaneously with the celebrations two engineers on attachment to the 347th were injured — fortunately, not seriously—when their Caterpillar bulldozer hit a German anti-tank mine.

The timing of the wedding could not have been better. The very next day, the 347th were given another urgent order: to complete the reopening of the 18 miles of double-track line between Vire and Flers, which would eventually be part of a northern alternate route eastward that avoided the bottleneck at Le Mans. The order came through on the morning of the twenty-first, and by the evening, the line had been reconnoitered; it was decided four companies would be needed to complete the task within the two-day time frame. Two companies started carrying out track repairs from Clairefougère, a village halfway between the two towns, and the others, respectively, from each end.

This relatively small but urgent task illustrates the complexity the railway engineers faced as they worked their way through France bringing the railways back into life. Here, the difficulties in coordinating the arrival of equipment at a time of mass movement of troops and matériel, proximity of the enemy, and a constantly changing strategic situation are all too apparent, as is the improvisation of the engineers. This short project, for example, involved the repair of several small bridges and, according to the regimental report, "materials for three bridges were being hauled by truck from Valognes, from a distance of 65 to 85 miles away over roads carrying an incessant traffic of motor convoys."[15] Such was the rush that one gap, where a bridge had collapsed over a road, was filled in to make a grade crossing where there had previously been an underpass. Another of the bridges was so badly damaged that part of its span was cut off and replaced with steel trestles; fortunately, the wreckage of German weaponry could be put to good use: "web and flanges of the girders were being strengthened with steel plate salvaged from destroyed German tanks in the vicinity."[16] By the afternoon of August 25, the bridge work was completed and the first train operated through to Flers, where it was greeted by the mayor and residents' cheers and applause.

As the Allies gained territory east of Le Mans, no time was wasted in preparing the railway route needed to maintain the line of communication to Paris. The Military Railway Service sent out teams of engineers to assess the work needed to bring the lines into use for heavy goods trains running at 20 miles per hour. Frequently dodging stragglers and snipers, they carried out thorough surveys and prepared new maps with precise details of the track, grades, and junctions, ensuring that the railways would be fully equipped for intensive use once the repairs were completed.

———————

In the main, the railways immediately east of Le Mans had suffered less damage thanks to the Germans' hasty retreat and the absence of key targets for the Allied bombers. Nevertheless, Allied commanders continued to deliberate over the delicate and complex issue of what to do about the railways in occupied areas of France. To bomb or not to bomb was a question for which there was no obvious answer. Destroy the railway and then find that the Allied army urgently needed the facilities, or leave the tracks intact for the Germans to bring in reinforcements. For the first couple of months after D-Day, Allied bombing of interdiction targets continued amid increasing doubts about its effectiveness. British officer Major Charles Benda, who conducted meticulous research on the effects of bombing, found that in the period from June 6 to September 30, 1944, French saboteurs destroyed 270 bridges and 1,750 locomotives and brought about 4,400 breaks of rail. The French author Sébastien Albertelli concludes: "While this did not altogether stop the Germans from using the railway, [according to Benda] 'it resulted in long delays, it forced the enemy to spread out and waste its manpower, and it improved the morale of the troops.'"[17] Benda noted that the aerial bombardment was aimed at the main lines, while the Resistance targeted secondary routes. In the South, which was more difficult for bombers to reach, undoubtedly the work of the saboteurs proved the more effective.

In the face of these concerns, the bombing campaign was scaled back as set out in a memo sent by the Supreme Headquarters Allied Expeditionary Force (SHAEF) on August 8 and authorized by Eisenhower: "The Director general of military railways has recommended that in view of the present rapid advance and in order to facilitate the quick reconstruction of rail lines and communications, air attacks on all rail targets west of the Seine, and north of the Loire should be discontinued at once, except attacks on stationary or moving trains."[18] The memo included a list of 70 specific structures in enemy hands, notably railway junctions and yards, the demolition of which should be avoided if possible. The document went on to recommend that rapid seizure of railway facilities, as well as actions to protect lines by the Resistance fighters, would reduce the likelihood of the Germans sabotaging the lines. Any remaining bombing attacks were to target only shorter bridges, which were—somewhat ironically—easier to repair.

Unfortunately, it took some time for these orders to get through to the Allied air forces because they were concentrating the majority of their attacks on targets farther south and in Belgium. And even though bombing raids on railway facilities were being scaled back, there were still civilian casualties. Moreover, many raids failed in their primary objective, and worse, the lack of coordination with ground forces increased the risk of "blue on blue" casualties.

Zuckerman had traveled to Caen to see firsthand the effects of the carpet bombing that preceded the land attack. He had not been impressed and came away questioning the effectiveness of such attacks. He reported that the aerial bombing had done little to "soften up" the enemy and merely sowed confusion among the troops. He concluded that the air support given to Montgomery ultimately "had not helped him get through Caen."[19] Zuckerman, therefore, advised that indiscriminate bombing should be stopped in favor of well-targeted and coordinated attacks when the infantry was already in position to move forward.

Eventually, the campaign was reined in, but not before, on August 13, a US bombing raid on Crest in the Drôme department just south of Valence killed 38 local people and destroyed or damaged 107 buildings. The effect, according to the historian of the French railway resistance, Vincent Cuny, was devastating and yet ineffective: "A thousand people were made homeless....But the bridge was left intact....Worse, the FFI [French Forces of the Interior] had taken care a few days earlier to remove the rails, paralysing the rail traffic over the bridge."[20] Three days later, a similar attack at nearby Saint-Vallier that failed to destroy the targeted bridge over the Rhône killed 74 local people.

The lack of success of these raids all but ended these types of attacks. Consequently, when the chief engineer, ETOUSA, Major General Cecil R. Moore, took to the air on August 18 to reconnoiter the state of the line to Chartres, the next staging point, he was pleased to find that damage was far less than had been encountered in Normandy. One small bridge had collapsed and several bomb craters pitted around the track, but he reckoned repairs could be effected quickly: "I estimate that the battalion can open a single track line from Le Mans to Chartres within 48 hours after getting on the job and distributing men and equipment."[21] He predicted that the line would be opened on August 23, but as it happened, the engineers managed to beat that deadline by a day.

And so, on the twenty-second, the first military train carrying ammunition and gasoline left Le Mans for Brou, 50 miles away and the new headquarters of the Third Army. The engineers had to drive blind on the single-track, with no signaling of external support, hoping the trackmen had successfully cleared the railway of any hazards. The level of activity increased daily to ensure the supply line to Paris would be available once the capital was captured. Engineers from a newly arrived battalion, the 712th, were repairing the second track from Le Mans through to Brou, which soon became the railhead for the final assault on Paris. Meanwhile, an alternate route from Le Mans to Chartres via La Loupe was being repaired, but its opening was held up by the replacement of three bridges.

Despite all the progress in track work, there was no time to install signaling on the reconstructed lines, which meant that the heavy traffic had to be controlled by a primitive system of "permissive working" involving flags and boards. According to John Livingstone of the 740th battalion, until the end of August, "trains were operated and switching performed at night by the men signaling with personal flashlights, cigarette lighters and lighted cigarettes."[22]

Improvements were coming, however. At the same time as local signaling systems were being rebuilt, a more sophisticated form of communications between the various railway centers and stations was already in the works. Because it was not possible to restore the wires alongside the railway tracks fast enough, the Military Railway Service created a whole new wireless communications system to replace the large numbers of messengers careening down the rural roads in jeeps. Starting in mid-August, as the invading troops rapidly headed east, 500-watt radio transmitting and receiving units were installed on the backs of trucks and set up at key locations along the line between Cherbourg and Le Mans, and later on, Chartres and Paris. Provided with their own power sources, these sets were totally

self-sufficient. To train operators, the Military Railway Service established a radio school. The system was fully functional by August 31
and greatly eased the communications problems by knitting together
the various headquarters into a coordinated unit.

Five days after Chartres and Dreux were captured on August 17,
the headquarters of ADSEC moved to Le Mans, but the speed of
the advance meant it remained there for only 18 days. Aerial reconnaissance had revealed that the damage from either Allied bombing
or German sabotage farther east was not extensive. Though several
bridges were missing, including all those over the Seine, this was easier territory to move through, and because German resistance was
feeble by this point, progress eastward was much faster.

Typical of this period was the progress of the 332nd Engineer
General Service Regiment, which established several temporary
camps by the side of the railway where they were working on sections of line. Alan Latta, a sergeant in the 332nd, was part of the
group sent to Mayenne right after arriving in France. After helping to reopen the line there, his unit quickly headed east, taking
with them salvaged rails from parts of the track that were no longer in use. Remaining at all times just a couple of days behind the
fast-moving front line, the team worked toward Chartres and then
Dreux. Their numbers were boosted by hastily recruited French
locals, who were initially sullen, worried they would be at risk if
the Germans returned—a quite rational fear after four years of
occupation. Fortunately, Latta's captain, Jop, spoke a bit of French
and managed to win them over. One told him he had worked on
this section of line for 35 years, and when Jop offered him tools to
work, the man became more accommodating. In his book *A Thousand Letters Away*, inspired by letters he wrote home during the war,
Latta recalled how the American railwaymen worked till nightfall to make a good single-track out of the formerly double-track

line. Relations between the two groups further improved when the Americans handed out K rations to the locals and, when their shift ended, were delighted to be offered wine and cognac in return. Latta noted that a camaraderie developed between engineers, despite the language barrier: "It was not much different from [working with] the British, except the difficulty of communicating.... Hard work is a universal language. However, it seemed funny that the French once worked side by side with the Germans."[23]

Alas, the Germans were never far away. When the Americans arrived outside Dreux, a key staging post just 50 miles east of the capital, they found that the enemy was still active in the area. The first night there, Latta and his colleague Crowley dug themselves shallow foxholes and were awakened by gunfire. Unsurprisingly, they vowed they would dig deeper trenches to sleep in the following evening.

At the morning briefing, Captain Jop reported there were no casualties but there had been several contacts with pockets of resistance, and it was unclear whether they were native sympathizers or Germans. However, as soon as they started work on the line, shots rang out and a French worker, hit in the neck, collapsed dead instantly without even letting out a scream. According to Latta, "The squad bent low and dashed to a covering woodline and took positions... the squad spread ten meters apart and moved forward to circle the entire perimeter of the job site."[24] The worksite briefly turned into a battleground. Latta lay flat and heard the sound of rustling as someone ran through the forest. His colleague Valdez then shouted from the trees: "I got him." Indeed, Valdez had caught up with the sniper and killed him in a medieval fashion, plunging his bayonet into the man's abdomen: "The corpse had a blood stained civilian shirt and German army trousers," but no gun was found.[25] Latta was left hoping that they had got the right man.

At Dreux, the main line to Paris had been carried on the town's railway bridge over the Eure, a tributary of the Seine. The bridge was of such strategic importance that the French had destroyed it during the Blitzkrieg in order to slow the enemy's advance, but the Germans had ordered its reconstruction, replacing the masonry arches with steel beams and wooden piers. Then, in the run-up to D-Day, the French Resistance blew it up again after several Allied bombing attacks failed to bring it down amid widespread devastation and numerous casualties in the center of town. The absence of a crossing at Dreux until the bridge's reconstruction on September 9 forced trains to be diverted south to Chartres and then east to Rambouillet to reach Paris, adding 30 miles to their journey.

While the Americans were pushing toward Paris, progress by the British, who were opening lines farther north that ran parallel to the Channel, was steady but slower. To speed up rail services from Cherbourg, the main line from Bayeux was rebuilt, relieving the slow coastal route from Courseulles that had been the first line restored by the British. Clearing these tracks required the use of a huge 45-ton diesel-powered crane, brought over on a landing craft in early August. When a collapsed bridge was successfully replaced, a wrecked German ammunition train had to be cleared, and again, concerns about booby traps required testing the line with a locomotive pushing two railcars weighed down with ballast to ensure any mines would be safely detonated. And this was not the only precautionary measure the engineers used. They were concerned that rusty unused rails would become shiny when trains started running over them and might consequently attract air attacks on moonlit nights. Therefore, they limited shunting movements as much as possible and tried to use tracks that were the least visible from the air, even though these fears were largely unfounded as a result of the Allies' air dominance.

The British 181st Railway Operating Company's task of reinstating the tracks and other railway facilities at Caen was daunting. Though they were able to quickly restore water and electricity supplies, overall damage to the railway facilities—much of it carried out by the Resistance—was extensive. Both the depot and the workshops were completely destroyed by explosions, and the French saboteurs had toppled the coal hopper used to refill tenders. They also had run a large main-line locomotive into the turntable well, a widely used tactic that prevented the Germans from using the railway for escape. However, it wasn't all bad news. Among the dozen or so wrecked locomotives that were unrepairable, the Germans had, surprisingly, left a couple of undamaged freight engines. Other main-line locomotives also had not been efficiently sabotaged and were soon put to work.

But work to restore Caen was disrupted on August 6 when the sappers of the 181st were ordered to spend the night in slit trenches because of a major assault launched in nearby Falaise. Guns were placed behind a railway embankment to shell the Germans, but this resulted in a tragic mistake when, the following morning, a squadron of USAF Flying Fortresses bombed the steelworks at the nearby Fabrique de Normandie, killing a group of the 181st sappers who were in the factory seeking rail equipment. The attack ended only when an RAF Spitfire pilot shot down the squadron leader of the US flight.

It took until the end of August to open the docks at Caen. The port's principal role would be for coal imports, and soon a major store was built up that required close guarding to prevent local people from pilfering the black gold. Mezidon, 21 miles southeast of Caen, which had suffered extensive damage from Allied bombing, was the next major railway center to come into operation, but the reopening of the line through to Argentan, 25 miles farther south, did not take place until mid-September. This slow progress delayed the opening of the Channel ports of Dieppe, Boulogne, and Oostend, which meant continued reliance on the extremely crowded port of Cherbourg.

While the railway troops were working heroically and at times perilously to rehabilitate the railway, the collapsed bridges proved to be serious obstacles. Even when they were repaired, they often required trains to cross at slow speeds and with lighter loads, greatly reducing the overall capacity of the lines and resulting in a greater reliance on the overstretched motor transport service. Had the Allied ground troops maintained the slow forward movement envisaged by the Overlord planners, this would have allowed the railway troops to carry out their work in time to provide the required levels of supplies. However, the surprisingly rapid rout of the Germans west of the Seine and Patton's insistence on continuing the advance into eastern France meant that only motor transport could be used to maintain the line of communication. This situation led to the birth of the Red Ball Express, a much-vaunted and ultimately famous trucking operation that ran rather like a railway.

When the west bank of the Seine was cleared of Germans on August 24, it opened the possibility of rapid eastward progress in the South by avoiding the capital. However, railway capacity was limited by the destruction of key bridges that forced trains to use slow diversionary routes. Only two or three trains per day were able to move east from Chartres, and this created a supply bottleneck.

———————

Because the Germans had left large swathes of the country unprotected, no longer were enemy armies the constraining force preventing progress — rather, the basic logistics of supply for rapidly advancing armies was. The supply implications of crossing the Seine and heading for Paris were overwhelming, and it was clear that this demand could not be met by the railways, despite how rapidly they were being rebuilt. The planners estimated that 100,000 tons of supplies would be needed by September 1 to build up supplies at Dreux and Chartres west of the Seine to support the troops once they crossed the river. But the railways would be able to carry only a fifth of that and a conventional trucking operation would not be able to cope with the remainder. Instead, they devised an unprecedented scheme: the Red Ball Express — a name for the trucking operation that was oddly evocative of the railways because to "red ball" a consignment means to give it top priority on rail.

On August 23, at the instigation of Patton, who was concerned that failure of the supply line would prevent the Third Army from progressing farther east, Brigadier General Ewart G. Plank, the head of ADSEC, announced the launch of the Red Ball Express in two days. The aim, initially, was to deliver those 100,000 tons of supplies from Normandy to the front line by truck over the following week and then to continue with a similarly intense road service for a couple more months. Unlike normal trucking arrangements, the Red Ball Express convoys would be given absolute priority on a defined one-way route, effectively creating a railway system on roads. The idea of priority trucking routes had been first developed in the UK during the buildup to D-Day, when a similar loop connected the depots in southern England with the ports where troops and supplies were embarked. However, this system had operated for only a short time in a limited way, meaning that the planners of the Red Ball Express were effectively working in the dark.

To ensure its efficacy, all civilian and other military traffic was ordered to stay away from the Red Ball route. Portentous advertisements were placed in local papers: "At the front line, soldiers are awaiting weapons, gasoline, shells and bullets and a multitude of other indispensable supplies. The Red Ball convoys are transporting these supplies...this is why they need to drive fast...thousands of lives could be needlessly lost because of a few lost seconds...a single civilian vehicle could hold up a whole convoy....In the name of fighting men, we ask civilians not to interfere in any way with military traffic."[26] Furthermore, the notifications, which appeared on signposts crudely attached to any handy tree, were unequivocal and warned of prosecution: *"Route Reservée au trafic militaire. Interdiction absolue de circulation civile sous peine de poursuites"* (Route reserved for military traffic. Civilian use forbidden under threat of prosecution).

The Red Ball route was a 400-mile one-way loop linking Saint-Lô, just below the base of the Cotentin, where the consolidation and loading took place, with Chartres, 55 miles southeast of Paris. The northern route, carrying loaded trucks heading eastward, ran through Vire, Argentan, and Dreux, while the empty trucks returned through Alençon and Mortain. The rules were precise: the trucks, each with two drivers aboard, would be dispatched in groups of five vehicles (known as packets) at intervals of one minute, with a jeep or a truck identified with a blue pennant leading the way and one at the rear dealing with any slow-moving vehicles. Each convoy consisted of 40 vehicles that would keep 60 yards—or a half minute—apart, with the result that it took around 20 minutes for a convoy to pass. And the convoys were each to be two minutes apart. There would be no passing, although stragglers who had broken down or been otherwise delayed would rejoin at the back of a convoy that carried similar goods. All traffic would stop for a rest at 10 minutes to every hour and then resume travel precisely on the hour. In this era before bypasses and highways, the convoys were routed through small villages, where they were expected to slow to 25 miles per hour. The entire route was marked with the characteristic red ball signs, and marshals at every junction would ensure drivers did not get lost, though the shortage of military police meant this was not always the case. The truck engines were adjusted to prevent them exceeding 50 miles per hour on the open road, but many drivers tinkered with their carburetors to allow them to reach up to 70 miles per hour.

Though these regulations were quite rigid, they were often disobeyed. The mostly inexperienced young drivers were excited to enjoy the freedom of the road in control of a large vehicle with a powerful engine. The recruitment process, too, was totally random. Any soldier, even those who had never driven, could be commandeered to join the Red Ball convoys if they hadn't yet been assigned to a specific duty. These men were given two or three days training, which included basic operating mechanics, like how to use a gearbox and change a tire. Inevitably, they drove too fast, ignored the injunction not to pass other vehicles, and paid little heed to the locals. Unsurprisingly, it was at night when there were the most accidents, even though headlights were allowed. Rookie drivers ignored the speed limits, oblivious to the difficulties of driving on narrow and winding roads, which contrasted sharply with the long, straight roads back home. Sometimes their driving was so reckless that, according to an official US Army report, British troops joked about what to do when a convoy approached: "Among British units gossip had it that to avoid a U.S. convoy one must 'not only get off the road but climb a tree.'"[27] Sadly, it was not a joke as the high death toll of civilians, together with the closure of these roads to local users, began to attract hostility toward the Red Ball Express. Reliability, too, was an issue because the trucks had been mass-produced cheaply to meet wartime demand.

———————

For the transport planners, Red Ball Express relieved the immediate supply problem but created a host of others. Of ADSEC's 82 truck companies, each with around 45 vehicles, only the 5 considered essential for unloading supplies at ports were not allocated to Red Ball. A further 41 companies previously used by other sections of the army were quickly reallocated to Red Ball in its first few days of operation. Moreover, the whole concept was patched together so rapidly and in such an ad hoc way that the final route was not determined until the first trucks rolled out of Saint-Lô. As a result, marshals were often sent to the wrong place; for example, those allocated to Verneuil-sur-Avre, 120 miles from Saint-Lô, twiddled their thumbs for three days without any traffic only to discover that the convoys had been routed elsewhere.

Given the scale, urgency, and ambition of the scheme, it was inevitable that much did not go to plan. Although the convoys were supposed to stick to the predetermined route that ended in a triangle defined by Chartres, Dreux, and La Loupe, about 50 miles west of Paris, many were required to drive farther, as the official report explains: "Convoys often traveled an additional 50, 60, or even 100 miles before locating an appropriate dump." Consequently, average turnaround was five days—they were making a mere 80 miles per day—which explains why more than 50,000 men were needed for the project.

The priority given to the Red Ball Express, however, ensured that it was up and running on a large scale within days of the decision to establish it. More than 25,000 direction signs were laid on the route, and a circular red sign attached to each truck's radiator indicated it was part of the scheme. By August 29, the system comprised 5,958 vehicles—the army records were meticulous—distributed among 132 companies. Ultimately, the Red Ball Express fell 10 percent short of its target of 82,000 tons by September 1 but nevertheless was effectively providing 7,000 tons per day to the forward troops. According to the subsequent impact analysis: "There is no doubt that but for these special measures in marshaling the transportation resources in both the communications and combat zones the advance of the armies could not have been sustained as far as it was."[28]

Of the 50,000 men who took part in the Red Ball Express, nearly 80 percent were black GIs who served in separate units from white soldiers. These men suffered serious discrimination in almost every way, both trivial and serious. For example, despite black soldiers being in a strong majority, the numerous journalists covering Red Ball tended to speak only to white men, who were featured disproportionately in the photos accompanying articles. A typical company composed of 150 black men was commanded by 7 white noncommissioned officers, a structure determined by the military authorities, who were concerned that black officers would not have the requisite authority. Worse, the military authorities recruited the noncommissioned officers from southern states because they believed southerners were used to dealing with "coloured men." Consequently, as the French author of a history of the Red Ball Express put it, "the US army...recreated the worst type of rural American racial division," encapsulated by a quote the author heard from an officer who reckoned "my cleverest soldier had an IQ of a hundred. The average was eighty. Most of them could not read or write."[29] As Washington Rector, a veteran of the 3916th Quartermaster Truck Company, recalled: "You accepted discrimination. We were warned not to fraternize with whites for fear problems would arise."[30] Rector explained how the races were so efficiently separated that some white veterans of the Express were unaware that most of the Red Ball drivers were black.

The endeavor was also particularly hard on drivers. James Rookard, a Red Ball driver with the 514th Quartermaster Regiment, recounted how the front was at times just five miles away, putting convoys at serious risk: "My worst memories of the Red Ball Express were seeing trucks get blown up. There were dead bodies and dead horses on the highways after bombs dropped." Rookard spoke about additional hazards and delays of "wandering livestock, theft, and starving civilians who would stand in the trucks' path to beg for food."[31]

The whole basis of Red Ball was an attempt to mirror the advantages of railway transport without the tracks, but its difficulties highlighted why trains remained key to efficient logistics. Red Ball required galvanizing huge resources, notably but not only thousands of trucks whose removal from other duties paralyzed considerable swathes of the army. An additional problem with trucks was petty pilfering and downright theft, which was rife and simple to carry out. Many drivers recalled thieves simply taking food and drink from the back of their trucks for impromptu parties, and sometimes, this was done in a systematic way, with gangs organizing the hijacking of whole loads. Joseph Hunter, a black soldier, reckoned "some of the big high ranking officers got rich over there, selling gasoline, cigarettes, candy. You could go to jail for that. Some did go to jail." Hunter more happily recalled that Patton himself was eager to boost morale of the Red Ball drivers, and the general once led his convoy from a jeep to show that it could be done: "He was the type of guy you couldn't tell that something couldn't be done. He didn't believe in that. There was no such thing as couldn't.... He'd say 'we are going to get that damned ammo.'"[32]

Patton's aide, Richard Stillman, who later became a professor of management, recalled that Patton was not above the shenanigans that led to loads being misdirected if it ultimately helped his cause: "A colleague of mine stopped one convoy of gasoline and diverted it to the Third Army." He reckoned Patton would have approved because he told another general: "If only I could steal some gas, I could win this war."[33]

Patton's readiness to abuse the system for his military purpose demonstrated how supposedly strict military rules were often ignored—even by those at the highest levels of command. The unofficial "borrowing" of trucks and the wider abuse of the system were almost as legendary as the Red Ball itself. In some respects, the deployment of this huge fleet led to complete anarchy. Charles Stevenson, a lieutenant with the 3858th Gas Supply Company, who was in charge of a load of fuel, recalled coming face-to-face with a colonel, pistol in hand, who demanded that he hand over his load: "You are not going anywhere until we have these jerrycans." Stevenson was furious and threatened to report the colonel and his men, but to no avail: "We left with just enough gas to get back to our camp."[34] Some victims fared worse than Stevenson when the thieves would drain even the fuel from their victims' trucks. Such theft was made possible by the shortage of military police.

As well as theft, there was widespread misuse of trucks. Young soldiers, often mere teenagers, were wont to jump in a truck in the evening in search of the bright lights of the nearest town. Once Paris was opened up, it was not uncommon for unofficial convoys of dozens of Red Ball trucks to illicitly head into the capital, carrying groups of excited GIs seeking bars and female company. The commander of the Motor Transport Brigade, Colonel Richmond, attempted to stop these trips by issuing a despairing but pointless memo: "Hundreds of trucks drive around the towns and villages at night... I have no idea how they manage to leave the bivouac without the commanders knowing... no passes are to be issued even on an individual basis."[35] Nevertheless, in October, the infirmaries noted a rapid increase in venereal diseases among the troops.

In fact, the downsides and limitations of the Red Ball Express explain precisely why rebuilding the railways was given such prominence. The sheer complexity of loading and unloading thousands of individual trucks was a logistical nightmare. Loading a single truck could take up to 40 hours and averaged around half that. It was an inexact process carried out by men with little experience. The trucks were supposed to carry only up to about five and a half tons, and though this was later doubled, the sense of urgency tempted the men to overload lots of crates of heavy material that took up little space, such as shells. As a result, breakdowns were all too frequent, with almost 20 percent of the trucks off the road at any one time. Heavy use was made of the breakdown trucks, which were located in eight towns on the route and could be sent out to repair broken-down vehicles or, as a last resort, tow them to a garage.

As the report into the logistics put it: "Red Ball was carried out at a terrible cost. As early as Mid-September the mounting strain on both personnel and equipment was already evident."[36] This was neatly illustrated by the deterioration of tires, with 40,000 tires needing repair by the end of the Red Ball operation. Stocks in some depots ran out completely. As for hardships on the personnel, sometimes when a driver slumbered at the wheel, the driver behind would gently bump into his truck to wake him.[37] Extreme fatigue resulted in accidents and led to sabotage and malingering, when drivers would tamper with their engines to incapacitate their vehicles so they could drop out of a convoy.

The Red Ball Express was extended farther east in mid-September, adding to the confusion of some drivers running on roads that were not properly marked. This increase in distance also resulted in more gasoline used to carry what, in railway terms, were tiny loads. Drivers getting lost on these longer routes or being misrouted to the wrong depot placed an added burden on the limited resources available.

Although it was an impressive improvisation, many accounts of the transportation system after D-Day greatly exaggerate Red Ball's contribution in the delivery of supplies to the front, overemphasizing the importance of trucking in relation to the railways. After the war, the Red Ball Express was the subject of several documentaries and an eponymous film that, though it featured a young Sidney Poitier in one of his first major roles, masked the fact that Red Ball was very much a segregated operation. Ironically, by the time of the film's release in 1952, this was no longer the case because the army had been desegregated for four years. Furthermore, the rather romantic name of the operation helped perpetuate the scheme's importance as did America's love affair with motor vehicles, though rail did later get in on the act with its Toot Suite Express, described later.

Ultimately, as the report on logistics stated: "Red Ball bore many of the defects of an operation hastily organized under the pressure of events to meet an emergency: there had been insufficient time for planning; extensive use had to be made of hastily organized provisional units, with all the disadvantages inherent in such practice."[38]

The report concluded: "The crippling impact which logistic difficulties were to have on plans for future operations was only gradually realized, but it was fully comprehended by the end of September, when the 12th Army Group began to dole out supplies to the armies through a strict rationing system based on assigned missions. The shortages experienced during the pursuit had provided only a foretaste of the real difficulties to come. For the next two months supply limitations were to dominate operational plans, and the Allies were now to learn the real meaning of the tyranny of logistics."[39]

It would be gradual, but the shift from motor transport back to the railways would ensure that things could get moving again—but only after the Seine was crossed, which was the next major obstacle. Having amassed the huge quantity of supplies on the west bank through the Red Ball Express, the river, with all its bridges down, had to be traversed. Creating a new crossing was one of the most difficult operations of the post-D-Day advance.

6

RAILWAYS EVERYWHERE

By the end of August, the Allies had created a sizable railway network that was almost entirely devoted to military purposes. Indeed, the American Second Military Railway Service was about to become the biggest rail operator in the world. With the Germans flushed from the area west of the Seine, the railways could operate safely as the principal line of communication—however, major work was still needed in many places to bring the system up to standard for the intense use to which the move east would put it.

Throughout July and August, numerous American railway battalions, manned by railway workers from across the States, arrived at Cherbourg and the beaches, where they were immediately set to work. A snapshot of the time when Paris was being liberated would show four battalions still working in the Cotentin and five more operating east of Le Mans, with a further four nearer to Paris.

Moreover, arriving US troops took over lines around newly conquered Paris and farther east as areas were retaken. These men would remain in Europe for the rest of the conflict, reinstating, maintaining, and operating the ever-expanding Allied-controlled railway network. The British also brought over thousands of men to work on the lines under their responsibility—broadly, the sector north of the American forces along the Channel coast, including the various ports, such as Boulogne, Calais, and later, Dunkirk. To make use of these ports, however, required considerable repairs of the railways, a process that would take several weeks.

Paris, taken in late August, proved to be something of a distraction. Capturing the capital was a symbolic rather than a military objective. A great morale booster, but from a logistics point of view, Paris was merely a small step forward on the way to more substantial military objectives such as the German border, the Rhine, and the vital Albert Canal, which runs between Antwerp and Liège in Belgium. In the event, the troops rushed through and around Paris, and Patton continued his remarkable thrust eastward even faster than before. The clearance of the remaining German troops on the west bank of the Seine on August 24 theoretically marked "mission accomplished" for Operation Overlord 11 days earlier than planned.

The unexpectedly rapid eastward progress of the Allied forces meant that the Seine needed to be crossed long before the date the Overlord planners had anticipated. Originally, the idea was for the troops to pause for at least a month on the west side of the Seine to build up sufficient resources for the establishment of a stable line of communication, making heavy use of the Channel ports. This scenario envisaged the sustained drive into Germany would not occur until well into 1945. But, once again, plans had to be changed in response to events.

At this point, the armies' speed and efficiency were such that the notion of stopping at the Seine would have been considered a lost opportunity. Therefore, in mid-August, strategists decided to continue across the Seine without delay, which is why the Red Ball Express had been put into operation. One can understand the logic. Progress was so rapid that an earlier end to the war seemed possible. Yet, the logistical implications were enormous: the supply lines would be stretched both farther and faster than anyone could have expected. This raised doubts and the question of whether a halt might be the best option.

The Seine was the last obstacle in the way of the troops' push forward on the flat and poorly defended territory of eastern France. All the Seine crossings north and south of the capital had been destroyed. Although the Allies managed to capture the bridges in the city—and keep them intact—they lacked the capacity to cope with military traffic.

According to a British Army report, constructing a bridge over the Seine was regarded as "the principal engineering feature of the extension of the Line of Communication from Normandy to North East France."[1] By late August, the British troops had repaired the coastal line of the railway through Caen and advanced as far as Bourgtheroulde, just six miles southeast of the Seine. The issue was then to decide where exactly to cross the river, which runs through Rouen in a series of lengthy loops as it winds its way to the sea at Le Havre.

———

There were several potential locations to consider, and a hastily established group of 66 engineers, including 21 officers, was dispatched to reconnoiter them and recommend the best location for a bridge. Instead of using cars and other motorized vehicles, this mission was conducted almost exclusively on foot, with groups of men walking along 156 miles of railway tracks to assess their condition. They found that none of the previous bridge sites was suitable; according to the British Army's official report: "The reconstruction of a bridge over the Seine on the alignment of any of the five original rail crossings would have involved very heavy work in clearing the wreckage of the demolished bridge, a task in itself greater than the building of a new bridge."[2]

Expediency was the priority, and the group was to select the route that would be the easiest to repair. They chose an alignment that went south to Louviers before crossing the Seine at Le Manoir, which sat right next to the former bridge, Le Pont de l'Arche. The line then continued northeast to a junction with the main line connecting Rouen and Amiens at Serqueux, which provided a rapid connection with the capital.

Although the reconnaissance team deemed this the easiest option, building the bridge was by no means a simple task. A tunnel blocked by an enormous wrecked steel door that had protected a rail-mounted battery of two guns had to be restored. The wreckage could be cleared, but the two guns were so big that the track in the tunnel had to be diverted around them.

The railway on both sides of the Seine also needed considerable attention. On the western side, a new section of line and an embankment were created to avoid two heavily damaged viaducts that would have taken too long to rebuild, and the line through the Fôret de la Londe, nestled within a bend of the river, required complete reconstruction. On the east side, a bridge over the Eure at Gisors, just 15 miles from the Seine, had to be replaced. And, finally, before the crucial line of communication to Belgium and the Albert Canal could be established, the British railway troops would have to reconstruct two bridges over the Somme.

Construction on the railway bridge over the Seine started on September 6 and was prioritized over other projects. The new bridge consisted of six 75-foot Bailey bridge sections and two shorter 40-foot spans, for a total of 530 feet. The 197th Railway Construction Company carried out this critically important work using the design developed by Colonel Everall on the Melbourne Military

Railway in Derbyshire between the wars. Within 16 days, the 197th not only reconstructed the bridge but also created embankments on the approaches to the bridge, which involved heavy earthmoving equipment.

Within two weeks of work starting, test trains safely ran across the bridge, which had been fitted with a central section that could be raised to allow barges to sail through. As soon as the bridge was fully open on September 22, it became the key route for shipping supplies and fuel for the forces in the North and the principal line of communication until the opening of the Port of Antwerp in November. Remarkably, in the fall, the bridge withstood the worst flood conditions experienced in the region since before the First World War. The bridge remained open throughout this perilous stage by keeping different sets of fully loaded freight cars in place on the central section that were then pushed or pulled by locomotives working on the banks. In other words, the bridge was weighted down with sufficient railcars to ensure it could withstand the flood and avoid being swept away by the rushing waters.

While the British took charge of opening this northern route, the Americans focused on establishing a railway route over the Seine at Juvisy, 10 miles south of Paris. The task was allocated to the 347th, whose commander, Colonel Hulen, took personal charge of this top-priority project: "Speed was essential because until the bridge was in, the Third Army operation east of Metz could not be supplied."[3] The plan, announced on August 25, was that Hulen would then supervise the reopening of the line all the way to Metz, 200 miles east of Paris and less than 20 miles from the German border, "as quickly as the tactical situation would permit."[4]

A detailed account of this bridge's reopening by the historian of the 347th, who called it "the most important bridge of this campaign," provides a deep insight into the difficulties the railroad

reconstruction teams faced. Water crossings were their greatest challenges. The account neatly highlights how, despite the popular image
of military precision, the process was somewhat haphazard, relying
on initiative, courage, extensive searches for equipment, and cooperation with the British military and the French civilians, as well as
more than a healthy slice of good luck. The men of the 347th had no
idea they'd be taking part in such an important endeavor until Hulen
announced on August 25 that they, together with the 377th, another
engineering regiment, and a dump truck company, the 412th, would
be responsible for rebuilding the bridge. The deadline was set for September 8.

Hulen's colleague Lieutenant Davison surveyed the collapsed
bridge at Juvisy and discovered that the second and fifth of the five
spans over the river, which was about 500 feet wide, had collapsed.
Nevertheless, unlike the British, who had resolved to build an entirely
new bridge, Hulen's team decided that making good the existing
bridge would be the easiest option. Davison reported that parts of
the road to the site and the right bank of the Seine were still in enemy
hands. He therefore devised a longer but safe route to Juvisy, which
was some 125 miles east of Le Mans, for the two companies working
on the bridge.

Davison also organized a hasty search for resources in the
Allied-occupied area, particularly in depots at Bayeux, Carentan,
and Valognes, which was the main engineering store just 10 miles
south of Cherbourg. Hulen sent a rather cheeky note to the quartermaster there, asking for 330 tons of bridge steel, stating it was for the
"most important bridge in this campaign."[5] Then, referring to Lieutenant Pierson, who had flown in to seek out the bridging materials,
he added, "Can you help us to eliminate this bottleneck by giving
him a lift [back]. It will save one day. Anyway you blew it [the bridge]
out."[6] In fact, that was not true. As the engineers started work on the

bridge, they realized that most of the demolition had, in fact, been carried out by the retreating enemy.

The initial mission of the 347th was to restore a single railway track over the bridge, ensuring, too, that a second line could be added later. At 8:00 p.m. on the evening of August 26, Companies C and D charged with the task arrived at their bivouac site in Savigny-sur-Orge, a couple of miles from the bridge, and found themselves at the center of locals' attention. Describing it as "the wildest demonstration of welcome by French citizens the men had ever seen," the official report author forgets formal military tone for a moment and states: "It just seemed that everybody in the town was on the street, waving, cheering, throwing flowers and offering wine and fruit to the soldiers in the vehicles. Pretty girls, smartly dressed, were very much in evidence, too, and one could readily see that the men enjoyed this reception no end."[7]

The following day, the men started removing the old bridge, which necessitated cutting it into manageable pieces. Though the Allies had control of the territory, the area was not completely secure, and that day two men were injured by a hand grenade thrown by a group of enemy stragglers. In response, several members of the 347th, along with a platoon from a fighting unit sent to protect them, sought out the group of German soldiers responsible, killing one and taking five prisoners. Further searches, using information obtained from the prisoners, resulted in the capture of two more groups, including two French women who were hiding with them.

There were also sporadic air attacks. The worst occurred on the thirtieth, when enemy aircraft dropped "innumerable" flares on and around the bridge, but fortunately, the bombs all missed the actual worksite. Nevertheless, as the history of the 347th recounts, it was "a spectacular sight as AA [antiaircraft] tracer bullets streamed upwards and flares from the plane overhead slowly settled to the ground."[8]

Spectacular it may have been, but the work around the clock was halted for only 45 minutes until the all-clear was given.

Work on major structures like bridges required much cooperation with other units and, crucially, local workers and suppliers. The senior officers spent much of that first day in negotiation with French contractors, who agreed to provide several barges, two floating cranes, tugs, rowboats, and even diving equipment. A major cultural gulf came to light in how these deals were conducted, a practice to which Americans had to become accustomed. One of Patton's officers, Captain Edwin Coker, who was responsible for obtaining equipment for the Signal Construction Battalion, later recalled: "I did business the way the French do. I would drop into an office, and accept a glass of wine, discuss its merits and then, when they found I would accept it, a little bread and cheese—also subject to discussion. In fact for a week or ten days there, wine, bread and cheese was all I got to eat! Then after we were a bit acquainted, we got down to business."[9]

The lengthy and extensive preparation for rebuilding bridges carried out as part of Operation Overlord now paid dividends because much of the required material had already been brought across the Channel and stored in military dumps. But it was not always clear where this material could be found—particularly when it came to prefabricated steelwork that could be used for missing sections of bridge. Here, luck as well as the curious ways of the military intervened. These crucial sections could not be found at the main depot in Valognes, and strangely, there was no clear inventory of what material was available at other army stores. Then, at Le Mans, Lieutenant Pierson, the officer sent to seek equipment back in Normandy, discovered a train loaded with two construction units of sufficient length to replace the wrecked east span of the bridge at Juvisy. Essentially, according to the history of the 347th, he just took them: "Unable to obtain information concerning the destination of the train and knowing that no other units were constructing railway bridges in the area, Lt Pierson decided to bring his convoy to this point and haul the materials to Juvisy by truck."[10] No questions were asked.

However, complexities and challenges ensued. Divers were sent to find suitable footings and clear debris, but there was a lack of underwater welding torches. Most seriously, the delivery of key construction materials was delayed by the shortage of gasoline, which at one point threatened to halt work completely. Fuel was scrounged from the British at Bayeux, 180 miles away, and they also provided the only available bridge-launching equipment in France, which was needed to push the new completed sections onto the piers. The driving of piles proceeded well, and the last one was only just completed as the sections were readied for fitting. In a last-minute panic over the ability of the crane to lift the sections, the crane's French owners claimed it would only be able to handle 25 tons, whereas the complete 60-foot span weighed 30. All were relieved when the section was lifted into place safely.

As the project neared completion two days before the deadline, a visit by the chief engineer of ETOUSA, General Cecil R. Moore, seemed to galvanize the men, despite the torrential rain that greeted him. The subsequent account of the opening by the historian of the 347th is worth reproducing in full because there were undoubtedly countless other similar occasions that did not have such an enthusiastic chronicler and whose stories are thus lost to us. The ceremony was somewhat redolent of the famous driving-in of the last spike on the Transcontinental Railroad at Promontory Point in Utah in 1869:

The visit of Major General Moore seemed to spur the men on to even greater efforts. A singleness of thought prevailed as they diligently carried out each individual task unmindful of the rain and approaching darkness. The men were now aware that there were no more obstacles in their path and the bridge across the Seine River would soon eliminate a gap in the supply line to the armies at the front. As the regiment's special train arrived at the west approach in the bridge at about 2230 hours, tired men were now carrying ties and rail into position on the last span. They showed no concern for the risk involved as they walked confidently on wet steel girders bolting ties in place and spiking down rail. As the last section rail was spiked into place at 2400 hours, Major Morrison started his train slowly over the bridge. Even now men were still working checking each tie carefully to be certain that each section of rail was firmly spiked into position. Tired men now smiled in satisfaction of the job they had done as the train passed over the last span of the 580 foot bridge. The bridge was now ready for traffic a full 48 hrs ahead of the target date, another noteworthy accomplishment for the 347th and a fine tribute to the ability, loyalty and courage of the men whose untiring efforts got this job done.[11]

Two days later, there was a formal ceremony with a regimental band performing on a flat railcar at the head of the train, ushering in a clutch of VIPs, including Colonel Hulen. Behind the diesel engine followed 12 flat cars carrying all the personnel involved in the reconstruction, who sat on lumber, rails, and the like. According to the unit's historian: "As the train approached Juvisy railroad station, with the band 'sounding off' in fine style, men, women and children came rushing to the tracks from all corners."[12] Even the French workmen dropped their tools to greet the train, and many locals jumped aboard, not without risk to life and limb. The impact of this project was not lost on anyone; both new routes over the Seine were to enable the forces—the British in the North and the Americans in the South—to bypass Paris. Next up, they set out for the Rhine and the Albert Canal in Belgium.

———————

The decision, on Patton's insistence, to drive rapidly eastward following the Avranches breakout, as opposed to focusing on Brittany, was vindicated with a major tactical victory. But the chickens had come home to roost. The rapid progress caused a massive logistics problem as the shape and extent of the invasion changed so comprehensively in such a short period of time. According to the official report on D-Day and its aftermath, this decision "had already involved at least a temporary subordination of logistic factors, and the difficulties over supply which the armies began to experience as they crossed the Seine foreshadowed serious complications later."[13]

On August 25, the most forward forces were a mere 10 days ahead of schedule, having reached the line that Overlord expected them to be on D plus 90 (September 14). But then, the advancing armies surpassed the planning. By September 12, the Third Army was, astonishingly, at the line set to be reached on D plus 350—late May 1945—as 260 days of progress envisaged by the plan had been achieved in a mere three weeks. The record was actually more impressive than even these figures suggest because of that initial delay of 30 days in breaking out of the lodgment. Even so, with barely so much as a halt at the Seine, Paris had been taken a full 55 days ahead of schedule. Afterward, the speed of the advance only accelerated. As the logistical report puts it (with some understatement): "The progress of the armies in the six weeks following the breakout on 1st August appears to have invalidated the conservative estimate of logistical capabilities."[14]

In fact, these logistical issues caused more problems and delay than anyone anticipated. As well as crossing the Seine north and south of Paris, the railway was creeping toward the capital, but many obstacles remained. With downed bridges at Dreux and Maintenon, the route between Le Mans and Paris took a tortuous path that doubled the normal mileage between the two cities. Matters improved somewhat once the bridge over the steep ravine at Dreux was completed on September 6 because it shortened the route to Paris from Normandy through to Versailles, which became a key railhead.

Paris was taken on August 25 without a major battle, thanks to the Germans disobeying Hitler's instructions to destroy the city. The French were given the honor of being the first to enter the capital, though General Leclerc's army had been delayed by poor roads and German resistance. An advance party had entered Paris the previous night—eight weeks earlier than scheduled in Overlord—and the Germans surrendered the following day, although they mounted sporadic resistance over the following week.

After a test train reached Paris on August 29, the first military rail convoy arrived at the Batignolles yard the following day, having followed a complicated route via Le Mans, Dreux, and Versailles. The train was met by the president general of the SNCF, M. Le Mesueray, who then hosted a celebratory lunch attended by none other than the head of the Military Railway Service, Brigadier General Clarence Burpee.

There was indeed cause for celebration. The ban on civilian services imposed by the military was relaxed, and on that first day a train full of potatoes, the first to trundle over the restored bridge at Laval, west of Le Mans, reached the capital. As the history of the 706th reports proudly: "The grand rush to get trains into Paris bad been accomplished in 14 days after the first train had pulled in to Le Mans, to the amazement of all Army Supply men, and freight poured into the capital city bringing not only supplies for the army but also food and coal to starving civilians."[15] The demand for food and the other necessities of life in Paris was so great that the transport system quickly became overwhelmed, and at times military deliveries were delayed even though they were given priority.

In a postwar interview, Itschner stressed how desperate the Allied forces were to ensure that the bridges in the capital were left intact: "We studied very carefully the maps and found that if we could just get these bridges across the Seine in Paris intact, we could take small trains and back them into passenger railroad stations... and you could work your way around the other railroads and then out of Paris to the east."[16] As with many capital cities across the world, Paris was the hub of the national rail network, with lines emanating in all directions and a belt line (La Petite Ceinture) connecting the various stations through the suburbs. Gaining control of Paris and its railway system was of great symbolic importance but by no means did it solve the transport issues the Allies faced.

Itschner went into Paris to assess the situation in a jeep, which almost disappeared under the countless flower bouquets thrown his way by the cheering crowds. He soon realized that his idea of routing the big freight trains through the capital was unworkable because of the intricate inner-city tracks and the meandering belt line's lack of capacity. Briefly, a line through the city was patched up to connect with the belt line, but such was the complexity of the trackwork that only a handful of trains per day could pass through Paris. Thus, the Batignolles depot, north of Paris, became an incredibly busy railhead for goods arriving in the capital and was also used as a yard for locomotive maintenance and repair. Despite its efficiency, Itschner thought it best that trains crossing the country avoid the capital altogether. Freight for eastern France was quickly channeled south of Paris via the Juvisy Seine bridge, a route that became available by

September 11. The line to the north, completed by the British, which would soon reach the key railway junction and freight yard of Liège, also became usable around the same time.

As Patton's Third Army and Bradley's First Army were advancing east, both required functioning railways with considerable capacity to ensure their continued progress. As a result, major railway activity ensued throughout Allied-liberated France, and according to the report on logistics: "At the end of August, more than 18,000 men, including 5,000 prisoners of war, were engaged in rail reconstruction projects," while thousands of other specialist servicemen ran the trains in very difficult circumstances.[17]

Despite all the difficulties, the Second Military Railway Service and the other engineers, both American and British, had exceeded expectations. The original Overlord schedule envisaged that by the first week of September (D-Day +90), the railways would be operating efficiently only to Le Mans, with very limited service beyond that. In fact, according to the report on the performance of the Transportation Corps: "Actually, on that date, railways were in operation in Paris and were on the verge of pushing east to the German border and northeast to Belgium."[18]

Meanwhile, promising news came from the South. As per plan, a new front had been opened when the US Seventh Army, with remarkably little resistance, landed on the famous sands and shingle of the Côte d'Azur on August 15 — fittingly, Assumption Day, always a big holiday in France. Code-named Dragoon (originally Anvil but changed in case the name had been compromised in secret communications), the plan was quite similar to Overlord but on a far smaller scale, with landings from the sea in enemy territory. Nevertheless, more than 500,000 troops and 100,000 vehicles would be landed during a two-month seaborne operation. In fact, matters proved easier than expected; German resistance was incredibly weak because their troop numbers had been greatly depleted by demands in other theaters. Brief fierce fighting flared up around the key ports of Toulon and Marseille, the immediate targets of the invading forces, and both were taken within a week.

The principal aim of Dragoon was to create a new supply route for the advancing troops in eastern France and Belgium, given the limited capacity of the Normandy ports and the decision not to make use of those in Brittany. Originally, Overlord and Dragoon were to have been launched simultaneously, but that idea proved to be logistically impossible because of a shortage of landing craft and other equipment. However, as the supply difficulties in northern France became apparent, opening up a new front in the South, using French troops as well as US forces, became an attractive option to maintain the line of communication for the Allied assault on Germany.

Militarily, Operation Dragoon exceeded expectations. Supported by very active French Resistance groups and a large contingent of regular forces, the Allies enjoyed quick success, rapidly moving north after capturing Toulon and Marseille. Within a week of the landing, they had chased the Germans up the Rhône valley and much of Provence was in Allied hands. In less than a month, Dijon, 300 miles from the Mediterranean and another crucial rail junction, had been taken, and Lyon soon followed.

The railways, again, proved vital for the supply line, which had become too extended for efficient truck transport. It took only two days for the Allies to assume control of the first railway line, a narrow-gauge railway along the coast between Saint-Tropez and Cogolin, 15 miles away. In their hasty retreat, the Germans had not destroyed the railways near the coast. Moreover, the Allied troops entrusted with restoring the railway soon found a dozen locomotives and 80 cars the enemy had left intact. This equipment enabled the men to establish a service on the main coastal line between Fréjus and Sainte-Maxime, a distance of 15 miles; the first train ran on the night of August 23 carrying 300 tons of fuel, rations, and ammunition.

Upon capturing Marseille in late August, soldiers were delighted to find that the railway facilities were in remarkably good condition, having suffered only light war damage. They found a further 30 usable locomotives and 450 freight cars as well, along with good quantities of coal. However, the rehabilitation of the rail network in this important port was marred by a deadly accident a few days later. A train carrying ammunition—including 500-pound bombs and chemical warfare matériel—blew up in the Marseille–Canet station. The cause was attributed to a group of French civilians smoking in a train near a leak of inflammable material, and the subsequent explosion caused 20 deaths, half of them American soldiers, and a large number of injuries. In the rush to clear the area, with no shunting engines available, tanks were used to pull trains away from the site, thanks to quick thinking by Lieutenant Colonel George Glass, an ammunitions expert whose action prevented the fire from reaching a nearby ammunition dump.

Not all facilities were in such good shape as those in Marseilles. Farther north, the destruction was much more extensive, because the retreating Nazis had more time to sabotage railway facilities. Parts of southern France that had been controlled by the Nazi-supporting Vichy government were fertile ground for the French Resistance, which, with logistical and equipment support from the British, had launched numerous attacks aimed at disrupting the railways in the run-up to the invasion.

Attacks by the Resistance continued after the initial landings and were then better coordinated with bombing raids, thanks to lessons learned from Normandy. The combined air force worked in conjunction with the French on the ground to select targets, ensuring actions were more effectively allocated between sabotage on the ground and attack from the air. According to a December 1944 report on the effectiveness of sabotage in southern France, British officer Major K. Henderson reported: "In the area of Lyon, Dijon and Besançon, air attacks and sabotage against the mainline necessitated diversion of traffic to secondary routes, which were kept continuously blocked by the Résistance. There was a general hold up of ten to fifteen days per train. From 20th August no trains at all left Lyon, all exits being closed, principally by trains derailed in tunnels."[19] In the valley of the Rhône, a crucial south–north artery, all the bridges over the river on the section up to Lyon, 200 miles north of Marseille, had been destroyed. North of Lyon, the situation was no better for the Germans because the air force had destroyed numerous bridges and reduced freight yards to rubble. The sabotage by the Resistance proved particularly effective in southwestern France, where the main line from Toulouse to Paris was disrupted almost continuously after D-Day with attacks and the destruction of two crucial viaducts. The specialty of the local Maquisards was to derail trains in tunnels, which caused particularly long delays. According to Henderson, "It was the general opinion in the South East area that the Maquis helped to prevent ten to twelve enemy divisions from escaping to the North."[20]

With the retreating Germans sabotaging key points of the railway, there was no shortage of work for the incoming railway teams. At times, they were overwhelmed, starting a job only to be quickly redeployed to a more urgent one. Moreover, the planners had mistakenly scheduled the arrival of the railway battalions for mid-September, expecting they would not be needed until then. That left the general engineer battalions of the Seventh Army, who were not railway specialists, so far less efficient, to carry out the initial repair work on the railways, learning as they went along.

In response to the obvious need, the introduction of the railway units was expedited, with the 703rd Railway Grand Division and the 713th Railway Operating Battalion brought over two weeks ahead of schedule. Several other railway battalions followed over the next four weeks. Given the inevitable shortage of locomotives, several oil-burning locomotives and diesel shunting engines, along with a thousand freight cars, were also imported from North Africa, though the numbers remained insufficient to make up the deficit.

As ever, scarcity of supplies meant improvisation and speed were essential. At Aix-en-Provence, a crucial rail junction where tracks heading northward split to lines running on both sides of the Rhône, the 343rd Engineer General Service Regiment used the base of a handy abandoned 270 mm German railway gun to span two missing 50-foot sections on a railway bridge, allowing the first train to cross on August 29. After hauling the gun to the site, the engineers levered the base along with a steel extension across the gap as a kind of make-shift Bailey bridge. Remarkably, this improvisation worked safely.

While the main route along the Rhône was unavailable, a diversionary route to the north through Sisteron and Grenoble and the foothills of the Alps on the eastern side of the river was developed. Improvisation, as ever, was the order of the day. To create this stop-gap route, a bridge over the Durance was hastily replaced using Bailey sections and local lumber and steel, and it opened on September 17. This enabled supplies to travel by rail from the Mediterranean coast all the way to Meyrargues, where they were transferred by truck to Sisteron, where the track needed to be fixed, and then back on rail to Grenoble. Repairing the diversionary route was initially given priority because it could be restored to service — albeit limited — more quickly than the main line. However, the steep inclines on the route limited the capacity to just 125 tons per train; routinely, trains carried at least 1,000 tons on main-line tracks. Obviously, this was only going to be a temporary solution because, in addition to its limitations caused by the incline, the line was frequently blocked by deep snows in winter. Consequently, once the temporary line was up and running, there was a rush to repair the main line along the Rhône and through to Lyon by the late autumn.

Given the urgency, railway specialists were allocated to various projects as soon as they arrived. After the usual period of confusion and uncertainty, and within two days of landing on the beach, the 713th was sent to Arles to rebuild the famous elegant railway bridge of 31 arches which stretched 80 feet above two canals. The men — who had been working on railways in North Africa and briefly in Italy — were delighted to be in France with "its neat villages, vineyards and pretty bicycling Mademoiselles. To see a town with people dressed much like the folks back home put new life into everyone and once again there was a cheerful happy smile to be seen almost everywhere you turned."[21]

They had their work cut out. The Germans had collapsed three of the arches over one of the canals and two adjoining arches were cracked. The 713th had arrived without their tools, which were still en route from the battalion's former station in Italy, and therefore: "It was necessary to borrow from the French. Picks, shovels, an air compressor, an antiquated pile driver and several other pieces of equipment, which could have dated back to 1800, were obtained from the French until our equipment arrived from Italy." To accelerate their progress, 200 local SNCF men were drafted and the design of the bridge was simplified. Working continuously, "the days rolled by almost unnoticed and at the end of two weeks a locomotive decorated with French and American flags rolled over the completed structure."[22]

The First Military Railway Service operating in the South of France had repaired lines up through Italy while the Second Military Railway Service was in charge of the US-operated services running in the northern half of France, Belgium, Holland, and Germany. Rather belatedly, Brigadier General Carl R. Gray Jr., the director general of the First Military Railway Service, arrived by air from Rome on September 14 and established his headquarters in Lyon, at the heart of the rail network that was being rehabilitated. Gray immediately set to work figuring out which projects to prioritize. Bridges were, as ever, the main obstacle and most important was to ensure that the high-capacity dual-track railway up the Rhône was fully functional. After three bridges over the rivers flowing fast with snowmelt from the Alps were completed, a Bailey bridge over the Doubs at Dole enabled a railhead to be established at Vesoul, just 135 miles south of Metz, by October 2.

After completing the work at Arles, the 713th headed to Dijon on September 21 to finish work on a bridge started by the French. Afterward, they were needed for a major reconstruction of the lines at Genlis, 10 miles east of Dijon, where an ammunition train had been blown up in an air raid. Just as an aura of calm descended with news of the Germans' retreat, disaster struck. The work at Genlis involved reinstating more than a half mile of track and, in the cold and wet weather on September 29, a fire had been lit. While the men were warming themselves, the heat triggered an explosion of a previously undiscovered shell, killing two and injuring six others.

Such accidents were not allowed to delay the vital task of reinstating lines. The 713th was quickly relocated to Langres, 50 miles north of Dijon, where the unit was scheduled to stay for a month to repair the extensive damage in several locations. The men were housed in strange but apposite accommodations: boxcars parked on a sidetrack marked with the infamous *"40 hommes, 8 chevaux"* (40 men, 8 horses, which were, fortunately, alternatives) notation on the side. Many soldiers of the First World War had become all too familiar with these railcars, the ubiquitous mainstay of the French rail freight system. The men were fed from a kitchen in a small outbuilding, and the more resourceful men transformed their boxcars into a home away from home, as the historian of the 713th recounts: "Each car had a stove with a smokestack poked out through the roof. Inside, with the skill and ingenuity of typical Americans, comforts and decorations of all varieties were installed. Some had a rug here and there on the floor. Many had armchairs and radios purchased from the French. There were pin up girls adorning the walls, a collection comparable to none." Some went even further: "Occasionally, there was a fancy porcelain wash bowl installed with a drain running out through the floor.... All this made the cars almost a palace on wheels." Others lined their new home with cardboard for warmth and appearance. The task of repairing this railway was demanding, but fortunately, there were no further fatal mishaps. The soldiers focused on raising the double-tracked sections of the bridge over the Marne–Saone Canal and fabricating deck girders for the engineers restoring a bridge near Epinal, which was on the main line to Metz, some 80 miles northeast of Langres and where the 713th would next go.

All the while, a combination of trucks and trains delivered supplies to the now static US Army units farther north. The decision to establish a southern supply route in mid-August before all of Italy was in Allied hands was controversial. In particular, the British opposed it, arguing that opening another front overstretched the Allies' resources. The principal purpose of the landings on the south coast had been to bring supplies to the front, but the reliance on truck transport because of the extensively damaged southern French network restricted the quantity of supplies being delivered. Gradually, as lines were repaired, this situation improved. In September, trucks carried 222,000 tons of supplies compared with just 63,000 tons by rail. Gradually, almost daily, rail capacity increased, thereby reversing these roles. The units at the front, notably, were keen for rail to be used because of its speed and reliability. From September 26, a kind of auction for space on rail took place every week for what would be delivered using the most northerly railhead — Besançon, then later, Vesoul. Army units in need of supplies bid against each other for the daily capacity, which was initially 5,000 tons, rising to 12,000 in October and 16,000 in November.

The urgent need to increase the capacity of railways feeding the front prompted the military authorities to take on ever more demanding projects. The most challenging was the reconstruction of a bridge that soared over the Durance, a tributary of the Rhône, between Orgon and Cheval Blanc, about 20 miles southeast of Avignon. The work started in the late autumn, and the reporter for *Railway Age* wrote how the weather affected progress: "An engineer unit started to work on one side of the bridge and a railway construction unit began building from the opposite side. The spot was isolated, high in the mountains. The icy Mistral [a local wind that sends cold air down the Rhône valley toward the Mediterranean] blew constantly, whipping the river into a fine spray which formed a glassy ice over everything underneath." At times, the men could not stand up against the "terrific force of the wind." Eventually, however, "the engineers and railroaders joined in the centre of the span."[23]

As well as track work, increasing the capacity of the network required significant numbers of new rolling stock, which started arriving at Marseille in October. The lines reopened by the railway troops, who were soon reinforced by several newly arrived railway battalions, offered a rapid and effective network for supplies heading north. At the end of 1944, the First Military Railway Service was in control of 4,000 miles of track. By that time, it had reopened four tunnels, repaired 800 miles of track, and reinstated 42 bridges. In the New Year, its battalions started the process of replacing the temporary Bailey arrangements with more permanent arrangements.

However, although Dragoon was successful and was effectively bringing supplies to the frontline troops in time for the push eastward, the overall situation had deteriorated. As the planners had feared, the lines of communication had become overextended and caused a hiatus in the northern European theater.

7

LIFESAVERS — BUT NOT ALWAYS

Operation Dragoon was accomplished swiftly and made a strong contribution to Allied victory, but it was in a secondary war zone. The main Allied force was committed to northern France, and a successful assault was needed there for Germany to be defeated. By the end of August 1944, with Paris firmly under the Allies' control and much of southern France abandoned by the enemy, the military controlled nearly the whole French rail network. Although the priority for most of the reopened lines was to carry supplies to the frontline troops, rail services also helped move the men themselves, both to the front and for leave. The troops rarely traveled in comfort, as they were usually bundled into the *"40 hommes, 8 chevaux"* cars. In his account of the work of the 740th, John Livingstone described how, as soon as the lines east of Le Mans opened up, "troop movements by rail to the front were increasing every day," mostly in the claustrophobic freight cars. The first troop train ran through Le Mans on the evening of the twenty-seventh and returned two days later with prisoners of war.

Not only soldiers rode those trains. Livingstone explains that the most welcome arrival on September 1 was the Eighty-Sixth General Hospital, precisely "86 nurses and five Red Cross girls." The train had to stop for an engine change, and word got around quickly, meaning

that "GIs appeared mysteriously from everywhere." Three days later
another train passed through all too quickly, this time carrying a
"frowzy-headed, sleepy eyed group but honest to God American
women from Virginia, West Virginia, Maryland, Pennsylvania and
South Carolina. Again, GIs seemed to spring up from between the
railroad ties."[1]

Livingstone was witnessing the rapid rise of the hospital train
service, which was made all the more necessary by the increased
length of the line of communication, which stretched over 400 miles
between eastern France and Cherbourg. There was no possibility of
using road ambulances for such distances; military authorities had
determined that for both practical and medical reasons no ambulance should undertake a journey of more than 25 miles. Rail was
therefore the only possibility and hospital trains (known by the
British as ambulance trains), with their onboard medical facilities,
offered injured soldiers a far greater chance of survival than conventional passenger trains.

Hospital trains had been widely used in the First World War,
parked just behind the lines and fully staffed in the run-up to major
attacks. Colonel Bingham, the serial innovator who had devised a
way for landing craft to deliver railway stock directly onto rails on
the Normandy beaches, was instrumental in creating a modern version of the hospital train. Bingham designed the basic hospital train
to have 14 cars, with 7 acting as ward coaches, and to carry up to
317 casualties, depending on how many were able to sit or needed
to lie on stretchers. The other coaches included a pharmacy, medical
facilities, and space for staff accommodation and baggage. Each ward
car was self-contained, with bathrooms, a mess, and heating, and was
fully staffed by a nurse and three orderlies. By September 1943, 15
hospital trains were running on British tracks, both to move patients
arriving by ship from the various theaters of war in North Africa and

Many French railworkers sabotaged the railways despite concerns over the impact on their own people, which the pro-German Vichy government exploited with propaganda like this poster which reads: "Sabotage of equipment? Sabotage of provisions!—who can protect the equipment and the life of your friends? You, railwayworker."

Below: The Resistance posted notices encouraging railworkers to stop German troop and freight movements. This one suggests that all paperwork associated with German trains should be destroyed and, where possible, replaced with documents citing fake destinations. It also says heating systems on train cars carrying Germans should be sabotaged with sand and finally warns "be careful, but act quickly and strongly."

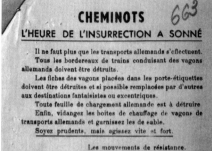

Above: With the rail network yet to be repaired, a trucking system, the Red Ball Express, was introduced to support the invading Allied troops but, while successful for a time, showed that railways were essential in the line of communication.

Truck companies, which were mostly manned by black drivers, required enormous numbers of personnel and needed a huge support network, such as this makeshift service station near Saint-Denis on the outskirts of Paris.

More than 1,000 locomotives built in the US were brought across the Atlantic, serving first in the UK as shown here in a ceremony at Paddington marking the arrival of the first engine on December 11, 1942, and later taken over the Channel to France.

Colonel Emerson C. Itschner oversaw the reconstruction of railways, roads, and ports as the chief engineer, ADSEC (Advance Section, Communications Zone), and was in charge of the remarkable reconstruction of the Avranches–Le Mans line on the orders of General Patton.

Most of the locomotives brought over from the US were Austerity class engines that were hastily built, occasionally leading to boiler explosions with tragic consequences.

A recruitment poster targeted at American railworkers who made up the vast majority of the specialist railway operating battalions.

Men of the Stormont, Dundas, and Glengarry Highlanders enjoying a break at the station in Caen, an important railway town where the lines were among the first to be brought back into use by British troops.

This swing bridge at Cherbourg was destroyed by the retreating Germans but rapidly brought back into use by American engineers from the 333rd regiment.

Airan, 10 miles southeast of Caen, was the site of one of the earliest and also the deadliest acts of sabotage by members of the French Resistance, when in April 1942 they derailed this train, which resulted in the death of 28 German servicemen and injured scores more. In reprisal to this incident, and another in which 10 German soldiers died two weeks later, more than 50 prisoners were executed and many others deported to Auschwitz.

The devastated state of Cherbourg when Allied troops first arrived to start repairing the port and railway facilities in early July 1944.

A key innovation used by the Allies was to fit tank landing ships with rails, which allowed them to deliver locomotives and loaded wagons straight onto tracks built on the beach and connected with the rail network, greatly speeding up the delivery of supplies.

General Patton reviewing his troops of the Third Army before embarking with them across the English Channel to lead the sweep through France.

Below: Repairing the tracks to restore the railway was a labor-intensive task often carried out just behind the front line.

Above: The heavy and prolonged fighting around Caen resulted in extensive damage to the railway, such as this collapsed bridge in the Faubourg de Vaucelles to the south of the town, which the British sappers later repaired.

The repair of the Coutances viaduct in Normandy over the Soulle River was the first time American engineers used the British Bailey bridge system.

A serviceman in charge of a maneuver in a rail yard run by the US Military Railway Service.

Above: Improvisation was the order of the day as shown by these men cooking a meal by the side of the tracks. Many railworkers had to survive on military K rations for several days as they took trains deep into rural France.

Left: It was not only tracks that required repairing. Keeping locomotives, which had often been poorly maintained, was an essential part of the work of the military railworkers, as illustrated by this repair being carried out in eastern France.

In the absence of available prayer facilities, train cars were turned into temporary churches and taken around to various army camps.

The first trains run by the military in France operated along the coast in Normandy and were proudly advertised on this train station schedule board as well as in a specially produced leaflet.

Hospital trains were a vital part of the military effort as the roads were too crowded and poorly maintained for long ambulance journeys, and eventually 50 trains carried nearly 200,000 injured men in the second half of 1944 alone.

Servicemen keeping warm just below a bridge they had hastily reconstructed.

Above: Roll-on roll-off ferries like HMS *Twickenham* shown here were commandeered for army use and several were sunk by the Germans.

Left: Rebuilding railways often involved starting from scratch by laying railroad ties.

The jokingly named Toot Sweet Express was a premier train service from Cherbourg to Paris and beyond that had priority over other services as it carried urgently needed material and mail for the men.

The Germans towed this fearsome machine, the *Schienenwolf*, or track ripper, at the back of a train to destroy the track and rip up the railroad ties.

Repaired bridges were often the quickest route for civilians to cross rivers, avoiding the roads crowded with military traffic.

These jeeps with flanged wheels were widely used for reconnaissance purposes by the troops who arrived first to assess the condition of a railway route.

Stations like here at Argentan were often in this wrecked state as they were frequently the last holdout of the Germans.

Left: No matter how much of a town was wrecked, trains had to get through, and the local railroad tracks were often the first part to be brought back into use, such as here at Saint-Lô, scene of the breakout from the initial lodgment.

Below: Verdun station, a vital rail hub in eastern France, was completely destroyed by the departing Germans.

At Saint-Valéry-en-Caux, a runaway train with inadequate brakes smashed into the station in an accident that killed 89 GIs and injured 152 in January 1945.

All the bridges over the Seine had been destroyed by Allied bombing so effectively that the British sappers decided to erect a completely new crossing rather than attempt to try to raise the collapsed structure.

Above: Several bridges, including this one at Wesel, were constructed across the Rhine for trains to provide supplies for the troops taking over the rest of Germany.

Left: Trains were used to transport prisoners of war under guard.

Tanks were carried whenever possible by rail as they consumed vast amounts of fuel on the road and often broke down.

Locomotives kept on arriving across the English Channel well into 1945, such as this one at Cherbourg, which was greeted with a celebratory bottle of champagne.

southern Europe and to train staff because the authorities realized there would a far greater need for them after D-Day. The trains were painted in drab colors, but, crucially, each featured a big sign of the Geneva Convention — the Red Cross — painted on the roof, with smaller ones on the sides. Unlike the ambulance trains used in the First World War, which merely transported injured men to hospitals, this new generation was more akin to a rolling hospital, with facilities for treatment onboard.

After D-Day, casualties started being brought immediately by ship to the southern ports in England, where they were transferred to hospitals across the country on ambulance trains — or, when necessary, on individual coaches fitted out with medical facilities that were attached to normal passenger services. In the first three weeks of the initial landings, these trains carried 23,000 casualties from the English Channel ports to hospitals around the UK. This proved to be a dry run for what would be a much larger operation on the Continent. After the Saint-Lô breakout in mid-July, casualties had to be transported longer distances to Cherbourg for embarkation.

The need for hospital trains was apparent as soon as the breakout began. Even before Bingham's trains were introduced into service, an improvised affair started operating on August 4. This consisted of 20 French freight cars adapted from boxcars that had been sent in kit form for medical use. Within days, a complete purpose-built 14-coach train of Bingham's design was brought over on the roll-on roll-off Southern Railways' *Twickenham* ferry at Cherbourg; another swiftly followed. They were the first of 23 sets of such trains, which the US authorities decided should be built at the Great Western works in Swindon, Wiltshire, in order to save space in the Liberty ships crossing the Atlantic.

The first two were quickly put into service in Normandy taking patients to the docks at Cherbourg, where they were loaded onto passenger vessels. After the railways to Paris and farther east were opened in early September, the work for the hospital trains expanded enormously. Typically, patients taken by rail were transferred from evacuation or field hospitals in the forward areas to the coast via Paris. In the first two weeks of September alone, 2,700 men were carried by hospital trains, and these numbers only increased as railway lines through to Liège and Metz were opened. By late November, all 23 British-built trains had been delivered, and a further 2 were assembled from French rolling stock. However, even with 25 trains operating, medical authorities complained about a shortage, so another 15, mostly improvised locally, were put into use by the end of 1944. The demand was such that hospital trains were kept as close to the front as possible.

Despite the shortage of rolling stock, the Military Railway Service prided itself on its ability to move trains rapidly to where they were needed. According to a contemporary report: "A Transportation Corps railway operating crew drove an Army Hospital Train into Belgium just two days after the first reconnaissance train crossed the Franco-Belgian border."[2] Considerable resources were allocated to keep the trains on the tracks: 10 special hospital train maintenance platoons were posted at receiving stations and depots.

Although fitted out with better medical facilities than their predecessors, there was still nothing luxurious about these trains. Heating and lighting were sparse, leading to frequent grumblings from the medical staff, and there were few facilities onboard beyond the bare minimum. The British trains were constructed from wood, which posed fire risks and offered little protection in accidents or attacks, which occurred both in Liège and in Paris. The more modern French cars were undoubtedly superior because they were steel-based and consequently far more likely to survive such events. Although the painted red crosses prevented deliberate direct attacks, the injured men could not always be guaranteed safety. In February 1945, at the port of Ostend, a torpedo being loaded onto a boat blew up, setting off other explosions. Spotting the risk to a nearby hospital train, Sergeant Page of the 181st Railway Company jumped into a switcher locomotive and towed it away from danger, an action for which he later received the British Empire Medal.

The trains were slow, often running at reduced speed to lessen the risk of further injuring patients. After the capture of Paris, the trains from the capital took about 48 hours to reach Cherbourg, a journey of just 220 miles for a trip which during peacetime would normally take only six hours. At times, the journey stretched longer because of military traffic on the rails, but timings gradually improved as the lines became less congested as more routes opened or double-tracked, and trains were subjected to fewer stops. Initially, all patients were transferred across the Channel to Britain, but soon the numbers became too large for the British authorities to cope with, and many injured GIs were sent across the Atlantic.

Literally thousands of soldiers owed their lives to these hospital trains because the alternatives — road transport or field hospitals — had far higher mortality rates. The story of just one of these trains is illustrative of the vital role they played. In August 1944, the first hospital train put into service made 15 return trips between Cherbourg and Lison, and although this was a mere 44 miles, the train provided a quicker and safer journey for the wounded than a road ambulance. In the remaining four months of the year, this same train made 19 trips between Paris and the railway hub in Liège and carried out another 20 trips on various routes in the first three months of 1945, including one run down as far south as Aix-en-Provence. Then, after a period of routine maintenance, the train made an additional 3 trips in April and ended its tenure after VE Day with several journeys from Cherbourg repatriating German and Russian casualties.

On June 29, 1945, after 10 months of hard work, the staff of the US Army Forty-Third Hospital Train Unit were finally allowed to return home.

The numbers needing these trains were staggering. In the six months between D-Day and the end of 1944, the Transportation Corps moved 194,842 patients by rail. As a result, toward the end of this period, during the Battle of the Bulge, there was a shortage of hospital trains because a large number of them were sidetracked for repairs but also the fierce wintry conditions slowed them down. After the Nazis were repulsed in January 1945 and Allied troops entered Germany, hospital trains ran across the border, and ultimately, by the spring of 1945, no fewer than 47 of these trains were in operation across the European Theater of Operations.

Near the end of the war, local civilian populations began to seek out the hospital trains because of a shortage of medical facilities, resulting once in a rather unusual "theft" of a train. Robin Wilson, a British officer who served with the 181st railway regiment, was in charge of movement and stores in Düsseldorf just after VE Day. He had been ordered to leave a hospital train parked in a sidetrack overnight to await further orders, but when he returned the next morning, it had disappeared. Because the train had been staffed by the Dutch Red Cross and had taken wounded Germans to and from the American zone, Wilson surmised that the crew wanted to use it for their own people: "I suspect that the hijack was organised by the Dutch as they were themselves desperately short of medical supplies."[3] Whatever their intentions, they failed to get the train to Holland. It was stopped on the Dutch frontier and returned to Wilson's team, much to his relief because he was concerned he would be court-martialed.

Given the intensive use of the rail network, and the primitive conditions for railroading, it was not surprising that, at times, the railways themselves were a source of risk when corners were cut. Operating units were forced to forgo many of the safety features taken for granted in peacetime and instead adopted makeshift arrangements, particularly for signaling and the condition of the track. As the history of Allied logistics in Europe puts it: "Operations often resembled those of a third-class Toonerville Trolley more than model railroading. Under those conditions the ghost of Casey Jones shadowed many an engineer on the forward runs."[4] And it was these primitive conditions, with crude signaling systems and limited communication "ship to shore" — train to control — as well as the high traffic and frequent blackout conditions that made accidents inevitable.

Despite these conditions, it was never clear why, in the early hours of September 5, a train carrying high-octane aviation fuel hurtled out of control toward two stationary trains, which had stopped on the line near Rambouillet, 37 miles east of Paris. The rear train was carrying ammunition and had a caboose that was protected by two extra railcars loaded with diesel fuel — a kind of safety for the conductor, given the fear of rear-end collisions in wartime. The engineers and conductors, all from the 740th, of the two motionless trains were chatting by the side of the tracks when the silhouette of the fast-running train appeared, hurtling toward them on a downward incline. They instantly recognized it was a runaway and that a collision was inevitable. The three men in the front diesel engine of the moving train jumped out just before the crash, but the last to try to escape, the driver, was too late, becoming the only fatality of this accident.

The courage of two railmen who had been by the side of the track prevented a far greater death toll. As soon as the diesel locomotive smashed into the stopped train, the first six cars carrying the highly flammable aviation fuel stored in unprotected jerry cans blew up, creating an instant inferno. Burning jerry cans were everywhere, and some were sent flying high into the air only to explode like enormous fireworks. Most of the men who had been operating the two stopped trains ran for their lives, expecting the whole lot to blow up. However, Sergeant Arthur MacDonald and Private Edward Russell noticed that only one car at a time was catching fire and ran to the sixth car behind the inferno to split the train. They shouted to the engineers, who had courageously stayed in the locomotive at the rear of the burning train, to reverse and pull the surviving cars away. But the pair did not leave it there. They were convinced they could save three more cars and again signaled to the engineers to pull those cars away. As a result, they saved about 50 percent of the fuel, and the inferno burned itself out. MacDonald and Russell rightly received awards for their bravery.

Meanwhile, Sergeant Frank Moore, the conductor of the first stopped train, faced a rather different type of risk. As the collision was happening, he ran to the second conductor's car, which fortunately was empty, but then fell into a deep bomb crater. Villagers pulled him out, but because Moore had been fleeing the scene, the locals suspected him of being a German saboteur. He was rescued only when other GIs intervened to explain.

Similar acts of heroism took place in other incidents across the rail network. In Paris, just days after the Allies gained control, Major William Derr, the superintendent of the yard north of the capital, discovered a fire gaining momentum among 15 boxcars filled with captured German ammunition. Just before the inevitable explosion, Derr, at great risk to himself, managed to disconnect a further 19 cars also loaded with ammunition, preventing the whole yard from blowing up.

It was perhaps only because of such heroic acts that these incidents were ever recorded. Few accounts of accidents appear in the records, but that does not mean there were not many other similar serious mishaps but rather signifies that the authorities were unwilling to release negative news, even in later reports. Railroading is inherently a dangerous undertaking; even in peacetime, there were hundreds of deaths annually on the British tracks, mostly of trackworkers and switcher drivers in yards—the job with the highest fatality rate. Given the difficult conditions in which the wartime railways were operating, doubtless many similar incidents resulted in fatalities that, in the fog of war, could be put down to enemy action or simply censored.

Certainly, censorship was the reason very little publicity accorded the most deadly accident involving the railways after the D-Day landings. The 782nd Tank Battalion and several other units in a cramped Liberty ship landed at Le Havre on January 16, 1945, and were transferred quickly to the Lucky Strike camp near Saint-Valéry-en-Caux, which had been the scene of fierce fighting during the 1940 retreat of the British Expeditionary Force. After a few days, the troops were deployed to join the advance into Germany, but many of these men unfortunately never reached the front line.

The plan was to move the GIs by truck or rail from the port to the camp, where they would spend six weeks assembling equipment and preparing for movement to the front. According to Russell C. Eustice, an officer who had arrived at Lucky Strike on an earlier train: "Hard-driving Maj. Gen. Frank S. Ross, the ETO's [European Theater of Operations] chief of transportation, demanded that the troop trains move quickly. Any delay had to be explained in detail to transportation officials."[5] The train taking the troops to Saint-Valéry, a small terminus station on the coast, consisted of 43 freight cars hauled by an Austerity engine recently brought over from England

and operated by a French crew. Around half of these were the old cars with "40 men, 8 horses" painted on their sides, but such was the rush to take these men to the front that several greatly exceeded their 40-man limit. Packing in 2,000 troops and all their equipment, the massively overloaded train departed at 2:00 a.m. on January 18 and initially crawled along the coast at the line-speed maximum of 12 miles per hour, taking six hours to cover just 32 miles en route to Motteville. According to the later investigation, at Motteville, a soldier expressed concern about the lack of sufficient brakes on such a heavy train: "During the pause, one engineer took a moment to protest about what he considered the engine's poor brakes, but he was reassured by his superior that there was nothing to worry about and sent on his way to St. Vaast. The stop at St. Vaast brought additional queries from the concerned engineer about brake safety, but he was again ignored and told to head for St. Valéry."[6]

The final few miles to Saint-Valéry were a gradual but relentless downward slope, and the train started to pick up speed. The men had opened the sliding freight car doors to allow in air despite the cool breeze, and as dawn began to break, they sat with their legs hanging out. As the train accelerated through the tiny stations of Ocqueville and Neville, a few onboard realized the speed was excessive. In the engine cab at the front, the French engineers desperately tried to put the throttle into reverse to slow the train, but to no avail. Only around half the cars were fitted with air brakes and the rest were running loose, pushing the train down the incline ever faster. The acceleration on the poorly laid track made the cars start to rock as the snowbound countryside flew by. The whole train pitched and lurched as it reached an estimated speed of 50 miles per hour as it crashed into the buffers at Saint-Valéry.

The carnage was devastating. Ten cars piled over each other as high as the station roof, while, in the rear, wreckage formed an even higher pyramid, leaving injured men dangling from splintered cars. Numerous men suffered spontaneous amputations as, on impact, the doors slid shut so fast that they were, according to the French newspaper report, "acting as a guillotine."[7] Many survivors would never walk again.

Eustice later described the scene to *World War II* magazine: "Near the pile of debris lay two long rows of bodies — one row for the dead, one for the injured. The able-bodied scurried about and searched frantically for blankets and first-aid kits. It was, no doubt, a sight commonplace on the battlefield, but this was not a scene of combat. This scene of death and destruction was a train wreck, and these were the bodies of men who had been on the Continent for only about six hours."[8] Both the engine driver and fireman, protected by their locomotive, which had hurtled right through the station, survived and were able to explain to investigators how they had tried in vain to slow the train. One bit of good fortune amid the tragedy: no locals were killed, even though the locomotive ended up in the street beyond the station.

The final toll was 89 dead and 152 injured, many of whom had lost limbs. Even so, many of the survivors, notably several from the tank regiment that lost the most men, were soon in action at the front. Although the French later conducted an inquiry, the US Army did little to investigate the tragedy. The Transportation Corps diary of that day mentions the wreck at Saint-Valéry only in passing, concentrating instead on the more mundane reports of the day's quantity of shipped goods. The only official army account was tucked into a report on logistics, which simply states: "A troop train wreck occurred at St. Valery in District 'A' on 17 January 1945, at 10:30 hours in which 89 were killed and 152 injured."[9]

George Shirk, who was aboard the train with the 1471st Engineer Maintenance Company, tried for years to get the US government to honor those who died in the crash. He told a reporter in 2008: "As severe and nasty as it was, the US government hasn't admitted it ever happened. This has stuck in my craw for 60 years. I've written to everybody, including Rep. Jack Murtha, and nobody would do anything." Interestingly, the newspaper report continues: "Shirk said he believed the cover-up after the wreck was to cover for the general, rather than to keep the Germans from taking consolation in American losses." In another account sent to the newspaper, Sergeant Lowell Sell of Ohio wrote: "We had heard that Gen. Patton was in desperate need of replacements due to recent heavy losses, as the Battle of the Bulge was winding down. He had sent a colonel to the port of La Havre to meet a tank replacement company that was vitally needed at the front lines, and they were on our train. Initially the crew refused to drive this train as it was in poor repair. The brakes were worn out, the engine had no acceleration gauge or speedometer, as well as other undependable items of equipment. However, the colonel ordered — at gunpoint — the French crew to get the train under way."[10]

Writing in 2001, Eustice concluded: "It was a tragedy based on ignorance and poor judgment, for which there was no alternative or satisfactory outcome." Like Shirk, Eustice lamented the lack of recognition of the accident: "While those killed at St. Valery have been remembered in France [with a plaque in the village], there has not been any recognition of the incident by the U.S. government to this date. Some survivors of the wreck have even been refused treatment at Veterans Administration hospitals in recent years on the basis that there was no train wreck involving U.S. soldiers at St. Valéry."[11]

By some measures, the Allies were lucky there were not more railway disasters, given the railway's perilous wartime conditions. In fact, this disaster followed a pattern as many previous wartime rail accidents equally went virtually unreported. Two of Europe's worst rail disasters in history both involved similar overcrowded runaway trains in the First World War: one in Romania in January 1917, which resulted in the death of an estimated 800 to 1,000 troops, and another at Saint-Jean-de-Maurienne in the French Alps in December 1917, when 435 troops returning for Christmas leave perished. In Britain, too, the country's worst-ever rail disaster resulted in the death of more than 200 Scottish troops on their way to Gallipoli, when three trains crashed at Quintinshill on the English-Scottish border in 1915. Italy, too, suffered its worst rail accident during the Second World War, when a steam-hauled train stalled in a tunnel in the southeastern town of Balvano, resulting in the carbon monoxide asphyxiation of more than 500 people.

But such disasters never stopped the railways. Or even resulted in a moment's hesitation about their use. Railways were essential to the military's cause, and in the final months of World War II they were at the center of the surge that ultimately led to victory. At this point, the eastward push to win the war in Europe hinged on the opening of a port that was an alternative to Cherbourg. It would reduce the line of communications by several hundred miles and facilitate the final phase of the conflict.

8

WAITING FOR ANTWERP

Patton's rush east was unsustainable. This became apparent in September 1944, when the strain on the supply lines could no longer be ignored. For Itschner, chief engineer of ADSEC responsible for the line of communication, autumn was the busiest part of the whole war. His work included everything from improving the northern ports and helping the British open Antwerp to large-scale reconstruction of facilities such as hospitals and military headquarters. But, as he put it in a later interview, "the rail work was probably our major job."[1] And making sure that the railways were able to support the final push into Germany was top of his agenda.

The progress toward the German border had been, up to that point, nothing short of remarkable. It was as if central France barely existed. Movement had been so rapid and unstoppable that, to an amateur observer, it seemed the whole conflict might soon be over. The leap from being weeks behind Overlord to months ahead meant that by the end of September the Allies occupied virtually all of France, Luxembourg, and much of Belgium, providing a continuous front from the North Sea to Switzerland. And every time more territory was taken, the railway battalions and engineer regiments were sent in almost immediately to bring the tracks back into use.

Despite the speed of progress, our amateur observer would have been wrong to draw any conclusion about the imminence of the end of the war. Taking over occupied land was a very different matter from conquering the enemy's home country. The speed at which the railways were being rebuilt was to ensure they could cope with the enormous supply demands of the planned assault on Germany. But because the work could not be completed overnight, inevitably there would be a period of what Patton hated: a static army. Moreover, unbeknownst to him and the military command, the infamous German counterattack later known as the Battle of the Bulge would be mounted at the end of the year, which for a time reversed the Allies' progress.

Beyond the Seine, the railway picture was considerably brighter than it had been on the way to Paris. For one thing, a much more robust network crisscrossed the Northeast, a legacy of the area's historic role as an industrial center focused on coal. The railway in this region, now being overrun by Allied forces, included several key main lines that had been kept in much better shape than those farther west, not least because the Germans had used them to connect France with the fatherland. Additionally, although the railways east of Paris had been targeted by both the Resistance and the Allied bombs, the Allied troops were pleased to find that much of the damage was nowhere near as comprehensive as the destruction in Normandy. Immediately east of Paris, the enemy's rapid retreat had reduced the opportunity for them to inflict major damage; in some cases, getting the lines running was just a matter of installing a few operational staff. Even so, overall there was still considerable work to do, notably replacing countless key bridges. Closer to the German border, the destruction was worse as a result of the Germans' infamous wrecking device, which had torn up many miles of track.

American-controlled railway operations east of Paris began on September 4 with a decision that was not greeted warmly by all elements of the local population. The US Military Railway Service decided to take over all the French rail network lines east and northeast of the capital on the grounds that no other arrangement would have been workable. The Transportation Corps explained: "It was found during operations west of Paris that the Military Railway Service could not predict with any degree of certainty when a proposed line would be open to supply. There were too many unexpected factors to contend with. Main lines were often badly destroyed at strategic points and a secondary or round-about route had to be used."[2] This, in fact, had been envisaged as part of the three phases of railway reconstruction, but even the most supportive locals felt some dismay at losing their rail network, albeit temporarily.

However, the military's ability to make all construction and operational decisions undoubtedly sped up the rehabilitation of the network. The huge amount of reconstruction work, with thousands of men located at numerous sites, quickly paid off. Crucial routes were patched up and diversions onto secondary lines were made to avoid collapsed bridges. By the end of September 1944, three railway lines extended east of Paris: one from the Batignolles yard north of Paris to Valenciennes and through to Liège in Belgium; a second to Charleroi, also in Belgium; and a third, from the Valognes yard south of Paris to Nancy. A north–south line in eastern France linked these routes, which at the time terminated in Verdun, just 62 miles from the German border.

It was in this eastern region near the border that the destruction was greatest, mostly a result of enemy sabotage rather than Allied bombing. The lines had to be brought into working order for the assault on Germany, but their proximity to the front line made it difficult to start the repair work, which was substantial around the strategic cities of Liège, Nancy, and Metz. In particular, according to a Transportation Corps summary: "Close to Germany in the area east of Metz, 'the track ripper' had been used. This was the first time its devastating effects on railroads had been encountered since the Italian front."[3] The Germans' use of this device, which involved targeted explosions and a huge hook dragged behind a train to tear up the sleepers, was so effective that 90 percent of the line needed rebuilding. Fortunately, only a few lines in the area where the German retreat had been protracted were affected.

———————

The scale of the railway reparations program was staggering since the number of miles under Allied military command virtually doubled in the final three months of 1944. The workload of the railway battalions was varied, effectively re-creating the French rail network east of Paris and then operating it. Even if a captured part of the track was operational, almost invariably it still needed repairs and rerailing to increase the line speed, which was crucial to boosting the capacity of the network and ensuring the safety of the network. Communications and signaling also routinely needed reinstating; facilities at yards and stations required rebuilding. Even where the Germans had departed rapidly, they had amused themselves by smashing up signal boxes, telecommunication switchboards, and easily accessible lineside equipment. Making good all this destruction was unsung and banal work but essential in establishing an efficient and safe line of communication.

As the Allied forces poured into eastern France, the number of tasks for the railway battalions increased, and new units, both British and American, continued to arrive to repair and run the ever-growing mileage in Allied hands. As new troops arrived, the more experienced men tended to move eastward, closer to the front line.

Given this huge catalog of work, it was impossible to ignore the fundamental difficulties caused by the rapid progress eastward, and it became clear the lines of communication had become so stretched that the Allied armies could progress no farther. Until the railways were able to operate at full capacity, there was no reliable line of communication to supply the forward positions because the roads were incapable of making up the shortfall. The Red Ball Express had proved its worth as a temporary stopgap but also highlighted the inadequacies of relying on trucks.

The rush eastward had put enormous strain on the army's equipment, notably resulting in a huge backlog of maintenance for trucks and other vehicles; for example, only 75 of the Third Army's original stock of 232 vehicles were in working order at this point. With the Brittany ports still in enemy hands—and, in any case, too distant to be useful—and the limited capacity of the Channel ports, a growing number of ships were waiting to unload. By the time Antwerp reopened in late November, the logjam of waiting ships had reached a peak of 240. These unloading difficulties might have been overcome had it not been for the lack of capacity further down the line, which put a halt to all progress by mid-September. The army report provides an apt analogy: "The whirlwind advances of August and early September thus left the Communications Zone in the condition of an immature athlete who has overexerted himself in his first test of endurance. And there was no time for true recovery."[4]

These supply blockages were particularly frustrating because they scuttled any hope that the war might quickly be brought to an end. Instead, within a matter of days, the deteriorating transport situation led to what the report author called "one of the most reluctantly made, and most debated, decisions of the war."⁵ In late September, Eisenhower was forced "to halt offensive operations on a large part of the front and to concentrate the bulk of the Allied resources on a relatively narrow front in the north." And this supply famine was to have serious and long-term implications: "For a period of almost three months logistic limitations largely dominated tactical planning, and U.S. forces learned to their dismay how supply, instead of holding her rightful position as the handmaiden of battle, could become war's mistress."

Eisenhower's decision put an end to what was building up to be a major fight between the two antagonistic generals, Bradley and Patton. After the crossing of the Seine and the capture of Paris, two armies, Bradley's First and Patton's Third, had swept east in almost parallel lines, but there was still great indecision at army HQ about which of the two should be given priority. Each had a railway line serving it. The First Army was supplied from trains operating northeast out of the Batignolles yard in the northern suburbs of Paris; eastbound trains ran from the Valenton yard on the southeastern side of the city to support the Third Army. However, the capacity of both lines was limited as repairs were still being undertaken and the signaling systems had yet to be established. Certainly, neither general, between whom no love was lost, was going to go out of their way to help the other.

Initially, both made substantial progress, but now running low on gasoline and meeting regrouped German forces, the troops stuttered to a halt. Patton's Third Army was heading toward Metz and Nancy in the middle of the country, taking towns such as Reims and Chalons, with the eventual aim of reaching the Meuse River. However, by August 29, the army's momentum was slowed by a shortage of gasoline, and a couple of weeks later it was forced into a complete halt.

Similarly, to the north, Bradley reached the Belgian border and took the key town of Liège, but then he, too, was forced to stop, having outrun his line of communication. There, the Allies faced the strong defenses of the Siegfried Line, and to the south, enemy resistance prevented the Americans from crossing the Moselle. By September 15, the railway lines to Liège, just 35 miles east of Aachen across the German border, had been opened by the Allied forces. Nevertheless, considerable work was required to expand the capacity of the eastern French network. Many of the reopened lines were single-tracked, and collapsed bridges often meant diversions on circuitous routes, which often required the time-wasting process of reversing. Despite the continuing work of the railway troops bringing tracks back into use, the railways were still overstretched. As Nicolas Aubin, the French historian of this campaign, puts it: "Whereas the months June to August had been ones of successful improvisation, those of September to November were those of disillusion. [None] of the armies found solutions to the multiple points of congestion. The supply chain became stuck and the American generals were reduced to playing a waiting game,"[6] and, as we see later, blamed Montgomery for failing to open up the port of Antwerp earlier.

The additional difficulty was that the network under the control of the military had expanded so rapidly that there was a lack of men to operate the tracks. Consequently, the Military Railway Service appealed to railroaders in the United States to come immediately to Paris and join a railway battalion. An article in *Railway Age* reported that after the call for additional trained officers was made in October, men began arriving a few days later and "within a few hours thereafter shouldered their share of the terrible physical and mental burden that our railway officials were carrying at the time."[7] And they did this with relatively little military training.

Certainly, the railway GIs had their work cut out for them. For example, the 706th Grand Division, after having brought the yards at Le Mans back into use, relocated 325 miles east across France to Toul on the Moselle River. Toul had become the key railhead in eastern France for the Third Army because the routes farther east and north were blocked. Upon their arrival on September 20, the 706th discovered themselves to be the only railway battalion between Toul and Paris. Fortunately, finding accommodation in Toul was no problem; they simply fitted out the train in which they had arrived. Unlike at Le Mans, the local yard—which was to become a huge supply base for the winter offensive into Germany—had survived the war relatively unscathed, but the neighboring lines were so damaged that Toul essentially became a dead end. The northern lines toward Metz were blocked by the destruction of five bridges, and on the line south to Nancy, a lengthy bridge over the Moselle was still in the process of being reconstructed. Other eastward lines were either too close to enemy lines or also blocked by fallen bridges. Although there was a healthy stock of French locomotives ready to use and a local SNCF workforce ready and eager to run the trains, they were barred from doing so because running the railways was still considered a military operation under the rules set out by the US Army. Moreover, the railway's primary purpose—supplying the troops headed for Germany—took precedence over all else, including passenger services, which did not please the locals newly liberated from the German yoke.

Because it took time to repair the lines beyond Toul and the advance had been halted, the task of the 706th was notably different from their work at Le Mans. The historian of the battalion explains: "This time it was not a race to get supplies further ahead because the Army had stopped. It was a terminal operation, thousands of cars came in and after being unloaded they were dispatched back to the ports for more supplies."[8] It was also dull, repetitive work, as railway operations often are, but essential nonetheless. The proportion of supplies going by rail as opposed to by road was increasing every month. The lessons of Red Ball had been learned. As the logistics report emphasizes: "While motor transport operated with greater and greater efficiency and gave a much-desired flexibility to the theater's transportation system, it constituted no substitute for the railways in the sustained movement of large tonnages over great distances. In the long run the railroad was the main workhorse of the transportation system, handling the great bulk of the tonnages."[9]

Even the senior officers preferred traveling by rail, as it was safer and quicker than using the roads, which were constantly congested by military traffic. The 706th found a couple of modern diesel inspection cars, the characteristic French red-and-white Autorails run by engines attached underneath. The commanding officer of the 706th, Lieutenant Colonel Louis G. Jamison, had one refurbished for the personal use of Brigadier General Ewart G. Plank, the head of ADSEC. This was such a success that another car was fitted out for General Patton complete with cooking facilities, beds, and a desk. The gleaming little train was presented to him at an informal ceremony at Nancy on October 24, and he promptly rode in it to Toul, where he dined with Jamison after an inspection of the rail facilities.

Because the army was now static and supplies sent farther east needed to be expedited, Jamison decided to establish a regular freight train that would serve four railheads near the front line. This daily run, which was given priority over other rail traffic, became known as the "Three Star Special" in honor of the three-star General Patton, and it was later expanded to take in other railheads so that it replaced truck movements across a swathe of eastern France. The 706th at Toul also handled numerous hospital trains, loading patients from ambulances and transporting them to general hospitals in Paris.

Although the headquarters of the 706th moved to the newly captured city of Nancy at the end of October, the rail operations out
of Toul continued to be intensive. Nancy was a better headquarters,
not least because it was already a key SNCF regional facility; therefore, closer cooperation with the SNCF could be established. But
the railway remained very much a military operation with all that
entailed—the SNCF was no longer in charge of its own national rail
network until the Americans started handing back sections as military demands reduced. Following the capture of Aachen on October
20, a significant network of lines to the rear were opened to create an
adequate supply line for the future advance into Germany. All these
lines were firmly under US control, and it was the US military that
selected routes to prioritize for repair.

For the 347th, there was no respite after they reconstructed the
bridge over the Seine at Juvisy. Within 48 hours of the opening ceremony for the new Seine crossing, four companies of the 347th were
relocated to Bar-le-Duc, 140 miles east of Paris. According to the
unit's log, this was not welcomed by the men, who "were just a bit
reluctant to leave the beauty and wonders of Paris."[10] One company
was tasked with rebuilding a hundred-foot railroad bridge in Bar-le-
Duc over the Marne River that had partly collapsed. Another was
sent to Verdun, a similar distance northeast of Paris, to carry out
the most demanding of these early jobs: the replacement of a key
railway bridge over the Meuse River to Metz. Three of this bridge's
masonry arches had been destroyed as well as two intermediate piers.
The work, however, was delayed by the lack of heavy cranes and the
difficulty of finding steel sections to replace the missing masonry.

Similarly, soon after the Rambouillet accident involving the
runaway train, the 740th was relocated to Laon, 100 miles northeast of Paris, as German resistance in eastern France crumbled.
Various other railway battalions were also sent eastward as summer

folded into autumn. Progress for the Allies was fast—too fast, as it turned out.

The farther east these armies ventured, the greater danger they faced from proximity to the enemy, especially because the rapidity of the advance meant the precise location of the front line was not always clear. Reconnaissance was hampered by uncertainty of who was in control of an area. One patrol, sent in a jeep to investigate the lines from Verdun to Metz, found themselves under artillery shells at a point 14 miles from the city and had to retreat after being pinned down by small-arms fire. Another, heading out of Bar-le-Duc, managed to find a French locomotive to take them to Amanvillers, just 8 miles from Metz, where they came under fire and had to retreat on foot. A third patrol entered an eerily quiet village called Hagondange, 11 miles north of the city, when a German tank rumbled past them, fortunately without noticing their uniforms. Later, an officer and a private of the 347th sent on foot to inspect a railway line to Sarralbe, some 20 miles south of Saarbrucken, disappeared, and despite several attempts to locate them, their fate was never discovered. Such reconnaissance trips were among the most dangerous tasks carried out by these railwaymen.

This type of incident was fortunately not the norm because, for the most part, the railroaders were able to carry out their work without being attacked, but in parts of eastern France there remained a danger of lurking hostile Germans, who could easily melt into the countryside. This border region of France, Lorraine, had long been disputed territory between the two nations. Many thousands of man-hours that could have been usefully deployed for engineering work instead had to be used for guard duty to fend off the constant threat of sabotage. And there were spies, too, whose stories could have come straight out of a war movie. An observant GI, Dwight Reed, was in a café in the small town of Champigneulles one evening when the man next to him pulled out his wallet and a photograph dropped to the floor. Reed instantly noticed that it featured a German soldier. Fortunately, Reed carried a pistol, which enabled him to arrest the man and his companion, who were taken to Third Army headquarters.

Whenever there was a lull in railway reconstruction work, the engineers were quickly allocated to other tasks, such as turning an abandoned enemy camp into a thousand-bed hospital. But it was not all work. There was some time for play. Toward the end of 1944, the Military Railway Service was running leave trains for troops who had a few days off and invariably headed for the bright lights of the capital or other big towns. The trains were notoriously basic, often without any restroom facilities, and consequently were required to stop at regular intervals.

Meanwhile, the 347th created its own entertainment. A regimental band played at various locations in the evenings and had, according to the log, "improved considerably." The band was led by a corporal with the appropriate name of Metz and had "through long hours of rehearsing developed into a first class musical combination."[11] Or at least that was the view of the diarist. Armistice Day, on November 11, was marked by ceremonies in two small towns just a few miles southwest of Nancy, Neuves Maisons and Pont-Saint-Vincent, where Colonel Hulan laid a wreath at the war memorial—an event made all the more poignant by the fact that Hulan, along with several of his senior officers, had fought in that war. Two weeks later, on Thanksgiving, the caterers ensured there was enough turkey to go round so that every member of the 347th received a portion. Indeed, the queues at the messes that day moved slowly as soldiers filled up their plates like never before. There was, too, another wedding—this time featuring a local mademoiselle, Gilberte Coasne, who had fallen for an officer, Lieutenant Wiley

Landrum. The chaplain conducted the ceremony, with Hulan as best man, and the bride's mother then provided a huge and welcome feast for the guests.

This snapshot of the 347th engineers' work—and fun—in mid-September could be replicated to represent the similar stories of other units during that autumn. Though lines still needed to be repaired and bridges still needed to be replaced, troops focused on expanding the capacity of the network beyond its prewar level to cope with the volume of supplies the attack on Germany required. Single-line tracks were doubled, new junctions were created to facilitate efficiency, and speed limits were removed by improvements to the track. The various companies of the 347th faced an almost infinite task list, even as other engineer and railway battalions were brought in to help them carry out this work. But it paid off. With each bridge that was replaced, each section of line that was reinstated, and each yard of track brought back into use, the capacity of the railway increased. That was the key. Railways are a network whose capacity is limited by their weakest link. Almost every section of line could now be used to help supply the army. There were big, major depots and railheads but also dozens of smaller ones that could be used to unload a train or two, and possibly closer to the front than some of the larger ones.

The role of the 740th, sent to run the lines just north of the territory of the 706th, was to back up the First Army. They initially operated from the recently liberated Laon, a key railway junction 325 miles northeast of Le Mans, but left Le Mans on September 14 in a ragbag train with a variety of rolling stock and all the men's possessions, which Livingstone described: "Company C had a circus-like atmosphere: one man carrying a bicycle; another a box containing a chicken and a duck, squawking and quacking; and still another with a bed on his back and a box of ten-in-one rations under his arm." The train consisted of a set of German boxcars, which the men reckoned would make useful accommodations at their posting in Laon, and Livingstone had snaffled an old German office car, "quite old and shot up, but in running condition." The journey across France took two and a half days due to track congestion and the chaotic state of the railways.

Livingstone's description of the trip around Paris is particularly revealing about the state of the network. It took a day for the train to reach the capital from Le Mans, a distance of just 115 miles, because there was no functioning signaling system and therefore only one train could be allowed on a long section of track at a time. Around the capital, there was utter chaos: "Passing through Paris by rail was similar to negotiating a maze. Incoming rail routes could be likened to fourteen spokes of a giant wheel connected by two rims, an inner and outer. Only the inner circle was in operating condition. Through the city French *cheminots* piloted military trains, and, in addition, MRS personnel were stationed at important junction switches."[12] The men, though, were heartened by the train's reception at almost every station, where crowds of local people cheered them on, with the women blowing kisses and passing out foodstuffs and wine to the beaming soldiers. Sometimes they offered fruit in exchange for K rations, which were sought after for their meat content. It was indeed the Liberation Line.

Upon his arrival, though, Livingstone found an even worse situation than he had faced at Le Mans: "Railway facilities and the adjacent newer business and residential sections down on the flat [section of town] were virtually obliterated by allied airmen. While the yard was not comparable in size with Le Mans, the aerial bombing had been more destructive, if that were possible. Rails curled in to pretzels were on top of cars, and cars on top of locomotives and vice versa. Deep bomb craters abounded. One freak result of the bombing was two lengths of rail driven lengthwise through a locomotive."[13]

Laon was a junction with an engine house rather than a yard, but there was plenty for the men of the 740th and the joining battalions to do repairing the tracks around the town and reinstating the railway to the east. The work was perilous, and a track foreman, Corporal Harrison Wilson, was injured soon after arriving when a shell he was removing from a bomb crater blew up. The division commander, Lieutenant Colonel Samuel Pulliam, and Captain A. Schofield had an even more dangerous dance with death. On September 20, they left in a jeep on reconnaissance to locate yards suitable for future railheads. They came to a deserted town in the extreme northeastern corner of Belgium but were unaware of its name because every road sign had been removed. All the houses were firmly shuttered, leaving an eerie silence in the empty streets. The two officers finally stumbled upon a local man whom they asked in French for the name of the town, but he only answered when they requested it again in German. He replied that they were in "Gemmenich," a town just five miles south of Aachen, which had yet to be captured. The two grew concerned, even more so after a huge German tank lumbered past them in the road. Fortunately, the tank's occupants failed to notice the markings on their jeep. Pulliam roared: "Turn around and get the hell out of here!" Somehow, they had blundered through their own infantry and the German front line without being challenged. Rather more amusingly, Livingstone reports how "I don't know whatever happened to it, but on 23 September some T&S [telecommunications and signaling] men showed up with a two-man German tank they proposed to use as a line truck."[14]

The at times delicate relationship between the local French railworkers and the American military men running the network is encapsulated by one of Livingstone's stories. Yes, they were repairing

the railway and investing considerable resources into it, but there
were sensibilities at stake and failing to recognize them could impact
the performance of the fragile railway. Livingstone relates how, on his
arrival at Laon, one of his officers, Lieutenant Bill Mason, took over
the responsibility of dispatching the trains only to find that the officer of another US Army regiment that had previously been in charge
had thrown all the French staff out of the office and confiscated their
"switch wrenches." As a result, the station was a bottleneck and only
two trains had gotten through on the previous night because of the
atmosphere of "constant bickering." The French were brought back
and the nightman, Lieutenant O. Draper, discussed the situation
with the Chef de Gare. As Livingstone reports, Draper "explained
that he would merely tell the French what the military required and
let them run the railroad. To establish amicable relations, a few packs
of cigarettes and chocolate bars were passed to the Chef," and that
night, 10 trains moved through the terminal rather than 2.[15] A similar discussion sorted out another delicate situation in the engine
house, where, again, an officer of a different battalion had antago-
nized the French staff.

Livingstone and his officers understood that getting things done
was all about establishing an entente cordiale and setting out clear
demarcation lines. It worked best when the US Army officers specified what was required and the French undertook the bulk of the
work. For the most part, the local railworkers were friendly and
supportive, but there were exceptions. Livingstone describes how
"difficulties were encountered with some of the French 'roadmen,'"
who had caused many trains to be delayed. One French engine was
"secured at the point of a carbine." There was looting, too, with a
couple of his men discovering 15 full gasoline tank cars shunted onto
a sidetrack "for no accountable reason." Both rations and clothing
were also being stolen from trains, and to prevent this, armed GIs

always accompanied the French crews "with orders to shoot if necessary."[16] However, by and large, there was cooperation in the joint goal
of defeating the Nazis.

Laon soon became extremely busy with military traffic operating
in both directions. Vast numbers of German prisoners, largely teenagers and men in their forties, were heading west, with as many as
6,000 passing through on the busiest day, September 20. In the same
direction, hospital trains, which each required two locomotives, were
taking their precious cargo to Paris. The vast bulk of traffic, however, was in the other direction, as supplies for the front were building up and demand was so great that there was a shortage of crews.
Occasionally, a train was given absolute priority, effectively pushing
the other services onto sidetracks, as happened on September 23,
when "a hot-shot gasoline and ammunition" train, as Livingstone
described it, with orders from the 708th Grand Division to be moved
to the front without delay to maintain the assault on Germany came
through. By mid-September, the 740th had 48 crews running trains,
but even with the help of French *cheminots*, there was still a shortage,
and GI railroaders found themselves on shift for seven or eight days
consecutively.

In early October, the 740th moved again, this time 115 miles
northeast to Liège. Liège had been liberated on September 8, and
by the middle of the month, much of Belgium was in Allied hands.
Soon after the Allies captured the city, the 708th Grand Division set
up its headquarters in the city, which was to become the key hub of
railroad supply routes as it had lines running in all four points of the
compass. The importance of Liège as a railway center increased as all
supplies heading east had to be routed through the Guillemins valley
in which the city nestles.

But the capacity of the line was initially limited because of damage to the tracks around it. The main yard on the outskirts was

deemed unrepairable, and consequently, the principal supply depot was established next to Liège–Guillemins, the passenger station, which included only a few tracks for loading and unloading. Worse, only one route out toward the German border was usable until late November when a key bridge was repaired. This led to potentially dangerous congestion, with vulnerable trains from France left immobile on the tracks for many hours. The 40-mile journey from Namur to Liège, a trip that would normally be completed in a couple of hours, at times took up to two or three days. Through October and November, a logjam of trains stretched along the tracks almost all the way to Namur.

When the 740th arrived, the situation was so chaotic that a train sent 20 miles east toward Herbesthal, where the headquarters of Company A would be established, ended up on the wrong line and found itself in enemy territory en route to German-controlled Vise. After several miles, the crew and the Company A passengers realized the mistake and slowly backed up to Liège, where their train was routed correctly, with the Germans none the wiser. The 740th was soon joined by a large contingent from the 741st. Their main work was reconnoitering and repairing lines to the east, which would be used to reach Holland and Germany. The effort was necessary because Antwerp was still not available and the Channel ports did not have the capacity. Therefore, trains had to run huge stretches—430 miles from Cherbourg to Metz, 400 miles to Liège—making massive hauls on a network that was in far worse condition than the one that had existed before the war.

Improving the railways in and around Liège was difficult and perilous work even when there was a lull in the fighting in the area. Numerous mishaps occurred, such as derailments, collisions of trains—which were traveling slowly because of the poor condition of the track—and even, at grade crossings, military trucks colliding with passing trains. And the problems didn't stop there. Another friendly-fire attack, like the one before the Saint-Lô breakout, only by luck did not cost soldiers' lives. Two GIs, Martin Malone and Michael Potts, had been sent 20 miles east to Verviers to inspect a damaged section of track when five planes flew over dropping bombs and returned to strafe the station. Potts attempted to set up a machine gun but—fortunately—did not have sufficient time to fire. The pair dived for cover and then found a shelter full of civilians who pointed out furiously that the planes were *"Avions Americains."* Two days later, a colonel of the Air Corps called at the headquarters of the 708th Grand Division and apologized for bombing Verviers, explaining that the bombs had been intended for Aachen. Livingstone could not understand how such a mistake could be made, given the fighting was around Aachen, not Verviers, and the town was far larger.

The local population, too, posed a potential risk, and there were constant reminders that the train service was being operated amid a major conflict in the middle of a population who were not necessarily all supportive of the invading troops. There were doubts, for example, about whether local track workers could be employed given that areas of Belgium had been German territory until the end of the First World War. Support from the local German-speaking population could by no means be guaranteed. Even after several weeks of Allied occupation, both overt and subtle sabotage occurred, such as newly laid phone wires being cut and the flow of goods being diverted. Mysterious red lanterns, a mandatory stop signal for any railwayman in the world, also appeared on platforms at night, even though the local station staff denied any knowledge. Normally, such lights were stamped with a station name, but these were not, suggesting a clear attempt at wrecking the train service. Strange anonymous phone calls, sometimes using American-sounding voices, suggested that "orders are to hold up all trains to the railheads tonight." Livingstone himself received such a message, but the caller immediately hung up when asked for his name. Local German sympathizers deployed direct methods of sabotage, too. On December 1, brake hoses were cut on two railcars that had just returned from Maastricht.

Then, there was the local "Mata Hari." At the yard where the conductors' cars were kept, railwaymen found themselves being chatted up by a woman Livingstone described as "a pretty, well-stacked, stylishly dressed and intelligent blond[e] who spoke English with very little accent."[17] In her conversations with the trainmen, she showed an unusual interest in the content and quantity of freight being moved to the forward supply dumps, but her approaches did not fool the men, who alerted the Belgian authorities. Two Belgian policemen turned up in Livingstone's office, and their visit prompted him to recall that she had once come into his office seeking information. The investigators were convinced that she was a German spy. Livingstone reckoned that the information she and her fellow informants provided might have explained "why the Germans in the Ardennes offensive had the capture of supply depots at Liège and eastward as one of their prime objectives."[18]

As more and more trains headed into Germany and Holland, Liège remained a key junction and supply depot, even after Antwerp reopened. The Germans were well aware of its importance and made it the principal target of their newest weapon, the V-1 rocket (Vergeltungswaffe 1, or Vengeance Weapon 1), which they hoped would destroy the Allied line of communication. The rocket was Hitler's pet project, and because he considered it his last hope of winning the war, he had devoted vast amounts of financial resources to its development.

As a response to the Normandy landings, the first V-1s were fired a week after D-Day, targeting southeast England and, particularly, London. Over the next four months, nearly 10,000 were sent over the

Channel until October, when the Allies captured the last launch site within range of Britain. Thereafter, V-1 bombs were aimed at targets in Belgium, notably the two key strategic cities: Liège and the Allies' new Port of Antwerp. In terms of V-1 attacks per square mile, Liège became the most intensely attacked city of the rocket campaign.

The first V-1 in Liège landed midafternoon on November 20. Railworkers did not recognize that this was a new type of weapon, even though it caused a big explosion near the main railway station. They would soon learn. Over the next quarter of an hour, three more landed, the prelude to a sustained attempt to wreck the railway facilities at the heart of Allied logistics.

Life in Liège changed rapidly under the assault. According to a reporter from an army journal, before the attack "there wasn't a thing you couldn't buy" because all the upmarket stores were open "displaying all kinds of clothing and nearly all kinds of food."[19] There was even an ice cream shop with 22 "delicious" flavors, "but not for long. Soon the horrors of war overtook Liège." The Germans tried to make up for their mistake in leaving a key railway hub intact by launching a full-out assault with their new weapon.

The strategic importance of Liège could not be exaggerated. According to the army reporter, what had previously been a quiet station mostly serving the surrounding countryside was now "destined to become one of the most important railway points in this war. The commanding officers of the rail units knew that their mission in moving to Liège was to supply the First and Ninth Armies. On them depended whether the two armies would have enough supplies to resist counterattacks and enough supplies to move farther into Germany."

The damage wreaked by this sustained attack was considerable. In the Guillemins yard, the control tower was put out of action, the bridge leading to the roundhouse where locomotives were stored collapsed, tracks were uprooted, and not a single pane of glass was left intact. The Germans then hit Liège with a few V-2 rockets, a more sophisticated and powerful weapon with a longer range and greater accuracy, but most of these rockets would later be aimed at Antwerp as part of the counterattack. Though the railways in Liège were the main target, much of the city suffered the fate of towns farther east such as Caen and Rouen, with large parts reduced to rubble. During the final eight days of November, a remarkable 331 rocket bombs landed in and around Liège, more than 40 a day. The deadliest day was November 20, when a girls school was hit, killing all pupils in one classroom and most in another, as well as several of the nuns running it.

Amid these attacks, by and large, the railways kept running, supplying the forward positions, including Aachen, the first major German town to be captured, which fell to the Allies on October 21 after a fierce three-week battle. Several battalions of railway troops were ready to carry out the repairs rapidly, at times putting their lives at risk. Guards were posted throughout the yards to alert the authorities of fires, and every man at some point carried out these duties.

For a two-week period at the beginning of December, the deadly fireworks suddenly stopped, only to restart on December 16 with the launch of the German counterattack, known as the Battle of the Bulge. In the midst of the initial rocket attack, and before the counterattack, the 740th enjoyed a triumph. After all the unit's hard work since D-Day, often undertaken close to enemy lines, Livingstone knew there was a strong desire among his men to be the first to operate a US military train into Germany. He recognized the crucial importance of the esprit de corps that had built up and the pride his men felt as part of what they called a "railhead battalion." After various relatively minor track repairs, a works train run by men of the 740th crossed the Siegfried Line and entered

Germany on November 7 to support the repair of the line. A week later, with one of the two tracks in working order, two trainloads of engineers' supplies destined for Walheim, more than 200 miles south of Aachen, were the first to reach the Allied troops in Germany by rail.

———————

Liège was vital as part of the supply route, but Antwerp was the big one because it was the only solution to the logistical problems the Allies faced once their forces stretched beyond Paris. As a deepwater inland port, connected to the North Sea by the 73-mile-long Scheldt estuary, Antwerp had long been recognized as the key for any army intending to attack Germany. Its importance was all the greater because the port facilities at Rotterdam, the only other major port on the North Sea coastline, had been destroyed by the Luftwaffe during the invasion of Holland four years earlier.

The bald statistics of Antwerp's port facilities set out by the French author Nicolas Aubin explain its significance and demonstrate its remarkable scale: "[Antwerp] could take the biggest ships in service at the time along its 50 km of quays, spread out within its 18 inner harbours. Its infrastructure was the dream of any logistics expert: 625 cranes, 900 warehouses, most of which were refrigerated, 495 petrol tanks."[20] Antwerp's advantages were all the greater because it was also blessed with excellent clearance facilities, with more than 500 miles of railway around the various docks and warehouses, as well as ample classification yards. It was the gateway to the excellent Belgian transportation network, with its 3,250 miles of railways and 1,370 miles of navigable waterways. Eisenhower had no doubts about its significance. In a message to George Marshall, the army's chief of staff, on October 23, he wrote, "The logistical problem had become

so acute that all plans had made Antwerp a sine qua non to the waging of the final all-out battle."[21]

Antwerp and its port were captured by a militarized wing of
the Belgian resistance known as the *witte brigade* (White Brigade),
which attacked the Germans before they could carry out their plan
to destroy its vital transport facilities. As a result, the British Elev-
enth Armoured Division faced little resistance when it took over
the town with its harbor intact on September 4. However, a fundamental failure of planning led to a lengthy and deeply damaging
delay of the port being put into operation for the Allies. The Port of
Antwerp can be reached only by the lengthy Scheldt estuary, whose
banks were still in German hands, preventing Allied shipping from
reaching the port. Moreover, the whole estuary was littered with
minefields, and the Germans had fortified the Walcheren peninsula at the mouth of the Western Scheldt. From there, they could
control access to the river and had established well-dug-in artillery positions impervious to air attack. This made it impossible for
Allied minesweepers to clear the river and open the port. The failure to address, let alone solve, this issue quickly became the source
of one of the fiercest disagreements between American and British
allies.

As soon as Antwerp was taken, Admiral Sir Bertram Ramsay,
the chief naval adviser to the Supreme Headquarters Allied Expeditionary Force (SHAEF), pressed Montgomery to make the Scheldt
his main priority, arguing that as long as the mouth of the river was
in German hands, the Port of Antwerp was impossible to access.
However, Montgomery was focused on preparations for the ill-fated
Operation Market Garden, which involved parachuting thousands of
men behind enemy lines to secure bridges around Arnhem in order
to create a new front against Germany from the north. Montgomery
argued this was the quickest way to end the war, but most of his

postwar critics argue he was grandstanding, pushing—in the face of American objections—a policy that was more rooted in the desire to see British boots set foot first on German territory. The French author Nicolas Aubin explains it in terms of the postwar realpolitik, writing that Operation Market Garden was an attempt to guarantee that the British would "hold the most advantageous position after the war. This was all about retaining the illusion of being a great imperial power, remaining an equal partner with the United States and not being relegated the level of a junior ally."[22] Montgomery, Aubin claims, apparently perceived clearing the Antwerp area as just a way of allowing the Americans to shine, something he was unwilling to do.

Aubin's critique is by no means an outlier. Postwar analysts almost universally agree that Montgomery's failure to prioritize the reopening of Antwerp was a fundamental error born of the British general's arrogance and nationalism. There is no doubt that Antwerp could have been opened sooner if Montgomery had given priority to clearing the approaches. If Montgomery had secured the Scheldt estuary as Admiral Ramsay had advised, Antwerp would have been opened to Allied shipping much earlier, and the escape of the German Fifteenth Army from France could have been stopped. Instead, the German forces were able to deploy defensively and prepare for the expected advance.

The failure of Operation Market Garden, which had wounded or killed 16,000 men just 10 days after its launch on September 17, only intensified pressure on Montgomery to concentrate on opening Antwerp. Despite Eisenhower telling Montgomery that "Antwerp is the most important [frontline operation] and needs all your attention," the British general prevaricated and refused to focus his main forces at the Scheldt.[23] Instead, the task of clearing the area was left principally to Canadian troops, who not only needed time to reach the estuary but also were already battle-worn, having endured considerable losses in taking Calais.

Montgomery's error meant that for a month after Antwerp fell into Allied hands nothing much happened. The shipping could not get through because the estuary was mined and German guns pointed at the river, and no concerted effort was made to flush out the enemy. Boulogne and Calais had been captured after Antwerp, on September 22 and 30, respectively, but they were so badly damaged that they were of no immediate use. Despite Montgomery's assertion that only one such minor port would have been enough to serve the supply needs of the Allied armies, even both together offered only a fraction of the potential of Antwerp, which, at the time, was the world's third-largest port.

By the time the Canadians were sent into the Battle of the Scheldt on October 8, the Germans had further reinforced their defenses and staged an effective delaying action, during which they flooded areas of land in the Scheldt estuary. This slowed the Allied advance and turned the battleground into a hell of marshes and mud. Only after numerous amphibious landings followed by perilous attacks over open ground were the German defenders finally dislodged. The victory came at a high cost in one of the trickiest campaigns after the Normandy landings: the five weeks of intense fighting resulted in 13,000 Allied troops killed or injured, half of whom were Canadian. It would have taken even longer had the Germans not undermined their own defenses with successive withdrawals of well-known units during the battle.

The German army withdrew on November 8, leaving more than 40,000 soldiers to be taken prisoner. Whereas the Germans had given up the Port of Antwerp with little resistance, having been taken by surprise by the Belgians, the enormous efforts they put into defending the Scheldt showed they were aware of its importance as the supply base for Allied troops. And therefore, as soon as it was liberated, they attacked it with rockets, and then, along with Liège, it became one of the key targets of the counterattack known as the Battle of the Bulge.

Though the port's shipping facilities were largely unscathed, the railways were not immediately usable because many tracks in the port had also been damaged by German bombs. The initial task was to bring these lines, the main means for taking supplies inland, into use. Unusually, running the railways out of Antwerp was a joint operation, with both British and American railway troops working together rather than being allocated to separate areas as had happened elsewhere. The British 181st Railway Operating Company arrived at Antwerp on November 3 and set to work repairing tracks in the docks and clearing the line to Roosendaal, the key route north to Holland. The line had been blocked by an explosion of an ammunition train that had taken out several hundred yards of track through an embankment; it took the troops a week to bring the line back into use.

The Americans in the 709th Grand Division arrived soon after and brought in the 743rd battalion for support. All available men were sent to clear mines from the docks, but the area was so vast and difficult to clear that a railwayman was injured when he stepped on a mine a few days later.

The arrangement between the British and the Americans applied to the allocation of supplies. The overall capacity of the port, estimated at around 44,000 tons per day—over twice Cherbourg's capacity— was distributed almost equally between the two armies. The Americans insisted on obtaining 5,500 tons more because of their greater numbers in the field. After three weeks while the minesweepers cleared the harbor and its approaches, the first convoy carrying Allied supplies successfully landed in Antwerp on November 29, 1944.

For two weeks after the port was opened, all onward transport was by truck. The ABC—American, British, and Canadian—haul, a rather more efficient version of the Red Ball Express, supplemented rail and canal transport in clearing supplies out of Antwerp. It was operated solely with American trucks and mostly took supplies to Liège but also to Mons and Charleroi. As with Red Ball, the ABC haul was given priority on key routes that restricted civilian traffic.

Only in early December, when the tracks had been cleared, did the railways operated by a combination of British and American troops become the mainstay of the transport system to Liège and other destinations nearer the front. The Antwerp docks area included the huge North yard, where the railcars were grouped into trains that soon were leaving at the rate of one every 20 minutes. Barges, used widely in this part of Europe on navigable rivers and canals, principally the Albert Canal in Belgium, were a third transport method used for less urgent matériel.

Once the railways were functioning, Antwerp became a game changer in every respect. It transformed the army's supply operation and proved essential in the advance into Germany. Antwerp could provide supplies for an army three times the size of one that Cherbourg, a smaller port far from the battlefields, could manage. The Channel ports, too, had very limited capacity even after they were brought into use, and those in Brittany were simply too far away. As Major A. G. Gregory, the historian of the 708th, puts it: "The utilization of the port of Antwerp, Belgium, meant a tremendous improvement over the original 'shoestring' method of supply from Western France because of its vast capacity and closeness to the enemy—at times too close."[24] Indeed, Antwerp was where the Liberation Line turned into the front line.

Accompanied by an occasional Luftwaffe raid, the cascade of rocket attacks on Antwerp was incessant, regularly causing civilian and military casualties, with the railroaders particularly at risk. The constant fear and, more practically, the frequent need to rush to shelters threatened to damage morale and effectiveness. The worst aspect, according to survivors, was the uncertainty and unpredictability of incoming rocket bombs. Whereas an artillery barrage, frightening as it was, followed a recognizable pattern, the rocket attacks were random and unscheduled. V-2s could come at any time during day or night, and as Mark S. Womack, a sergeant with the 743rd, recalled in an interview later: "You couldn't hear it until it hit."[25] Womack heard the explosion from the deadliest of these attacks, a direct hit on a cinema: "There was a motion picture theater maybe a mile from our barracks, billets, and I remember the impact. 'Bang!' I remember hearing that."

The cinema in the center of town was attacked on December 16, the very day that Hitler launched the Battle of Ardennes counterattack. Many British and American soldiers filled the cinema to well over capacity, with many men standing in the aisles, to watch *The Plainsman*, a movie about the legendary Buffalo Bill. As a result, the toll was horrific: 537 killed and 300 injured. Womack recalls several men of his battalion dying, some from the wider effects of the explosion: "[the dead] were the ones in the balcony, especially, as the shock got them. The battalion surgeon was in there killed...and so was one of our cooks in my company, Sichorello, Italian vintage...our Battalion dentist [who had] just filled some teeth a short time before, and he was killed. After that, they shut down the theaters so there wouldn't be so many people in one place." For a week, 200 men dug through the rubble to find survivors and victims.

Numerous additional rocket attacks in Antwerp that day brought the death toll to 667, changing the mood of the local population and the military. Beyond the physical devastation, the psychological impact, a feeling of constant dread, never went away for many soldiers after the Rex cinema attack. The US Army report puts it eloquently: "In many ways the bombing of Antwerp was more trying than actual combat, in which the individual soldier was able to shoot back, capture prisoners, go on raiding parties and participate in the general excitement, which gave vent to his personal feelings. It required stamina to bear up under the grueling uncertainty of everyday existence in Antwerp." Indeed, even some battle-hardened men who had served on the front line could not cope. They "left their bags at the station when they saw the V-bombs coming over and went AWOL."[26]

Responsibility for maintaining the port was now in the hands of the US Army's Fifth Engineer Brigade, headed by Colonel Doswell Gullatt, a native of Louisiana and a veteran of the D-Day landings. He had arrived on Omaha Beach just two hours after the first landing and was responsible for providing logistics support to the troops coming off the landing craft. According to an account of his role, "'Arrowhead' Gullatt with his calm, persuasive yet forceful personality, became the most popular man on the narrow beachhead."[27]

After serving in Cherbourg, in October he was given command of the two ports regiments, which were tasked with rehabilitating and operating Antwerp—the toughest assignment in the history of the Transportation Corps. Gullatt's calm demeanor was essential because Antwerp remained under constant attack for weeks, with the Germans seeking to disrupt the supply line at every opportunity.

The effect of the continuing attacks was devastating. The V-2s made life almost unbearable for the vast numbers working on the docks and the railways serving them. Antwerp suffered almost three times as many V-1 attacks as Liège—a total of nearly 8,700—and was the main target of the V-2 campaign by a remarkable margin. It could be said that the very raison d'être of the V-2 attacks was to destroy Antwerp's transportation facilities. A staggering 1,610 rockets, half the total of all V-2s launched, hit Antwerp, and only 54 were aimed elsewhere in Belgium, principally Liège. In the first two months of 1945, V-2s rained on Antwerp at the rate of one every 40 minutes. Three thousand civilians were killed during this period, and the US forces lost 86 men, mostly port and railway workers, to Hitler's revenge weapon. The constant attacks meant that ammunition had to be stored away from Antwerp to reduce the risk of a V-2 hitting a munitions dump. Ships carrying ammunition were redirected to the Channel ports, too, lengthening the line of communication.

The British military logged the almost daily damage to the railways, which had to be constantly repaired while always under threat of another bombing. The log relates a grim story. On January 1, three locomotives were damaged by enemy aircraft; five days later, the Antwerp–Esschen line was attacked as well as two tracks just outside the port area; on the tenth, both Antwerp and Kiel stations were hit, but with no damage to tracks; a further attack on the fifteenth destroyed a section of track near Antwerp, but repairs ensured traffic resumed the next day. The worst damage during this period was on January 19, when rockets hit a shed at Hoboken petrol installation and part of the Antwerp docks that blocked a line. Several more minor attacks occurred in the rest of January. In that month alone, which incidentally was one of the coldest on record with regular snowfall, 19 incidents affected the railway. A similar number occurred the following month, with the worst being on February 17 at Schijnport in Antwerp, where seven people, including three soldiers, were killed and the line shut down for a day.

When, finally, on March 31, the attacks ceased as the launch pads were overrun by the advancing Allied troops, the deputy commander of Antwerp, Colonel Edward O. Forsythe, summed up the feelings of his men about this lengthy onslaught: "It's like hitting yourself in the head with a hammer. When you stop, it feels good. It makes a difference when you are not subject to dying every couple of minutes."[28]

Of course, facing up to this barrage proved to be worthwhile. In addition to its size, Antwerp had numerous advantages when compared with Cherbourg. It was only 65 miles by rail from Liège, the key advance depot area, whereas Cherbourg was more than 400 miles away. Even Nancy, the forward depot area for the Third Army, was only 250 miles by rail from Antwerp, 150 fewer miles than from Cherbourg, a considerable savings. Possessing sufficient facilities to handle the bulk of the incoming cargo and located much closer to the fighting front, Antwerp helped the Allies solve the tight interior transport situation. Between November 1944 and April 1945, 2.5 million tons of supplies arrived in Antwerp, most of which was taken forward by rail.

As Eisenhower had rightly anticipated, opening Antwerp solved many of the supply difficulties. But the rapid dash across France prompted by Patton undoubtedly had a deleterious and lasting effect on keeping the line of communication running efficiently. Both the First and Third Armies simply overran their logistical support, which resulted in gasoline shortages of 6 and 12 weeks, respectively, for the two armies. Nicolas Aubin sums up the other consequences: "The rationing of ammunition introduced in mid-September was maintained for three months, up to the Ardennes counter-offensive. However, we can also add the obligation in August–September for the fighting men to eat only K rations that had insufficient calories and the lack of winter clothing, jackets and overshoes that continued up to January 1945 or the cigarette crisis in December."[29] This crisis in logistics posed a terrible missed opportunity. Without the breakdown in the supply chain, the war might well have ended earlier because the Germans would not have been able to regroup behind the Siegfried Line and successfully mount a counterattack. Aubin concludes: "It is obvious now that during the course of the summer, the American logistical chain failed. Under radiant summer skies, free of any Luftwaffe threat, thousands of GMC trucks had not been enough to supply the two American armies.... The price paid for this was very high."[30]

Opening Antwerp unblocked this logistical paralysis. However, the operation of Antwerp was tricky because, given its sheer size, the docks were always a bottleneck, despite the hive of activity and the 18,000 civilians eventually taken on to help run it. The railways serving the port were stretched to the limit. There was, as there invariably is in wartime, a shortage of railcars, and those that were recovered were allocated to three groups: the British Army, the US Army, and the civilian railway. However, these three organizations failed to coordinate use, so a wasteful system emerged: the Americans sent freight south from Antwerp into Belgium, civil traffic from southern Belgium pushed up to France, and the British directed loaded railcars from France to Antwerp. All these flows returned stock empty, but by combining and coordinating routes, more intensive use of the scarce pool of cars could have been made. An article in *Military Review* pointed out that, "by arranging for the British to give empties to the Americans, the Americans to civil traffic, and civil traffic to the British, the anti-clockwise movement was eliminated and everyone was able to have nearly twice as many cars as before. The moral is—car supply must be centrally controlled by experienced railwaymen."[31] Indeed, that was one of the rules set by Hermann Haupt, the American Civil War railroad expert who first developed a coherent strategy for the use of railways in wartime. It can make the difference between victory and defeat.

In many ways, it is impossible to quantify the contribution of the railway battalions and engineers to the war effort. They were vital in so many ways, and the extensive operation out of Antwerp is a good illustration. Although they may not reflect the wider importance of these men's role, the sheer numbers are impressive: by the end of 1944, the Second Military Railway Service encompassed 757 officers, 26 warrant officers, and 16,763 enlisted men (not including those in the South who belonged to the First Military Railway Service or the troops in engineering units that were allocated to repairing the railways or the British troops working in parallel). In addition to the headquarters, there were 5 railway Grand Divisions, 18 railway operating battalions and 2 detachments, 4 railway shop battalions, 5 railway workshop (mobile) units, and 10 hospital train maintenance platoons. Thanks to their combined efforts, US engineers rehabilitated "4,780 miles of double track and 3,050 of single track lines."[32] And there was more to come as new units of railroad troops entered Germany.

Many of these men, finding themselves unexpectedly on the front line and blitzed by a counterattack, were about to face a new challenge. Decisions about when to retreat, what equipment to leave, and what services to operate would have to be made—and quickly. The railwaymen who had joined up to build and operate railways now had to unexpectedly use their training as soldiers.

9

HITLER'S LAST THROW

By mid-December, the logistics crisis had largely been sorted. Goods were flowing through Antwerp despite the continuing V-2 rocket attacks, Liège had built up a phenomenal store of supplies, and the railway lines to Germany had mostly been rebuilt. It seemed like the Allies were poised for a victory early in the New Year. But then came a hammer blow. Hitler surprised the Allies with a counterattack — referred to as the Ardennes Offensive or Battle of the Bulge — that would lead to some of the fiercest fighting of the war and delay the Allies' march into the enemy's homeland.

The German counterattack was not about regaining territory because too much had already been lost. Instead, it was about destroying the supply base of the Allied forces and undermining their line of communication in order to prevent them from entering Germany. In the run-up to the launch of the Ardennes campaign, the Luftwaffe repeatedly strafed railheads and rail lines across eastern France as far west as Paris, an indication that the transport network was the ultimate target. This was well expressed in a book published as part of the US propaganda effort in Europe: "In effect, therefore, the German counteroffensive of 16 December was a blow at communications, as the key to the struggle."[1] The primary strategic aims of the German attack were to regain or destroy Liège, the chief supply base, and Antwerp, the principal port. Had one or both of those goals been achieved, the progress of the Allies into Germany would have been, at best, delayed or, at worst, halted. Antony Beevor quotes a German company commander presciently predicting "In twelve or fourteen days we will be in Antwerp — or we have lost the war."[2]

The attack took the Allies by surprise. Given the amount of intelligence available through Ultra and other sources, it is quite extraordinary that the counterattack was not expected. Indeed, many senior army staff had rejected such an idea as impossible, arguing that Hitler did not have the men or the resources to back up an initial attack, a prediction that actually proved to be correct but did not take into account the impetuous nature of the German leader.

Hitler selected the Ardennes as the focus of the attack because not only was the area thinly held by American forces but also the thick Eifel Forest shielded the buildup of troops and equipment from air reconnaissance. Despite the pleas of the few generals in the know, Hitler insisted on keeping the attack secret until the last possible moment; even his regimental commanders were not told anything until the day before. As much as possible, the German army's advance to the front was kept hidden: the troops marching into the Eifel Forest moved at night; charcoal, largely smoke-free, was provided instead of wood to burn for cooking; and radio silence was maintained until the last moment. Yet, despite these precautions, according to Anthony Beevor, "German officers were amazed that Allied air reconnaissance failed to spot villages and woods 'full to bursting point.'"[3]

To be fair, the weather was terrible in early December, which prevented regular aircraft patrols. But the Allies should have picked up other clues, notably the railway activity, which was as essential for the Germans as for the Allies. Altogether, 1,050 trains were needed to bring the attacking Germans to the front, 70 for each panzer division. The German buildup involved 1,400 tanks and 400,000 men, resulting in an intensive use of the rail network alone, which should have alerted the Allies but passed off unnoticed. According to Beevor, "The Allied Command had no idea of what was about to hit them on their weakest sector."[4] When the attack was finally launched on December 16, the Allies were shocked, the result of a fundamental failure of intelligence.

Surprise is always an attacker's biggest advantage and the initial assault, aided by the terrible weather conditions that had grounded the Allies' planes, met with some success. Seeing the German troops thundering toward their front lines was a rude awakening for the Allies, who had been largely static for months while preparing their own attack on Germany.

One immediate casualty was work on railway routes across the front line, which came to an abrupt halt. On the morning of the attack, Company B of the 341st Engineer General Service Regiment had just started repairs on yet another railway bridge at Bütgenbach but soon retreated when faced with a barrage of shells. As the morning progressed, several other units working on railway sites also withdrew when it became apparent to the Allies' high command that the Germans were launching a full-scale attack across a broad front.

The 706th Grand Division had been tasked with reconstructing lines to support Patton's advance and provide the Third Army's main line of communication. Although some of the forts around Metz were still not flushed out, the railway battalions under the 706th had been working in the area for a couple of weeks, repairing the extensive damage to the city's tracks caused by the Germans' track ripper and the Allied bombing. The lines in every direction out of the city had been wrecked, and all 269 switches at the terminal in town had been sabotaged by the enemy. It was, as the historian of the 706th

described it, "a maze of destruction." The 706th was working with
the 347th engineers to repair it. The Allied plan was to revitalize the
lines toward the Rhine so they could handle the huge loads needed
for the planned attack. But all this activity had to be stalled in order
to focus on stemming the advance of the Germans.

Indeed, the launch of the German counterattack, which targeted
the First Army's front between Saint-Vith and Stavelot in central Belgium, forced the Third Army to alter its entire tactical and supply
plan overnight. On Patton's insistence, the Third Army was given the
role of leading the counteroffensive against the German incursion,
and this involved a compete restructuring of the whole supply chain.
The task was made harder because the Germans had overrun the
lines from Luxembourg north to Gouvy and northeast to Namur,
which were both key supply routes. In particular, the break in the line
between Arlon and Namur disrupted the communications between
the First and the Third Armies and meant that the personnel, equipment, and freight on that line had to be evacuated via Arlon, on the
border with Luxembourg.

The Americans' ability to move troops around using a combination of trucks and trains prevented the Germans from crossing the
Meuse, and within a week, they were bogged down. Despite their
success on that first day, the Germans' progress fell well short of
what Hitler had hoped, thanks to pockets of sharp resistance and
the Allies' destruction of key road bridges. On December 23, the
improved weather allowed Allied planes to take to the air, which
forced the Germans to pull back. The farthest west the Germans
reached was the village of Foy-Nôtre-Dame on Christmas Eve, 50
miles into previously occupied Allied territory. Despite this progress, crucially they failed to take either of their main targets, Liège
and Antwerp. Although the offensive was only finally halted on
the twenty-seventh, by then the battle had long been lost by the

Germans. Nevertheless, the fighting continued for another month in conditions of extreme cold on what was very difficult terrain, at a high cost to both sides.

The railways were absolutely crucial in turning this situation around for the Allies. Trains running on a broadly east–west axis were the key means of rescuing vast stocks of supplies in advanced dumps that would likely be taken by the Germans. At the same time, these trains were used to establish and supply railheads as near as possible to the shifting front line. Importantly, they carried ammunition closer to the front than trucks could reach. The railways in the region on a roughly north–south alignment provided the most efficient and fastest way of moving reinforcement troops at key points and shifting supplies to key railheads. Thousands of trucks supplemented this rail activity, but whenever possible, the railways were used for the longer journeys, given the poor condition of the roads, which worsened as the Battle of the Bulge wore on.

The tasks of the Allied soldier-railwaymen were made harder as the Germans recaptured 225 miles of railway track in their push westward, creating uncertainty about the destinations to which trains could be safely dispatched. The impact on the supply chain was immediate, instantly reducing the amount of goods carried to the front by almost half. Had that reduction continued for long, the frontline troops would have found themselves short of ammunition and food, but fortunately, the offensive petered out.

Many of the railroad troops and engineers found themselves dangerously close to the front line. Although some longer-term projects rebuilding bridges and fixing broken lines were hastily abandoned, many railwaymen had to keep running the trains despite the enemy's proximity because these services were vital in ensuring the troops and supplies were in the right place. For railway battalions, this was both their finest and most perilous hour, as an article written shortly afterward put it: "Perhaps the most concentrated hell the GI railroaders ever caught was what the Germans threw at them during the Battle of the Bulge in December 1944. Transportation Corps troops in the advance section of the communication zone got exactly what the combat troops got. They were bombed and strafed by the Luftwaffe, night and day. They caught it from Nazi V-1 robot bombs, big guns and snipers."[5]

Inevitably, Patton's Third Army reacted the quickest to the change in circumstances; with the newly created Ninth having joined the First and the Third to prepare for the attack on Germany, the Third was the southernmost of the three armies. Luckily, Patton was ready—kind of. After taking Metz on December 13, his troops had a little time to regroup, and this gave him a chance to reconnect with the men. As one account puts it: "Patton could be seen everywhere in his army area addressing his troops and radiating optimism."[6] Moreover, "he made sure that guaranteed mail deliveries, hot chow and showers, plus liberal distribution of passes and unit rotations out of the line all contributed to high morale despite miserable weather."[7] He was also cheered by the fact that Eisenhower had just given him permission to break through over the Saar and to the Rhine on December 19, a move that was thwarted by the German attack. Interestingly, Patton was one of the few in high command who had anticipated the possibility of a counterattack, as on December 12, he had been asked for a report on what his Third Army might do in response to such an event.

Even though the breakthrough toward the Rhine was stymied by the counterattack, preparing for it meant that Patton—the man who thought that even one day in the same place was too long—had a comparatively long time to gear up for action. The supply bases had to be moved rapidly to prevent them from falling into the hands of the enemy but also to ensure they were in the right place for the Allies' troops. These confusing movements across the back of the front line had to be organized and carried out with remarkable haste. Because of the difficulties of shifting this equipment by road, railheads were established nearer to the front line than previously.

The supply dump Patton's troops established for the assault over the river Saar immediately had to be shifted farther behind the lines using a combination of truck and train. The units of the Third Army that had already crossed the Saar River into Germany with the expectation that the rest of the army would follow were forced to retreat. The transport function was carried out by the 718th, the railway battalion that had supported the Third Army's advance through France and that was operating a number of railways in eastern France and Belgium. In contrast, the main supply base at Verdun was moved 40 miles east to Longwy, closer to the defending troops along the Belgian and Luxembourgian borders. Longwy had good railway and road connections eastward and, from there, the 718th established railheads farther into Belgium, near the front line at Libramont, which involved going through Bastogne (the scene of a crucial siege during the Battle of the Bulge) and north to Saint-Vith. Throughout the course of the German advance, supplies flowed through Longwy and then on trucks to the frontline troops. Similarly, trains and trucks fully laden with fuel were dispatched from an existing storage facility north of Metz to Longwy, where a large fuel dump was rapidly set up on a hillside to support Patton's men.

Similar operations were carried out at various points along the 75-mile front, both defensive and offensive. In addition to supplies, the railways were used extensively to transfer troops across the front. Within the first two days of the counterattack, the 718th moved soldiers from four different divisions across the combat zone to reinforce key weak points. According to an article in the *Yankee Boomer*, the magazine produced by the Military Railway Service: "Assigned to the task of a railhead battalion in support of the Third Army, the 718th operated the advanced line in Patton's territory, moving as close to the front as possible.... During the period of the [battle] the 718th R.O.B. accomplished a rather remarkable feat in that they moved within forty-eight hours four divisions, including supply, of the Third Army laterally across the front into the south flank of the Bulge."[8]

The article concludes: "This movement was so successful that units withdrawing from the line in the south received their supplies at railheads and were returned to combat without delay. Third Army spokesmen consider this a primary factor in the repulse of the Bulge."[9] Indeed, so did the historian and military railway expert Admiral James Van Fleet, who recalled, "This feat was achieved against the handicap of heavy snow which had to be cleared by hand shovelling and against enemy air opposition. Ammunition was delivered sometimes right to the guns by rail."[10]

According to the historian of the 706th: "Stationmasters from the 706th set up headquarters at Arlon and Athus to expedite the evacuation of this First Army tonnage and also to handle the trains of the Third Army which were beginning to arrive in the new territory. Railheads opened up on a moment's notice, and cars were placed for unloading on every available track in the area south of the German salient."[11] He concludes: "Had it not been for the flexibility of rail operation and the careful and expeditious manner in which the 706th handled the Third Army tonnage the supply problem of the move northward might have been a serious one. As it was, everything worked smoothly, diversion orders were carried out to the letter, and placement of loads and handling of empties to the rear areas ran according to plan. General Patton's men soon had the German thrust stopped and began to turn them back."[12]

The launch of the German attack also intensified the already frenetic activity of railway troops behind the lines in their efforts to keep these trains running. At Aulnoye, a key railway junction in northern France where main lines crossed, Company B of the 716th had the task of ensuring sufficient numbers of locomotives were available to take supplies east and the unglamorous but essential task of returning the empties back toward Paris. The men were originally billeted in parked railway coaches, but the risks of these quarters were all too evident when, on December 26, soon after the troops' arrival, the carriages were targeted by a late-night strafing run by a marauding Messerschmitt. This led to a hasty move to safer accommodations in a school building some distance from the tracks. The historian of the unit recalled the intensity of the operation: "The locomotive men at Aulnoye within days of their arrival found themselves suddenly called upon to make available motive power in ever-increasing quantities. Once more, they worked long and difficult hours. Three Star Specials, priority trains, hospital trains…a never-ending stream of war materials demanded engines…engines…engines."[13]

The working conditions were never ideal. There was a shortage of tools — indeed, there was always a shortage of tools, an oft-repeated complaint in the accounts of the railway battalions. At one point, the gantry used for replenishing coal broke down, requiring the men to load the coal manually. Snow and freezing weather that terrible winter made repairs difficult because engines would literally freeze up, and by the time the maintenance men thawed them out, other parts would be frozen. The most dangerous work was at night because of the blackout conditions "when it appeared power demands were always the heaviest."[14] The risk of being killed by an engine shunting around the yard quadrupled; indeed, even in peacetime operation with no lighting restrictions, working in engine houses was always the most dangerous job on the railways.

The complexities of the work increased, too, because only some engines were equipped to provide steam heating on the trains, which was essential for hospital trains passing through Aulnoye, where the locomotives were changed. The 716th maintenance team also processed vast numbers of railcars for these trains, a daily average of nearly 2,000, which all needed checking and sometimes repairing. Even one car failing on a long train could result in major delay for subsequent services. Meanwhile, another Company B detachment of just 11 enginemen serviced 20 engines per day at the roundhouse in Lumes, the location of the biggest classification yard supporting the Third Army, 60 miles south of Aulnoye. This backroom work of repairing and maintaining locomotives, undertaken by thousands of men at numerous locations behind the front line, might have been unheralded but it was recognized as essential in keeping the army at the front supplied.

For the 718th, it was not an enemy attack but a train accident that caused a fatality that, had it not been for the bravery of the crew concerned, could have resulted in a major catastrophe. A Three Star Special, the priority freight service named after Patton's stars, was struck by an ammunition train that had been allowed to slide out of control down an incline. Seeing the ammunition train heading down toward him, the freight train engineer, Joe Cushman, who in civilian life was a fireman on the Baltimore & Ohio, attempted to cushion the impact by reversing and stayed in the engine instead of abandoning his post. He was killed after being trapped in the burning cab despite the efforts of his two colleagues, Private Oliver Smith and Robert Voss, to pull him out. Meanwhile, seeing the accident, Captain Anton Reider rushed to the scene and uncoupled the car behind the burning engine, allowing the 13 cars of the ammunition train to be safely pulled away from the conflagration by an engine driven by two engineers, Sergeants John Zabel and William Pierce. Zabel climbed to the top of the train to try to close the doors of a car where a shell exploded, which blew his helmet off but fortunately did not injure him. The two managed to pull the cars to a nearby yard, where the train was safely unloaded. All five men were given medals for their courage, with citations mentioning their "heroic service."

Not only were bombs and shells threatening Allied troops. There was also a bizarre attempt to undermine their efforts through subterfuge because a key German tactic in the Ardennes campaign was the infiltration of a fifth column behind Allied lines. The Germans had established a special regiment of mostly English speakers who would pass through the lines disguised as British or American soldiers, dressed in the uniforms of prisoners or dead soldiers. The so-called Operation Greif was the brainchild of Hitler, who thought it would be a good tactic to prevent the Allies from destroying bridges over the Meuse River that he needed for his advance. In the event, Hitler's special unit, led by Otto Skorzeny, was greatly undermanned, with only 150 men rather than the hoped-for 500. Moreover, despite wearing Allies' uniforms, the unit made only a few attempts to cross the lines using stolen US equipment such as jeeps and guns.

However, the fear engendered among the Allied troops by the very existence of this unit had a far greater impact than its attempts at sabotage. News of Skorzeny's unit caused widespread concern across the front, and sentries were made to ask arcane questions that only genuine Americans could answer in order to flush out the German infiltrators. But even Allied generals were stumped as soldiers manning checkpoints were all too eager to get one over on their officers by dreaming up ever more obscure Americana queries, mostly around baseball and presidents' names. Two days after the start of the counterattack, Itschner, on a visit to Patton at Arlon, on the border with Luxembourg, found himself having to answer "Who bats number four on the New York Yankees?" despite having given the correct password. Luckily, he was a sports fan who knew the answer, but others were less fortunate. At least two American GIs were shot by overeager sentries as a result of failed interrogations, and several others were marched away at gunpoint as a precautionary measure.

Itschner was there to discuss with Patton the importance of protecting Liège and Antwerp in the face of the German counter-offensive and the need to solidify their plans to cross the Rhine. In admiration, Itschner describes how, when the general appeared for the meeting, "striding down the aisle with his pearl-handled pistols, everybody was very apprehensive because the German Bulge attack had come as a great surprise" and they were concerned what his reaction would be. Instead of fuming, Patton instilled confidence, saying, "Gentlemen, this [Ardennes Offensive] is the stupidest thing those *blank-blank* Germans have ever done.... What a mistake they made. We're going to take advantage of it." According to Itschner, this allayed all nerves and "after that speech everybody was out to get em."[15]

The role of Liège as the key railway hub during the counterof-fensive cannot be exaggerated. The railway unit operating farthest east and nearest the German lines, the 740th, was based in Liège and operated railways across a large swathe of Belgium. Consequently, its men faced a particularly intricate set of tasks, evacuating forward positions while maintaining railheads close to the lines. Before the

German counteroffensive, the 740th's territory had stretched through to Raeren, the last station in eastern Belgium that had once been part of Germany and was now just a couple of miles from the border. Initially, the plan was to establish a rail yard in Raeren, but then it was decided this would be too risky. And so it proved, because the town was occupied on the first day of the German Ardennes Offensive. Instead, the 740th established the rail yard in Malmedy—a few days later the scene of a notorious massacre of US troops who had been taken prisoner—where two big fuel storage depots were built. An American train laden with fuel arrived at Malmedy station on the morning of December 17, but the engineer realized too late that the town was already in German hands and rapidly reversed before the Germans could block him in the station with tanks.

Liège was also the main supply point for all the operations east and the repository for a huge mountain of supplies of all types: food, ammunition, and fuel. The depot at Liège was expected to hold 40 days' rations and 13 days' fuel for the 925,000 men of the First and Ninth Armies. (The Ninth arrived in France in September and had been deployed as the northern flank of the US force.)

As the historian of the 708th Grand Division puts it: "In Liège, the ability of the military railway service was put to its severest test in supplying the combat armies butting against Germany's Siegfried Line and west Rhine defenses. Liège was like the palm of a many-fingered rail net that stretched in all directions."[16]

But it came at a cost. Some of these "non-combat" service troops lost 10 percent of their number to injuries—mostly resulting from rockets and bombs—which was very high for service units that were supposed to be behind the lines. The historian adds: "Little known or appreciated, except by the armies in the immediate area, these revelations mark one of the greatest chapters in military railway history. Almost legendary stories could be related of train crews evacuating supplies under the very nose of the enemy. Some, cut off and unable to get their trains out, had to escape through the snow-covered Ardennes, and many of the railway men joined combat units in the line along with other service troops caught in the area."[17]

During the first couple of days of the counterattack, the 740th lost a section of the railway it had been operating and quickly had to cope with the fact that the enemy was on their doorstep. They were working in unprecedented circumstances, and Livingstone, the ever perceptive author of the 740th's history, relates how one of his men put it neatly to him: "Any resemblance between military railroading on the continent and railroading back home is purely coincidental, accidental and illusory."[18] After several weeks of a lull, on the first day of the Ardennes Offensive, Liège's railway yards, which the Germans knew fed the supply line to the east, were targeted by rockets with all too deadly effects. A Stuka dive-bomber aimed its powerful load at the 708th's HQ, which was in a hotel near the station, but managed only to destroy the building next door, which killed several civilians. It was the start of a month of hell for the city's inhabitants and the hundreds of railroad troops operating and repairing the railway.

The one easy decision for Livingstone at the start of the German attack was to move the headquarters of the battalion back immediately to the safety of a basement where it had been at the height of the first round of rocket attacks. That move was immediately justified the following day when a pedestrian bridge over the Guillemins yard was hit by a V-1 rocket at 6:15 a.m. and the blazing railcars threatened to spread fire to a fully loaded hospital train. Colonel Pulliam, the commanding officer of the 740th, was quickly on the scene and in his limited French managed to persuade the courageous Belgian fireman in the cab of the hospital train to drive it to safety; the engineer was nowhere to be seen, having rapidly fled the scene.

Livingstone's situation report on the morning of December 19 was typical, revealing a series of overnight attacks on and around the railway, both from bombers and saboteurs: signaling cables had been cut on the line 25 miles east of the city, between Herbesthal and Eupen; just north of Eupen, a 500-pound bomb had landed but not exploded next to the track; a bomb had hit the line to Aachen close to the town of Birken; and worst of all, several bombs had damaged tracks and the interlocking (the connection between signaling and the tracks) at Montzen yard just north of Birken. None of these attacks, which were all to the east of Liège, was successful at disrupting the supply lines, but the intensity of attack clearly suggested the Germans intended to block the city's transport system. Every day over the next couple of weeks, Livingstone's diary lists similar attacks: a bomb here, sabotage there, V-1 rockets ever looming, and worst of all, the constant fear that the Germans might turn northward from their salient and mount a full-on attack of Liège. Fortunately, that full-on attack never happened, even though Livingstone was warned several times that it might be imminent.

While the men of the 740th were spread out safeguarding the integrity of the line of communication, their base in Liège came under continuous attack both from the renewed rocket launches but also from conventional air attacks. Suddenly, the entire battalion of the 740th was on a war footing. Rules were broken. Initiatives taken. Regulations about how many trains should have working brakes were forgotten. A train that was wrecked by a bomb was simply patched up and sent on its way.

Bombs as well as rockets hit the railway almost daily. On December 22, a section of track already damaged in a previous attack was destroyed at Longdoz, on the outskirts of the city; the next day, the roof of the hotel near the station housing the 708th Grand Division was hit and collapsed and two, fortunately empty, ambulance trains were strafed. On Christmas Eve, the barracks used by the 741st was bombed, killing nine GIs, a casualty rate that would have been far higher had not most of the battalion been working on the tracks. Then, three days later, the luck of the 740th in having suffered few casualties to that point and only one fatality—a man drowned in a bomb crater during a blackout—ran out. Company B's men sleeping in railway cars in the large Kinkenpois yard, just across the Meuse River from the Liège–Guillemins station, were hit by a V-1 that, unluckily, had been diverted by an attempt to bring it down. Livingstone rushed there and describes the scene where the flames lit up the night: "We found four bunk cars and the Medic's car (bunk and infirmary) to be on fire from a V-I that had exploded on the side of the hill just above them. Four dead and the injured were laid out in a row. The tops and sides of the wooden cars had been consumed and on the floors of two cars, one in one car and two in the other, were the partially incinerated bodies of three boys with flames leaping up around them. One can feel so damn helpless."[19] The death toll was 8, and a further 19 men were seriously injured.

The pressure under this assault was unbearable. Morale in the beleaguered city was so fragile. The men left in Liège found the psychological effects of the random rocket attacks worse than being on the front line. When a V-1 hit a hospital where many GIs were recovering from injuries—causing the death of only one patient, a German prisoner of war—a medical officer told Livingstone that the "wounded combat GIs were contending that they were simply easy targets with no way of fighting back as they could on the front line and demanded they move out of the city." Livingstone responded: "We have been sitting ducks for over a month but the damn railroad can't stop running because of bombs."[20]

In his diary, Livingstone notes further: "For more than a month we have been working under the strain of front line battle conditions.

Many days our life expectancy is one minute to the next, which often is the frequency of aerial and buzz bomb strikes. The trains have kept on moving through it all. The train crews and yard, engine house and track men have stuck it out and each one is deserving of a medal." He resisted calls for replacements to take over: "Some of the officers and men think we should be sent back to a rest camp. I don't agree. The more all pitch in the sooner this fracas will end and we can go home. Sure, we have had and are having it rough, and maybe some of the same is in the offing, but let's see it through quickly. And remember how much tougher the boys in the fox holes are finding it."[21]

The attacks continued—and even intensified—through the New Year. The targeting by the rocket bombs was relentless. On the worst day, in early January, 140 rockets fell on the city, one every 10 minutes. Livingstone recalled that when he had arrived in October, there was barely any war damage in Liège; however, upon leaving five months later, he reckoned not a single city block was left unaffected. By the time the V-1 attacks ceased in March 1945, 97 percent of the 82,700 dwellings in the province of Liège had been damaged or destroyed. And all this during the harshest Belgian winter in living memory.

Throughout this period of constant insecurity, the work of the 740th continued unabated. In his diary, Livingstone emphasizes that it was this feeling of uncertainty combined with the demands of the tasks at hand that made life so difficult for the railway soldiers, many of whom had probably not expected to find themselves on the front line. Hindsight offers a pattern of events that, in reality, could not have been predicted. The precise positions of the warring armies often were unclear, and every train dispatch required an assessment of whether the engineers were being sent into danger. Only several days into the German attack was Livingstone informed, wrongly as it happens, that the enemy was only 12 miles away. In response, he made numerous reconnaissance trips in a jeep around the wide 740th operating area, but even that left him none the wiser about the precise situation. At one point, the 740th was ordered to make preparations for emergency evacuation, although work continued unaffected. Important decisions had to be made with only partial information. Should Livingstone abandon parts of the railway to avoid his men being overrun by German troops? Which were the most important lines? And should he start removing supplies from the front line to secure them from enemy capture?

The historian of the 708th Grand Division was equally expressive of the horrors and uncertainties of the siege of Liège:

> *Mere words are highly inadequate to portray the terror and noise and death which all occur at the height of battle or bombing. In the two robot bomb sieges of Liège when more than a thousand V-bombs fell and detonated in the city... The Germans knew that every pound of rail freight for two American armies (the First and Ninth), and for all supporting troops east of the Meuse River, had to come through Liège across only one bridge. This fact alone was almost enough to cause the unprecedented V-1 attacks. Seldom has prolonged warfare been more indiscriminate and all-inclusive affecting the civilian non-combatant population as much as, if not more than, the uniformed Allied soldiers. Nothing was untouched—every aspect of life suffered. With great loss of life and untold misery, civilian men, women and children and Allied military personnel were caught in the city of terror.*[22]

It was a matter of not only supplying the Allied armies but also preventing the huge buildup of provisions in Liège from falling into enemy hands: "During this 'Belgian Bulge' period, the task of evacuating supplies from periled areas to save capture by the enemy was as important as the need for the infantry to close with the Nazi horde in hand-to-hand combat in the snow. Had the enemy captured sufficient food supplies and gasoline to keep his tanks and men going, the outcome might have been different. Evacuation of supplies was begun when intelligence reports indicated a massing of German troops in the area which later proved to be the path of the counterattack."[23]

Patton also discussed his counteroffensive that intended to cut off the salient, although this plan did not come to fruition. Instead, Patton's Third Army pushed the Germans back to their previous lines, thanks to his usual aggressiveness but also as a result of their own deep-rooted logistical failings and the Allies' attack on their transport system.

Colonel William Carr, the commanding officer of the 708th Grand Division (which included the 740th), was at one point told that he should move depots 50 miles behind the lines, but he decided to stall. Further up the command chain, Brigadier General Robert M. Littlejohn, the quartermaster general of the European Theater of Operations, received similar advice from Montgomery on three occasions, suggesting he should evacuate the depots at Liège. Littlejohn, too, turned a deaf ear to what he believed was the panicking Brit and responded by doing precisely the opposite, continuing to bring in more supplies. American logistics officers like Littlejohn had learned about the need for shorter lines of communication as a result of the difficulties following the Saint-Lô breakout in the summer of 1944 and therefore argued that maintaining supply dumps near the front line was worth the risk. They were proved correct. Keeping the railway going in and around Liège despite the attacks and the proximity

to the new battle lines was essential to stopping the enemy's advance
and then pushing it back. And Liège was far too well defended anyway. Livingstone, too, had been misinformed about the proximity of
the Germans. The intel was wrong—the enemy was never less than
20 miles away—and, in any case, those enemy troops were not heading toward Liège but seeking to bypass it to the south.

Antwerp, farther from the German salient, kept operating through
the Ardennes campaign. However, the British, who were responsible
for lines in northern Belgium and into Holland, had to move several
railheads 30 miles southeast to Aarschot, the headquarters of the British railway units and a key railway junction and yard. They had first
moved there in early November, handing over the operation of all the
railways in Normandy and east of Paris to their American counterparts. Aarschot had unfortunately been flattened by Allied bombers,
which left only a few facilities in working order. The turntable had
taken a direct hit and only 6 of the 38 locomotives were usable.

Within a couple of weeks, freight trains were operating under
the control of the 181st Railway Operating Company to and from
the depot, with around 20 locomotives having been repaired. The
crews, mostly Belgian, often worked shifts requiring three or four
days of continuous work because of the poor state of the lines.
Soon, British troops operated the railway out of a series of railheads
toward the German border and in Holland, but these had to be hastily evacuated following the launch of the German counterattack in
mid-December. Those sent to pick up the railway troops then had
to negotiate their way through the retreating British forces. But the
Germans never reached anywhere close to Antwerp and, despite
the constant rocket attacks, the port continued operating throughout
the Ardennes Offensive.

General Eisenhower saw the Germans' failure to capture either
Liège or Antwerp as the key point of the Battle of the Bulge: "The

professionals knew the jig was up on the third day after the Rundstedt offensive had started in the Ardennes. They knew then that they
could not go where they intended. If they could not get complete
surprise and drive clear through to Liège and then drive on behind
Antwerp, then there was not much they could do."[24] Ironically,
although the Germans never reached the Meuse, which was their primary target, the only major structure outside the battle area that was
destroyed during this attack was a bridge over the river. This bridge,
which had been rebuilt by US engineers in November, was prepared
for demolition in the event that a retreat was needed to the west of
the Meuse. During an air raid on Namur the night of December 26,
an unlucky hit set off the prepared charges and completely demolished the center and southern end spans.

Even before the launch of the Führer's last desperate attack,
the Allies had targeted the German transport system, particularly
the railways. In preparation for the aborted assault on Germany
that had been scheduled for December 19, five of the eight railway
bridges across the Rhine were put out of service, mostly as a result
of bomb damage to the bridge approaches. For the most part, German railworkers were unsuccessful in repairing them. According to
Hugh M. Cole, the author of the definitive account of the Ardennes
campaign: "Feeder rail lines in the Eifel had been so crippled by air
attack that through movement from the Rhine to the army railheads
was no longer possible and supplies were being moved by truck and
wagon between the 'traffic islands' where rail movement remained in
effect."[25]

This already enfeebled network was later subjected to a ferocious onslaught from the air, which further inhibited the Germans'
ability to advance. When the fog that had prevented the Allies
from renewing their bombing of railway facilities in the first week
of the German counteroffensive finally gave way to fairer weather,

the Allies launched a weeklong series of targeted attacks starting on Christmas Day, attacking rail lines, bridges, and classification yards on both sides of the Rhine. This time, the German engineers were completely overwhelmed and could not restore the damage quickly enough, further depleting their supplies. According to the official history:

> *German reports indicate that this transshipment from one mode of transport to another—and back again—cost at least forty-eight hours' delay. By the 26th railway bridges were out on the vital Ahr and Moselle lines, supporting the two southern armies.... On the 28th the rail center at Koblenz, supporting the German left wing, was put out of operation.... Allied air inflicted eighty-five breaks on the Army Group B rail lines west of the Rhine and fifty four of these were repaired. But in the last week before the Allied ground counteroffensive any hope of maintaining a satisfactory ratio between damage and repair had vanished.*[26]

Bridges over three crucial rivers had been put out of operation and it was taking the Germans as many as five days to make repairs: "The cumulative effect of this kind of damage simply saturated the German capabilities for rail repair."[27]

Crucially, the Allies managed to disable the logistics that would have enabled the German advance: "At one time the German armies had been able to rely on the railroad system as the backbone of army transport. From the beginning of good flying weather on 23 December this was no longer possible and by 27 December it may be concluded that the offensive in the main was fed and armed by a road transport system quite unequal to the load forced upon it."[28] From Christmas on, some of the supply trains from forward combat units headed back as far as Bonn, more than 80 miles behind the front lines, for ammunition and supplies. In particular, this led to a shortage of German ammunition: "The lack of ammunition should be charged to transport failure rather than to paucity of artillery shells at the Rhine dumps. The Panzer Lehr Division, for example, first reported that it had run out of gas, then on 28 December reported a shortage of ammunition because of the 'lack of transport.'"[29] In contrast, the Americans were never short of ammunition in this battle: "Most of the American ammunition stocks were put on wheels (trucks or railroad cars) after 19 December. The Third Army, for example, was able to move an average of 4,500 tons of ammunition per day during the last half of December and consumed, on the average, only 3,500 tons per day."[30]

In some respects, the Allies faced an enemy whose logistics was more suited to 1914 than 1944. Even in this big final campaign, the Germans were still using horse transport. The logistical superiority enjoyed by the United States was crucial: "Not only did the American divisions have a very large number of vehicles and trailers organic to the unit, but the number of line of communications trucks and trains available in the forward area was enormous. Perhaps even more important, the movement of American ground transport was unaffected by harassment and attack from the air."[31]

On New Year's Day, as the German assault began to peter out, a company of the 341st Engineer General Service Regiment was assigned to rehabilitate the railroads, yards, and engineer depot at Libramont, close to the front line. They had to stop work several times that day because the line was the target of artillery shells, but fortunately, none hit the railway facilities. As a result, Libramont became fully functional within two weeks. Another group of 341st men repaired the wrecked yards at Bastogne and were also repeatedly interrupted by shelling, but again with no casualties.

It was in Luxembourg City, where the men of the 718th and the 341st, who were repairing lines and bridges, found themselves closest to the enemy lines. The daily shelling forced frequent stoppages as the men labored in the very shadow of the German army. The company of the 341st repairing a line at Manternach in eastern Luxembourg on the border with Germany had to suspend work for a whole day because of heavy artillery fire. Later, when they were replacing two bridges less than two miles from the front line, the men came under fire again; still, they managed to complete the work within two weeks. Once the Germans began to retreat in early January, many of the railroad teams had to start all over, repairing lines they had previously worked on: "The lines that had been occupied by the enemy had been severely damaged and there was much work to be done. Between Ettelbruck and Gouvy on the main line [north of Luxembourg], 32 bridges had been destroyed by the retreating Germans as they pulled out."[32]

Most of the lines captured by the Germans in the Battle of the Bulge were reopened by the Allies in January, reconnecting, for example, Luxembourg with Namur to the northeast and Ettelbruck to the north, as well as key railheads such as Libramont. With those repairs completed, the Rhine and the rest of Germany beckoned.

10

TAKEOVER

Once Hitler's attack through the Ardennes had been halted and then reversed, the Allied invasion of Germany was a matter of when, not if. The war was effectively won, but numerous battles were still to come. Because the Allies needed to gain control of the German rail network to establish themselves as the ruling force, these last few months of the war — indeed, right up to the end of 1945 — were the busiest time for the Military Railway Service and their British counterparts. In fact, the largest movement of freight by rail occurred from February through April 1945 to support the rapidly advancing troops.

For the railway troops, these new circumstances drastically contrasted with those they had encountered in France and the Benelux. They were no longer chasing out an occupying force, welcomed by locals. Instead, they were the invading troops taking over a hostile country. And by no means did all the local people welcome being liberated from Hitler's yoke. Taking over and operating a railway in these circumstances required a different approach, as resentment against the Allied forces was a constant consideration. Moreover, there was considerable rebuilding to be done; the Germans had sabotaged the lines as they retreated and did so quite effectively, given their intimate knowledge of the territory.

The primary challenge was establishing a railway connection across the Rhine because the road capacity across the river, even when the bridges were rebuilt, would never be sufficient to meet the demand. In the meantime, British and American engineers carried out countless smaller but vital projects. Their work often encompassed both road and rail projects, and though the rail schemes were normally given priority, railroad engineers were occasionally dispatched to maintain roads suffering under the weight of military traffic. As parts of Germany were liberated, railway battalions moved swiftly to reestablish lines of communication. Engineering units not only worked on-site for these various projects but also frequently produced the building materials and steel sections required. In effect, these soldiers were re-creating the lost infrastructure of the countries they occupied. Behind every part of the front line, there was a railway unit hard at work, maintaining, rebuilding, and operating the railway.

Indeed, numerous major reconstruction projects needed immediate attention. The 332nd Engineer Regiment, for example, was a particularly busy unit. In early January, the men were assigned to build a large depot on the Isle de Monsin, an artificial island at the junction of the Meuse River and the Albert Canal. Goods arriving at Antwerp were transferred on this little island from the overworked railways and roads onto the 80-mile-long canal connecting Liège and Antwerp, as well as the Scheldt and Meuse Rivers. Here, the 332nd was joined by a couple of other units, making a total of around 200 GIs, manpower that was doubled by the addition of 200 Belgian civilians.

Hampered at first by the snow and ice on the ferocious river, the work on the depot was not completed until mid-March. Meanwhile, another company of the regiment worked on replacing a nearby single-track railway bridge on the Bilsen–Maastricht line across the

Albert Canal that had been destroyed by the retreating Germans in September 1944. Two other units were required, respectively, to run a cement factory to supply the various reconstruction projects and to produce steel at the Ougree steel plant in Belgium for railway bridge construction across numerous locations. This undertaking obviated the need to haul large bridge parts over the Channel and across long stretches of the European continent. In addition, on January 19, a platoon of Company A of the 332nd started reinstating a 220-foot-long section of a bridge that was on an important route between dumps in Belgium and Aachen. Removing the debris took four weeks alone and replacing the bridge was particularly treacherous because the center span stretched a hundred feet above the water. Snow and sleet continued through January, slowing down the work that was eventually completed on March 12.

Finally, the 332nd's most hazardous task was operating a fuel line at an airfield in Liège that was frequently attacked by V-1 rockets. Working next to fuel lines while threatened by random rocket attack was one of the most perilous jobs the engineers faced. Unsurprisingly, the civilians hired to help repeatedly failed to show up for work, especially as the rocket attacks intensified.

Apart from air attacks, mines were the greatest and most constant risk the GI engineers encountered. The sheer variety of mines taxed the skills of even the best sappers. A book by Chester Nichols on the exploits of the 332nd in which he served lists numerous types of devices: "box mines, schu mines [which were in a wooden box and therefore difficult to detect as they contained very little metal], teller mines, stick mines, and regal mines [which tended to be unstable] which were ingenious and distributed everywhere."[1] One site in the Roer valley where a bridge was being replaced took three days to demine, and even then, a sergeant, Andrew Vissers, and two Belgian civilians were killed when they triggered a teller mine, a particularly powerful mine that was designed as an anti-tank device.

All this is just a snapshot of the projects of a single engineering unit, among the dozens of railway and engineering teams working in the region. Some, such as the 341st, had built a couple of bridges in Germany before the German counteroffensive forced them to retreat. Now that the Battle of the Bulge had been won, this type of work restarted in earnest. The 341st was responsible for the devastated area that had been the German salient. According to one account, by their second retreat, the Germans' capabilities for destruction and sabotage had become much more effective. Although only 4 of the bridges the 341st had reconstructed before the Ardennes campaign had been destroyed, many others had been blown up—no fewer than 15 on the 45-mile line between Bastogne and Malmedy, an area at the center of fierce fighting in December: "As rapidly as the enemy withdrew from his costly salient, the railroad builders returned, and, with burning tanks, frozen bodies and snow-buried mines for a background, repaired the damage."[2]

Mines, as the 332nd experienced, were a vile hazard. In the Bulge areas, both sides had deployed them extensively. The Americans had first laid them alongside the railways when they retreated, and then the Germans mined the railways again when they, in turn, withdrew. In the two-week period from late January to early February, two companies of the 341st recovered 300 mines, each painstakingly removed by the sappers at great personal risk. When, at last, the cold weather relented, it only made matters worse: "In the midst of this busy and hazardous period came the thaw, and the complete break-down of the roads in eastern Belgium and the Siegfried belt." Nevertheless, "it was clear to all that only the railroads could sustain the American follow-up attack. Deployed all along the lines, building several bridges at once, the troops could not wait for the railroad to bring materials successively to each bridge."[3]

As troops moved into Germany, the scale and extent of the work expanded relentlessly, right up to Victory in Europe Day (May 8, 1945) and, in some cases, beyond. The almost unlimited demand for reconstruction depended on whether the railways could deliver building materials around the country, but, as the Allies took over more territory, the rail system was also required to cope with an influx of passengers. Military demands on the railway increasingly had to take into account humanitarian concerns, as millions of displaced people required transportation. Most civilian transportation was provided by the railways because the roads were clogged with military transport and suitable passenger vehicles were simply not available.

Another measure of the growth in demand for railway operations was the number of railheads, where supplies were transferred from rail to road. The Liège-based 708th Grand Division, which encompassed several battalions, was responsible for an ever-expanding network of lines stretching into Germany. By February, it operated 78 major railheads that were the unloading points for men and supplies for both the First and Ninth Armies and ADSEC. Each railhead supplied a military unit at the front line.

The Roer River bridge was recognized as one of the most important of these early projects in Germany because it enabled the Allies to cross the Rhine. The bridge was a six-span masonry construction on an 18-mile-long double-tracked line that stretched across the broad Roer valley. It had been completely destroyed by the Germans. Chester Nichols, a member of the 332nd, later recalled that when work started on the line, it was in a terrible state because it had been part of the defensive Siegfried Line: "There was damage caused by bombing, shelling, mortar-fire, and strafing," as well as booby traps and mines.[4]

Reconstruction of the bridge was undertaken 24 hours around the clock using floodlights at night and an air force plane nicknamed the "Black Widow" patrolling the sky, ever ready to warn the engineers of an impending attack by the Luftwaffe. As Nichols explains, the Black Widow could send "one radio signal [that] would turn out all the lights."[5] The reconstruction over the fast-running river, which made the task more perilous, started on March 2, and work was completed in merely nine days. This was achieved despite the fact that more than half the members of the 332nd had been called up for infantry duty to replace casualties at the front line, greatly depleting the unit's skill base. In recognition of the unit's varied accomplishments, the 332nd regimental train was given the honor of being the first to cross the line on a successful test run. The train was hauled by two American locomotives, more than a thousand of which had been delivered via Cherbourg. According to Nichols: "The deep-throated whistle of the American built locomotives in Europe created much comment among our European friends. The European engines squealed like 'stuck pigs' while the low-toned 'whoo-whoo' of the American built machine was quite a contrast. Thus the name 'whoo-whoo' became the name which stayed with us for the remainder of the time in Europe."[6] The following day, a train loaded with ammunition that had been waiting in the yard at Aachen safely crossed the bridge, and this line became the principal supply route through to the west bank of the Rhine.

The early trips deeper into Germany were not without danger. The risks of working in this uncertain environment were highlighted by an article in *Trains* magazine published in 1945: "A barracks train crawled forward into the blackness on newly captured tracks out of Aachen, the crew knowing only that their advance party was somewhere ahead and should probably flag them down when the new location was reached. The engineer could see nothing ahead of him. He had clearance through to Krefeld [just over 50 miles from Aachen], and he expected that his destination was somewhere in between, probably at Munchengladbach."[7] Because the embankment had been damaged by bombs, the ride was particularly bumpy and slow. As night fell, the soldiers drifted off, unaware of the forthcoming perils. Feeling a particularly heavy lurch, the driver stopped, took out his flashlight and discovered he was about to go over a trestle bridge that had all but disappeared, leaving only the tracks across the river. He realized he had gone past his intended destination and later learned that a repair team had left the points open to run northeast to Düsseldorf, which was still in enemy hands. When daylight came, a group of men from the train walked back along the tracks. The advance party had somehow missed the train, expecting it to arrive the following morning.

The crossing of the Roer valley opened the way to Mönchengladbach and eventually the Rhine, which runs across most of Germany from the Alps to the North Sea. How to cross this vast and fast-flowing river had long taxed the minds of the Allied commanders. The importance of reconstructing the Rhine River bridge was such that, in the weeks running up to the start, a special school was created to train the officers and men in the units destined to work on this key project and other crucial crossings. The Rhine River Training School, nicknamed the "River Rats," ran for around six weeks from mid-February at a school in Cheratte in Belgium on the Meuse River, where engineers and railwaymen were given a two-week course in rebuilding bridges. The existence of the school was testimony to the difficulty—and risk—of handling very large sections of bridge that needed to be floated carefully on barges and boats that had not been constructed for that purpose. The smallest mistake or misjudgment could easily capsize a barge and dump its load in the river.

After the Battle of the Bulge, the Allies' push eastward recovered its momentum. They were now moving rapidly toward the Rhine, the traditional barrier that had long protected Germany from invaders. Unsurprisingly, as the Germans were retreating to the east, they destroyed all the bridges over the Rhine and crossings over numerous smaller rivers, canals, and railway lines. In addition, the Germans tried to remove or destroy all the rolling stock left on tracks about to be captured, but the speed of the Allies' advance meant they were not always able to do so. As a result, in the late-February push to the Rhine, the Allies recovered thousands of railway cars and numerous locomotives in working order and put them into service as soon as the tracks were rehabilitated. This was fortunate because, as the lines of communication lengthened, trucking became increasingly unviable.

Because the military commanders recognized the Rhine as the key obstacle blocking their progress farther into Germany, they were delighted when one of the bridges over the river was captured in a usable state before it could be blown. Well, only just, as it proved to be a temporary passage over the river. The Ludendorff railway bridge at Remagen was taken on March 7, thanks to good luck and a crucial German error. Named after General Erich Ludendorff, Germany's military leader during the latter half of World War I, the quarter-mile-long bridge was comparatively new and solid, having been built by Russian prisoners of war during that earlier conflict. Now, in their retreat, German engineers had rigged the bridge with explosives, but the local commander had delayed blowing it in order to allow as many of his troops as possible to escape to the east bank. Unfortunately for him, he miscalculated and delayed the destruction a little too long. As a group of tanks led by Lieutenant Karl Timmermann, a platoon leader in the Ninth Armored Division, who by coincidence was of German origin, having been born in Frankfurt just after the First World War, approached the bridge, the Germans tried to blow up the central span, but the charges failed to detonate. One charge did explode, but the bridge seemed to rise in the air only to settle back down on its supporting piers. Although the Americans were quick to exploit this windfall, the damage from the explosions had so weakened the structure that it could only support road vehicles rather than the trains for which it was designed. Moreover, any hopes of finding another usable bridge soon dissipated when the Germans blew the remaining crossings in March.

The Ludendorff Bridge was so crucial to the war effort that the Germans' failure to destroy it was front-page news in America and fueled hopes that the war would end earlier than expected. Aware of the seriousness of their error, the Germans focused on destroying the stricken bridge using every type of weapon available. Artillery shells rained down on the Allied troops crossing the bridge, and a uniquely large mortar gun mounted on a nearby hill was a constant threat. Numerous mines also had to be cleared. The Americans counted 367 Luftwaffe aircraft attacking the bridge over the next 10 days and claimed to have shot down nearly 30 percent of them in what was later termed "the greatest anti-aircraft artillery battle in American history."[8] A daring attempt by seven German divers carrying explosives sent downriver to blow up the bridge was foiled, and they were all captured or killed. In their last and ultimately futile attempt, the Germans, on Hitler's direct orders, launched V-2 rockets at the bridge. Wholly unsuitable for the task, none of the 11 rockets came within 500 yards of the bridge, though they did kill six Americans and numerous local citizens.

As it happens, the Germans need not have bothered. After General Itschner inspected the bridge, he issued an all too prescient warning to the local commander about the precariousness of the structure.

In a postwar interview, Itschner said that he had expressed concerns about the heavy decking that had been put on the bridge: "I talked to [Colonel] Bill Carter [engineer, First Army, who was in charge] and I think he really felt so, too, that they were taking a great risk with that added weight. But he said, 'It's already on and I don't think I should tell them to take it off because, after all, we don't know and the bridge is badly needed.'" As Itschner predicted, 10 days after the bridge was captured, it collapsed—killing 28 engineers and injuring nearly a hundred others on the bridge, which had fortunately been closed as a precaution because it had begun to sag. Itschner subsequently blamed himself for not being sufficiently forceful: "I was later sorry I hadn't urged him [Carter] more. But I couldn't order him to remove it. All I could do was to try to convince him."[9]

However, by the time of the collapse, the bridge had proved its worth. Elements of five divisions crossed the Rhine, and two temporary structures were built next to it; as a result, around 25,000 men and thousands of vehicles successfully reached the east bank of the Rhine and established a bridgehead to begin the assault on the Ruhr, Germany's key industrial region. Over the following weeks, temporary pontoon bridges were installed at various points along the Rhine, but no railway crossing was available until April.

Nevertheless, the railway engineers were among the advance group using the crossing as they endeavored to establish control of the railway running along the eastern bank of the Rhine. This proved a fruitful exercise. Just three days after the Ludendorff Bridge was captured, the first railway personnel to cross the Rhine were a reconnaissance team in a jeep led by Lieutenant Colonel John D. Drury. They were rewarded with rich pickings, according to the 708th's historian: "East of the Rhine the reconnaissance party discovered enemy trains made up and apparently ready to pull out, but which never rolled due to the fast moving First United States Army. In one sector

of the railroad yards at Erpel they found trains and locomotives cam-
ouflaged so well that they were difficult to see with the naked eye.
Complete trains of coal and many other valuable materials needed
for the war were captured intact."[10]

The unexpected availability of this bridgehead proved to be an
enormous boon to the Allied forces. It was, rightly, seen as a pivotal
moment in the war, having been established more than two weeks
ahead of the long-planned launch of Operation Plunder, the main
assault over the Rhine. Plunder, an operation almost on the scale of
the original D-Day landings that involved 1.2 million men, including almost 60,000 engineers, was launched on March 24 and justified the months of preparation. Within six weeks, the war in Europe
was over.

However, to successfully bring the conflict to a conclusion, the
Allies needed to establish permanent crossings of the Rhine that
would accommodate trains because relying on boats and barges
to take troops and equipment across could not meet the military's
requirements. The Ludendorff collapse meant they had to go back to
plan A: finding a suitable location for a railway crossing. Given the
width of the river and the difficulty of finding a suitable site, "bridging the Rhine proved to be one of the major engineering tasks of
the war in Europe, ranking with the engineer aspects of the Normandy assault and the reconstruction of the ports in magnitude and
complexity."[11]

After much discussion, Wesel, the northernmost option of the
four under consideration, was chosen — even though the project
would be technically difficult because it required the construction
of a second bridge, about a quarter of the Wesel bridge's length and
with six spans, over the neighboring Lippe River. The decisive factor
was that a bridgehead had already been established on the other side
of the Wesel that would make construction easier and faster. Even

with preparation, notably, bringing large sections of the proposed bridge as near to the front line as possible, the task was daunting. Supported by 23 separate spans, the bridge was more than a third of a mile long and required one and a half miles of new connecting railway line. Nevertheless, the construction, carried out by an engineering team led by the 1056th Port Construction and Repair Group working around the clock, was completed in just 10 days, on April 8, despite some (unsuccessful) raids by the Luftwaffe.

Two other railway bridges built for army use over the Rhine were the President Roosevelt Bridge at Mainz, completed in 10 days on April 14, and the Victory Bridge at Duisburg, which opened on May 8 and gave the Allies access to the vital Ruhr coal fields. Itschner, who organized the reconstruction of these bridges, was particularly proud of the one at Mainz because, as he later recalled, "the engineering unit doing the construction arranged that the white surrender flag left by the retreating Germans on one tower [of the destroyed bridge next to the new one] would be cut down as a signal to start the construction. Before it hit the water, they had a dozen pile drivers banging away."[12]

Itschner had hoped to be on the inaugural run across the Mainz Rhine bridge with Patton but had hurt his head in a minor airplane accident a few days earlier. He was up and about again by the opening date but did not dare to turn up because, as he later explained: "The only trouble was I could not be there because I was afraid to go up into his area without my helmet, and I couldn't get my helmet over the bandages." Patton, though, was so delighted by the speed of construction and the fanfare that he pinned a medal on the chest of Itschner's deputy, Colonel A. H. Davidson. The various engineering units building bridges competed vigorously with each other. For this bridge, crucially, they had been able to call on local materials, either taken from the Germans or manufactured by the army. Itschner admitted, "We could never have built these things we did without that help."[13]

The British were the recognized experts at railway bridges, and by the time their engineers reached the Rhine, they had built a total of 122, around four miles of bridging. On April 13, Montgomery attended a celebration marking the thousandth Bailey bridge—both road and railway—built by the US and UK forces over the Weser–Ems Canal near Recke. The British built a fourth bridge over the Rhine farther north between Spyck and Emmerich, almost the last to be constructed by British engineers—and undoubtedly the most challenging. Even before work could begin, a total of five miles of new rail line had to be built to bring the railway to the location of the new bridge as, again, there had been no previous crossing there. At this point, the water was 20 feet deep and the banks were around 600 yards apart, posing a tough challenge for the engineers, who raised great concern about the possible scouring effects of the fast-running water. The site was first inspected on April 2, when the last German forces had been flushed from the area, and work started five days later. The bridge, which eventually had 34 spans and stretched over 750 yards into nearby marshland, was built from both ends to speed up the work. It was completed in precisely a month, on May 8, the very day that "Victory in Europe" was declared. According to Brigadier Gage, this was something of an anticlimax for the 1,386 men who had worked on it, and they felt "to some extent cheated of their rewards for the bridge could not now be used for its primary purpose—the support of military operations against Germany."[14] Nevertheless, over the next few weeks, it was a vital route for military traffic, with 20 trains in each direction crossing the new bridge, which offered the quickest connection between parts of Germany and Holland and the Channel ports.

These initial bridges over the Rhine quickly became essential
components of the war effort and their completion undoubtedly has-
tened the end of the conflict. Rail traffic over the Rhine began on
April 8 and soon overtook motor transport as the main long-distance
carrier. Within 10 days, the railways were handling about 12,000
tons over the Rhine bridges, which approximately equaled the tonnage hauled by truck, and doubled it by VE Day. And yet that was
still not enough. The problem of lack of capacity in reaching the
Rhine's east bank remained throughout this final period of the conflict. Because of their limited number and capacity, these railway
bridges became terrible bottlenecks. Special controls had to be set up
to direct traffic over the Mainz and Wesel bridges, which both had
only a single-track. The backlog of loaded railway cars was particularly heavy on the west side of the Mainz bridge, where the situation
was complicated by the US Third Army's tendency to call forward
selected items of freight, which involved a lot of sorting in the
depots — typical of Patton to ensure he got precisely what he wanted.

The Americans were anxious to make as much use of these bridges
as possible, which provides a fascinating contrast with the British
approach to the transport issue. Lieutenant Andrew Gillitt, a British
officer responsible for locomotives for the 182nd Railway Operating
Company, later recalled how the American attitude toward operations was far more cavalier: "Unlike the Americans who ran 100
trains head to tail on the opening day, we observed strict Military
Railway Operating Rules which permitted just twelve paths in each
direction."[15] Actually, his recollection of the American operation was
a bit of an exaggeration; traffic over the Wesel bridge reached a peak
of 48 trains per day in each direction, but his point about the different operating techniques is still valid.

In relation to train operations, a key innovation made early in the
New Year was designed to speed up priority supplies. This was the

Toot Suite Express, which garnered almost as much attention as the road-based Red Ball Express, thanks to its canny name and excellent PR. The name *Toot Suite Express* was based on a corruption of the French *tout de suite*, meaning "immediately," and had been chosen in a vote of 620 Transportation Corps men, with the winners receiving a prize of leave time.

The Toot Suite Express was a daily train carrying priority freight from Cherbourg to Paris, where it would pick up more filled railcars to take through to Verdun or Namur—later extended to Liège and eastward into Germany. Various army units bid for space for their train consignments, and the train was given priority over other services. The best, most reliable equipment was specially marked for use only on the Toot Suite. Run by the 728th Railway Operating Battalion as part of the Military Railway Service, the express started operating on January 22 with an expectation that cargo unloaded at Cherbourg would reach the front within 36 hours.[16]

The service was given remarkable priority, including the ability to overtake other trains by going on the opposite line in double-tracked sections: "Outside Lison, Frashour [the engineer] stops the train and telephones to the operator. He gets orders to cross over to the westbound line and proceed against the current of traffic in order to by-pass other trains ahead. In spite of heavy traffic and the blackout, Toot Sweet, pampered lady of the Transportation Corps, must be kept on time."[17] In fact, that particular journey to Liège in February 1945 was completed in 32 hours, nearly 8 hours ahead of schedule.

The Toot Suite was important in bringing priority goods through France quickly and actually continued to run right into Germany after VE Day; however, in truth, the service was less significant in strategic terms than many of the numerous previously mentioned projects undertaken by British and American railway troops. Even so, it brought some welcome publicity to the role of the railways, which was mostly neglected in contemporaneous and subsequent reporting. Its success resulted in the inauguration of a similar special train in March 1945, the Meat Ball Express, which carried perishables — mostly meat — from Namur to the First and Ninth Armies in Germany.

In fact, Toot Suite Express did not just carry ammunition and K rations. Mail was a key part of its consignments and, arguably, its most important one. Receiving mail regularly from back home was perceived by the higher echelons to be an important component in improving the troops' morale on the line, so it was highly prioritized. The GIs on the front line were delighted to find that their mail was now getting to them within a week or so of being sent, or as the *Yankee Boomer* put it, "Weary doughfeet blinked at the postmark on their letters from home — they'd been mailed just a week before. Most of the rail had previously taken from three to six weeks in reaching combat troops."[18] There was another advantage, too. The Military Railway Service's decision to use the train for the delivery of mail meant that there was far less pilfering, and the GIs were far more likely to receive the presents they had been sent by friends and relatives at home.

This is a small insight into a phenomenon that was little discussed but was undoubtedly widespread. The railway battalions were not entirely staffed by angels, and the very nature of the job created great potential for thievery and corruption. Coal had always been a problem, given the local demand as well as the vast quantities needed to power the locomotives, and both the British and the American railway units installed armed guards on trains to prevent pilfering of this black gold.

There was, though, a much more serious crime issue, one that threatened the very supply chain that the railways were designed to provide. As the lines of communication extended, so did the opportunities for the bad guys. According to the official report on the activities of the Transportation Corps, "Thefts from U.S. Army supply trains and diversion of the loot into the French black market became a serious problem during the closing months of 1944. Every stolen item represented a dual loss, first in critical shipping space, and second to the military personnel for whom delivery was intended."[19] In the South of France, the First Military Railway Service had sufficient military police units to assign them as train guards, but manpower was scarcer in the North: "In both the Normandy and Channel Base Sections excessive and heavy losses caused by pilferage necessitated the detail of infantrymen and service troops as train guards. Both military personnel and native civilians pilfered, encouraged by the enormous black-market profits."[20] The rewards for the thieves were sufficient to tempt many impoverished and even not-so-impoverished soldiers: a 20-pound drum of coffee would go for $300 and a case of K rations for $100 (about $1,700 in today's money).

Theft of items such as cigarettes, rations, shoes, and mail reached such a scale that it was contributing to mass shortages. Blankets and uniforms were stolen from hospital trains, and 66 million packs of cigarettes — the most tradable item — disappeared in a single month. Antony Beevor reckoned Paris had become "Chicago sur Seine," but this was not the only example of troops diverting supplies into the black market. American deserters teamed up with local criminal gangs: "The profits were so large that even drug dealers were drawn into this new market. Up to half the jerry cans in continental Europe went missing."[21] The modus operandi was simple: the train would be stopped on a bend so that the military police at the end of the train could not see and then the supplies were unloaded to the train crew's confederates waiting by the tracks.

During the relatively quiet period, when vast quantities of supplies for the front line were being built up, the rate of loss became
so great as to attract the attention of the army's Counterintelligence
Division (CID). Undercover agents of the CID eventually uncovered a massive operation based in Paris but with tentacles reaching
across the Allied-occupied parts of France. It was systematic and centered around a particular battalion where corruption was allowed to
run rife. The investigators charged 8 officers and 190 enlisted men,
including the commanding officer of the 716th Railway Operating
Battalion (sponsored by the Southern Pacific Lines), Major Walter
Marlin, with black-marketing offenses.

A few men from the 724th (sponsored by the Pennsylvania
Railroad) were accused, but almost a quarter of the personnel of
the 716th were court-martialed, suggesting that the battalion had
been taken over by criminals. Major Marlin, who had only recently
joined, was clearly operating out of his depth and was unable to
prevent the situation from getting out of control. At his trial, he
claimed that he had told his men they could help themselves to
rations but they should only take enough for their own consump-
tion. Oddly, his naiveté was accepted as being in good faith and
the case against him was dismissed, though that was very much the
exception: of all the men charged, only 4 other officers and 17 men
were not convicted.

There was also an element of pour encourager les autres about
the sentences, which were remarkably harsh for stealing. However,
the military hierarchy saw theft as a conspiracy that threatened the
war effort and undermined the military's very ethos. More than a
hundred men who were convicted received prison sentences rang-
ing from 3 to 50 years, with nearly all receiving terms of 20 years
or more. The longest sentences of 45 to 50 years were imposed on a
group of four, who appeared to be ringleaders and were making deals

worth 100,000 francs ($2,000) in one night's theft from boxcars. Later, some of those convicted took advantage of an offer of clemency by the theater commander whereby they could be restored to duty in a special combat unit. After these trials, stricter supervision of the freight trains and railway installations, as well as other measures, such as putting dye in the diesel and enforcing stricter penalties, reduced but by no means eliminated malfeasance of this type. Pilfering by civilians from military trains and railway yards remained troublesome throughout the war.

As the Allies advanced through the Ruhr in April, the railroad troops soon took over the operation of the German rail network. Apart from rebuilding bridges and repairing tracks, one of their biggest tasks was the rehabilitation of the railway facilities at Hamm, just northeast of Dortmund, the biggest railway yard in Europe. It had been targeted regularly by Allied bombing and then repaired repeatedly by vast numbers of workers commandeered after each attack. However, when the 735th Railway Operating Battalion (sponsored by the Erie Railroad) arrived and was charged with bringing the yard back into use, the GIs found that most of the freight facilities had been sabotaged by the retreating Germans. Fortunately, much of the equipment had been left undamaged, including locomotives that proved to be more reliable than French or Belgian equipment. With the help of 300 local German railway workers—paid by the local *burgermeister* out of German government funds—sufficient tracks were brought back into use to provide a service of a dozen trains departing from Hamm daily. Most of these were passenger services, which carried around 3,000 "displaced persons," and as many as five prisoner-of-war trains, each with around 2,000 men.

Transporting prisoners of war was a key function of the railways because trucks were rarely available. One transport ended in a horrific—and little reported—incident in which dozens of German prisoners perished. On January 22, 1945, a train taking prisoners of war from Aachen to Belgium included two refrigerated cars with the cooling mechanism disconnected. However, according to Livingstone, the historian of the 740th: "The men in charge of loading the prisoners, not knowing that such cars are manufactured airtight, locked the doors."[22] When the doors of the train were opened at Charleroi after an overnight journey, all the prisoners in one car and three-quarters in the other had died of suffocation.

As the end of the war approached, the dominance of the Allied forces resulted in an almost total takeover of the German railway network. The system was managed day-to-day by the military, which was responsible for all aspects of service and required much improvisation. For example, according to a report in *Railway Age*, the headquarters of the 735th was operating from "a 50 car [static] train consisting of a complete office, chapel, dental laboratory, medical laboratory, orderly room, dispatcher's car, shower cars, mess supply and mail cars."[23] Similarly, in April, the 708th Grand Division moved to Warburg, 40 miles east of Dortmund, and took over a system that was operated by a haphazard collection of cars from across Europe, including France, Hungary, and Holland—all of which had been purloined by the Nazis. Though the locomotives were German, the local railwaymen were cooperative and ready to show troops how to drive them. It was only just before VE Day that a few US locomotives arrived to help provide traction.

The German rail network was in better condition overall than those in France and the Benelux—because it had been designed to withstand attack. As one rail battalion officer put it, "Even after six years of war, with accompanying manpower shortage, German railway maintenance was excellent."[24] As I wrote in my previous book, *Engines of War*, "While the French railways had been wrecked by a combination of the Résistance and Allied aircraft, the Allies had to rely on attacks from the air to destroy the German ones and that showed how difficult it was to wreck railways without the availability of precision-guided munitions. The Germans had, however, the advantage that they had been on a war footing throughout the 1930s and therefore their railway system was far better able to withstand attacks than those of Britain or France."[25]

A group of civil defense officers who visited Germany after the war were particularly impressed by "the large number of alternative routes available and the generous nature of the facilities provided and the spaciousness of the layouts on running lines at junctions in passenger stations and goods depots and marshalling yards." To enable the railways to recover quickly after an attack, huge stockpiles of materials were stored around the country and much of the network's infrastructure had been strengthened: "bridges, retaining walls, signal boxes, stations, and railway offices had all been built to resist bomb damage, and the officers noted that many of these were still standing, showing signs that they had withstood attacks."[26]

There was also ingenious subterfuge:

One clever tactic used across Germany throughout the war was to install railway camouflage: fake bomb craters were dug and flimsy artificial bridges were flung across rivers while mounds of earth and debris were left scattered to suggest that repairs had not been carried out. Decoy targets were provided at a number of less important yards and were deliberately lit to attract the bombers away from more significant areas. Another brilliant innovation which helped the speedy recovery of the railways was the mobile signal box. The Germans built 300 of these boxes, which were despatched with great speed on express passenger trains as soon as damage was reported. They resembled ordinary freight wagons and, placed on sleepers, could be set up within just five hours of their arrival.[27]

By and large, the Germans had kept their rail network operating, even under the intense attacks of Zuckerman's Transportation Plan, and this ultimately benefited the Americans troops who took over running the system. After the Allies' invasion, the well-disciplined German civilian railway workers usually cooperated with the Military Railway Service in restoring the railway system because they were eager to have regular paid employment. Although there were a few instances of sabotage, mostly the locals wanted a functioning railway.

As soon as the Allies crossed the Rhine, the rapid end to the war was inevitable. Without controlling the vast industrial complex of the Ruhr, the Germans were powerless. The war did not end in a flourish but rather with the collapse of Germany, invaded from both sides and with its leader stuck in a bunker from which he never emerged. Impressive as Patton's rush across France in the late summer and early autumn of 1944 had been, its speed was superseded by the final thrust of the Allied army in Germany. The railways, as ever, supported from behind the line, but in a final irony, the rapid advance was helped by Hitler's own great innovation, the *autobahnen* (divided highways), which had been conceived as a key military asset. These spacious roads enabled the advance troops to move forward swiftly, though these positions could not be sustained without railway support to bring in the supplies.

By VE Day in May 1945, more than 50 battalions had been formed, and ultimately the Military Railway Service encompassed 44,000 men, of whom 28,000 served in France, and nearly all were recruited from railway companies. According to a history of the Military Railway Service, "The 1,161 railroad men who served as MRS officers [across the world] between 1942 and 1946 had an average of 12 years' railroading experience,"[28] while the enlisted men averaged two and a half years each. In other words, these men whose efforts have been largely forgotten were effectively railwaymen first and soldiers second.

The statistics collected so meticulously by the US Army both tell and mask this story. The tens of thousands of men involved, the thousands of miles of railway, the number of locomotives and railcars, the lengths of rebuilt bridges—all these are impressive, staggering even, but do not reflect the fact that the conditions in which these men had to rebuild and operate the railways were truly extraordinary. Add to these numbers, too, the thousands of British engineers working on the railways in Holland, Belgium, and northern Germany and it is all the more surprising that the story of what these men achieved has been so ignored in accounts of this worldwide conflict.

It is difficult to account for this failure. The supply chain may seem like a particularly banal part of warfare, and it is no wonder that even when consideration is given to logistics, jeeps and trucks, indeed anything on four wheels, may seem at first more exciting than trains. After all, these vehicles are controlled and driven by individuals with the ability to go wherever they want, whereas running a railway is a huge cooperative undertaking. Besides the myth of the legendary Casey Jones, those who drive the trains are anonymous engineers who merely follow tracks whose direction is set by signalers on a route decided by operators. Of course the Red Ball Express, with drivers hurtling over muddy roads while pushing aside all other traffic, appears to be a far more exciting concept than the Toot Suite Express, which trundled slowly across France and Belgium. And though steam trains are photogenic, the rest of the train, a dull assortment of freight cars or perhaps a few unexciting passenger carriages like a bus on tracks, hardly offers an exciting vision. Given this context, it is quite easy to forget that a single train can haul a couple thousand tons farther, more quickly, more efficiently, and far more cheaply than a hundred or more trucks.

There are so many more exciting images of warfare — the movement of thousands of troops, the air battles, the arrival of huge ships into massive ports, tanks brushing aside all in front of them, men shooting each other and even killing the enemy with bayonets. Why would anyone focus on the supply chain in the face of all this derring-do? The Germans made the same mistake, as the author Jonathan Trigg notes in his book about how the Wehrmacht lost France: "By the end of August, the allied Fleet had landed no fewer than 2,052,099 men, 438,471 vehicles and 3,098,259 tons of supplies in Normandy — the Wehrmacht was losing the Materialschlacht (matériel war) so despised by the German General Staff — and with it, the campaign — and France."[29] In other words, the Allies won because they understood the importance of supply chains, logistics, transport facilities, and quite possibly above all, railways. When it comes to winning a war, it's never really about how flashy or cinematic the tactics are; it's ultimately about efficiency and sustainability.

The humble railways and those working them must be accorded the recognition they deserve. Certainly, the war in Ukraine has again highlighted the crucial role of the railways in warfare, to carry people to and from conflict zones but also to act as a fundamental part of the supply chain that so often is the key determinant of a conflict's outcome. This story is not just about railways or war or history or even railway workers. It's about all that and much more. Crucially, there are lessons in this story for today's military strategists.

EPILOGUE

PEACE — BUT THE WORK OF THE RAILWAYS NEVER STOPS

Adolf Hitler committed suicide on April 30 as the Russians approached Berlin, and his successor, Reichspräsident Karl Dönitz, authorized Germany's surrender a week later. The terms were negotiated near the Dutch border by two Allied officers who were taken across German lines on April 29 in Alive, the train Eisenhower used to travel around England before D-Day. It had been brought over from the UK and was moved to Germany in December 1944. A few days later, Eisenhower traveled in it to Paris and then used it to reach Reims in eastern France for the signing of the surrender documents with the German High Command. The hostilities ended at 11:00 p.m. the following day, May 8, VE Day.

Although some parts of the network were notionally handed over to German control after VE Day, the Allied railway operating battalions retained ultimate control and the military made all the decisions about which services could be run. As the historian of the 708th Grand Division put it very frankly: "In Germany, the rehabilitation of railway lines was based on the opening only of such lines as would be necessary in the U. S. military interest. Other lines were left to the Germans."[1] As an example of the amazing complexity of the task, after a reorganization in May 1945, one Grand Division was responsible for five battalions running services over 1,059 miles of railway. And similar arrangements were made across Germany with other Grand Divisions in charge, except in the areas occupied by the Russians.

In the absence of any national German government, the Allies, in their various zones—French, British, American, and Russian—took over. Not only did repair work on the railways continue, but it also expanded. The railways had to be kept going so that the reconstruction could continue and, crucially, displaced people, prisoners of war, and returning soldiers could be transported. Consequently, the basic jobs of repairing war damage and replacing bridges continued after VE Day. For example, the diary of the 341st Engineer Regiment reported that "fourteen bridges [were] opened from the 5th to the 12th of May: a total of 43 spans replaced: more than 2,160 feet of bridges reconstructed! That is the record of the last week on rail-roads in Germany. Eleven of these bridges, all double track, were started and completed in the last six days."[2] Indeed, a further 1,610 miles of railroad were brought into use and 35 bridges rebuilt in these months.

It might seem strange that the Allies carried out so much railway activity after VE Day, but the need for transport actually intensified following the end of the conflict. People were free to move about without the risk of being killed by one side or the other, and this put the transport system, notably, the partially functioning railways, under great strain.

The official role of the Military Railway Service in Europe did not end until early 1946. Even then, the US Military Government retained small units throughout Germany to ensure that military trains moved promptly and no unauthorized civilian goods were moved out of the US zone. The task of bringing the millions of soldiers in Europe back to their home countries was one only the railways could undertake. Huge camps, such as Lucky Strike near Saint-Valéry-en-Caux, the site of the infamous railway disaster, were created near the ports where men could rest while awaiting transport. But the GIs were so eager to return home that they organized a demonstration down the Champs-Élysées when a large number found themselves stuck in France after Christmas 1945.

Shockingly, black regiments were often given the lowest priority. According to the history of the Ninety-Fifth Engineer General Service Regiment, the unit of black soldiers who had arrived in France two weeks after D-Day to work on railways and bridges and then served in Liège during the Battle of the Bulge had to wait longer than others to return home: "They were kept at Lucky Strike for 45 days when most units spent at most a week in the camp." This was partly because combat units headed for the Pacific were given priority but also "they were waiting for a ship of the right size for the 95th as white soldiers did not want to share a ship with black troops."[3] They did not arrive home until August 12, far later than most units.

The British quickly organized the return of service members under the aegis of an organization called Medloc (Mediterranean Lines of Communication), which had been set up in the First World War. As soon as peace was declared, the organization arranged for the soldiers' return. First, it used convoys of a half dozen open-topped trucks, where the 20 men sitting on benches were exposed to the elements apart from the flimsy camouflage cover. For a few weeks, these convoys were a common sight but were clearly insufficient for the numbers involved.

However, by October 1945, it had been decided that all the men would be transported by train, and three routes to the Channel ports—starting from Toulon in southern France, Milan in Italy, and Villach in southern Austria—were established. Remarkably, the latter, serving British troops in Germany, operated all the way up until 1955. The service was, to say the least, patchy, as described in a booklet on the Medloc story: "Medloc was at the same time a resounding success moving millions of men and women to and fro, back to Britain... and a tale of trials and tribulations—according to some an inglorious episode in the history of the army... returning servicemen found themselves crammed uncomfortably into carriages on a seemingly interminable train ride through the war-ravaged landscapes of Europe on railway systems which had been bombed, sabotaged or otherwise destroyed by one set of belligerents after another."[4] Because the railways had been patched together for military purposes, it took more than a decade before services were restored to their prewar standard.

After the surviving soldiers were returned, there was one more final task for which the railways were uniquely suited: the grim duty of repatriating the remains of GIs killed in the European theater. On orders of the US government, the hastily buried bodies of American soldiers were disinterred from countless graveyards across Europe, placed in temporary metal coffins, and transported by train to the main ports through which they had arrived. In Europe, the coffins were transported in 118 specially adapted hospital trains, with all the windows blacked out and special secure locks fitted. All the railway transfers were escorted by veterans who were specially trained in military etiquette. When they reached America—five ships carrying up to 8,000 coffins each were used on the Atlantic crossings—the coffins were taken to the soldiers' hometowns also by train. This process started in 1946, when it was announced that relatives could request the body of their fallen soldier be transferred to a grave in the United States at no cost to the family, and ended in 1952. All told, 171,539 men were transported back to their homeland from all theaters of war. The remaining 108,328 killed in the conflict either had not been found or were not identified or the families had not asked for their return. The final cost of this program was a staggering $200 million (about $1.35 billion in today's dollars).

In operating these mortuary trains, the railways, again, proved their worth. Yet, as with all the stories told in this book, the railways' role across so many aspects of the conflict has been forgotten or ignored. There are a thousand more tales of these amazing railwaymen. I hope this book inspires further research into the last untold story of the Normandy landings.

APPENDIX A

UNITS SPONSORED BY RAILROAD COMPANIES

This list compiled by Nancy Cunningham shows the sponsorship of the railway battalions activated in World War II. The Grand Divisions each oversaw a group of battalions that were themselves divided into four companies broadly along functional lines with specific tasks such as operations and signaling. Most of the men were recruited from the sponsoring company, but some were enlisted without railway experience.

GRAND DIVISIONS

701st   New York Central Railroad
702nd   Union Pacific Railroad
703rd   Atlantic Coast Line Railroad
704th   Great Northern Railway
705th   Southern Pacific Lines
706th   Pennsylvania Railroad
707th   Southern Railway
708th   Baltimore and Ohio Railroad
709th   Association of American Railroads
710th   Atchison, Topeka and Santa Fe Railway

RAILWAY OPERATING BATTALIONS

712th Reading Railroad

713th Atchison, Topeka and Santa Fe Railway

714th Chicago, St. Paul, Minneapolis and Omaha Railway

715th Illinois Central Railroad

716th Southern Pacific Lines

717th Pennsylvania Railroad

718th Cleveland, Cincinnati, Chicago and St. Louis Railway

719th Texas and New Orleans Railroad

720th Chicago and North Western Railway

721st New York Central Railroad

722nd Seaboard Air Line Railroad

723rd Union Pacific Railroad

724th Pennsylvania Railroad

725th Chicago, Rock Island and Pacific Railroad

726th Wabash Railroad

727th Southern Railway

728th Louisville and Nashville Railroad

729th New York, New Haven and Hartford Railroad

730th Pennsylvania Railroad

732nd Great Northern Railway

733rd Central of Georgia Railway

734th Texas and New Orleans Railroad

735th Erie Railroad

737th New York Central

740th Chesapeake and Ohio Railway

741st Gulf, Mobile and Ohio Railroad

743rd Illinois Central Railroad

744th Chicago, Milwaukee, St. Paul and Pacific Railroad

745th Chicago, Burlington and Quincy Railroad

746th Missouri–Kansas–Texas Railroad

748th   Texas and Pacific Railway

749th   New York, New Haven and Hartford Railroad

750th   St. Louis–San Francisco Railway

752nd Boston and Maine Railroad

759th   Missouri Pacific Railroad

761st   Railway Transportation Company

RAILWAY SHOP BATTALIONS

753rd Cleveland, Cincinnati, Chicago and St. Louis Railway

754th Southern Pacific Lines

755th Norfolk and Western Railway

756th Pennsylvania Railroad

757th Chicago, Milwaukee, St. Paul and Pacific Railroad

758th Atchison, Topeka and Santa Fe Railway

763rd Delaware, Lackawanna and Western Railroad; Lehigh
         Valley Railroad

764th Boston and Maine Railroad

765th Erie Railroad

766th Association of American Railroads

A few more battalions were not sponsored and therefore recruited from various railways, and others were never activated.

APPENDIX B

LIST OF KNOWN DEATHS IN RAILWAY UNITS

This is the list of known deaths of members of the railway units killed during the conflict. Nancy Cunningham compiled this list from a wide range of official and unofficial sources; there are bound to be omissions. Most were killed in the European theater, but those who died in other locations have been included. Information about other casualties can be sent to Nancy via her website: militaryrailwayservice.com.

298   APPENDIX B

NAME	STATE ENLISTED	DATE OF DEATH	UNIT	PLACE OF DEATH	ARMY RANK
Wayne B. Agnew	IA	Dec. 5, 1944	713th Railway Operating Battalion	France	Private
Clarence J. Anderson	MS	Dec. 24, 1944	741st Railway Operating Battalion	Belgium	Private
John A. Auriemma	NJ	Dec. 12, 1944	741st Railway Operating Battalion	France	Private
Charles C. Bain	AL	Feb. 24, 1945	732nd Railway Operating Battalion	Belgium	Private
Lonnie W. Baker	AL	Dec. 14, 1944	722nd Railway Operating Battalion	France	Technician 5th Class
Leon R. Barter Jr.	WI	May 26, 1945	744th Railway Operating Battalion	Belgium	Technician 5th Class
Sam Belcastro	WV	Dec. 27, 1944	740th Railway Operating Battalion	France	Corporal
Elbert P. Bennett	MS	Apr. 7, 1945	750th Railway Operating Battalion	France	Unknown
Edward G. Billman	CA	Oct. 1, 1944	732nd Railway Operating Battalion	England	Corporal
James R. Black	MO	Aug. 27, 1945	749th Railway Operating Battalion	Manila	Private
Harvey N. Blank	ID	July 29, 1943	730th Railway Operating Battalion	Carthage, Tunis, Tunisia	Corporal
John H. Borkert	PA	Dec. 24, 1944	735th Railway Operating Battalion	France	Private
Robert L. Bourne	KY	July 26, 1945	746th Railway Operating Battalion	France	Technician 5th Class
Dalton R. Bradley	AR	Sept. 3, 1945	716th Railway Operating Battalion	France	Technician 5th Class
Adolph C. Brennecke	MO	Mar. 15, 1944	760th Railway Shop Battalion	Carthage, Tunis, Tunisia	Tech Sergeant
Harland J. Broussard	LA	Sept. 12, 1944	725th Railway Operating Battalion	India	Staff Sergeant
George Edward Brown	NY	Dec. 24, 1944	735th Railway Operating Battalion	France	Technician 4th Class

NAME	STATE ENLISTED	DATE OF DEATH	UNIT	PLACE OF DEATH	ARMY RANK
Carl E. Buckingham	KY	May 9, 1944	715th Railway Operating Battalion	Nettuno, Italy	Private
George B. Cash	OH	Sept. 30, 1944	756th Railway Shop Battalion	England	Private
John J. Catanzaro	NY	May 19, 1945	735th Railway Operating Battalion	Netherlands	Technician 5th Class
David O. Champagne	CT	July 18, 1943	729th Railway Operating Battalion	England	Tech Sergeant
Joe W. Chandler	OR	Feb. 9, 1945	732nd Railway Operating Battalion	Belgium	Technician 4th Class
Robert W. Ciarlelli	MO	Oct. 19, 1945	741st Railway Operating Battalion	Netherlands	Private
Willard E. Collette	OH	July 13, 1945	740th Railway Operating Battalion	France	Technician 4th Class
Clarence H. Creamer	AL	Dec. 24, 1944	741st Railway Operating Battalion	Belgium	Private
John L. Cronin	MA	June 20, 1945	752nd Railway Operating Battalion	Netherlands	Technician 4th Class
James J. Curd	PA	Apr. 7, 1945	750th Railway Operating Battalion	France	Technician 4th Class
Joseph M. Cushman	OH	Jan. 10, 1945	718th Railway Operating Battalion	Belgium	Technician 4th Class
James V. De Luca	NJ	Nov. 27, 1944	763rd Railway Shop Battalion	Belgium	Warrant Officer Junior Grade
Wayne Dister	CA	Apr. 26, 1943	713th Railway Operating Battalion	Carthage, Tunis, Tunisia	Private
Oscar W. Dixon	OH	Feb. 27, 1944	715th Railway Operating Battalion	Carthage, Tunis, Tunisia	Technician 4th Class
John Leonard Donahue	NE	Mar. 28, 1945	759th Railway Operating Battalion	France	Private
Harlan J. Dooley	ID	Apr. 5, 1944	711th Railway Operating Battalion	Carthage, Tunis, Tunisia	Private

NAME	STATE ENLISTED	DATE OF DEATH	UNIT	PLACE OF DEATH	ARMY RANK
Bernard R. Dougherty	OH	June 20, 1943	711th Railway Operating Battalion	Carthage, Tunis, Tunisia	Private
Leonard N. Ervine	WV	June 1, 1943	759th Railway Operating Battalion	Carthage, Tunis, Tunisia	Private
William L. Evans	NE	Oct. 31, 1944	711th Railway Operating Battalion	Carthage, Tunis, Tunisia	Private
James P. Fahey	IL	Nov. 21, 1944	712th Railway Operating Battalion	France	Sergeant
Eric E. Fall	NV	Oct. 31, 1944	711th Railway Operating Battalion	Carthage, Tunis, Tunisia	Private
Robert L. Freeman	IN	May 14, 1944	755th Railway Shop Battalion	England	Private
Berman W. Gallion	WI	June 20, 1944	719th Railway Operating Battalion	Nettuno, Italy	Sergeant
Donal R. Genovese	IL	Dec. 27, 1944	740th Railway Operating Battalion	France	Corporal
Rex C. Gill	KS	Sept. 27, 1945	750th Railway Operating Battalion	France	Lieutenant
Jack Valentine Gordon	UT	Sept. 4, 1943	719th Railway Operating Battalion	Rinehart, Tunisia	Corporal
Rito J. Greco	NY	Dec. 27, 1944	740th Railway Operating Battalion	Belgium	Private
George J. Grimm	CO	Jan. 9, 1945	735th Railway Operating Battalion	Belgium	Sergeant
James V.	TN	Mar. 31, 1945	723rd Railway Operating Battalion	Germany	Private
Robert D. Gugger	IL	Dec. 24, 1944	740th Railway Operating Battalion	Belgium	Technician 5th Class
Max R. Hall	CA	Nov. 2, 1944	735th Railway Operating Battalion	France	Private
Charles A. Harrison	N/A	Unknown	740th Railway Operating Battalion	Belgium	Unknown
Thomas A. Hawkins	WI	July 13, 1945	716th Railway Operating Battalion	France	Technician 5th Class

NAME	STATE ENLISTED	DATE OF DEATH	UNIT	PLACE OF DEATH	ARMY RANK
Francis P. Hearn Jr.	CT	May 16, 1943	730th Railway Operating Battalion	Carthage, Tunis, Tunisia	Private
William C. Hedin	MN	Nov. 8, 1944	718th Railway Operating Battalion	France	Technician 5th Class
George H. Herrmann Jr.	IL	Apr. 11, 1945	743rd Railway Operating Battalion	Belgium	Sergeant— Conductor of train crew
Miles R. Hicks	VA	Apr. 1, 1945	717th Railway Operating Battalion	Belgium	Private
Arthur J. Hitchler Jr.	NY	Aug. 16, 1945	757th Railway Shop Battalion	Kassel, Germany	Technician 4th Class
Howard O. Hoonsbeen	IL	Aug. 28, 1945	720th Railway Operating Battalion	Netherlands	Master Sergeant
Arthur R. Hoveland	MT	June 2, 1945	723rd Railway Operating Battalion	Netherlands	Private
Claude W. Hovis	KS	Oct. 26, 1943	762nd Railway Shop Battalion	Carthage, Tunis, Tunisia	Lieutenant
Arthur R. Ivester	SC	Aug. 6, 1945	713th Railway Operating Battalion	Belgium	Private
Hilmar H. Jacobson	TX	Mar. 17, 1944	719th Railway Operating Battalion	Lazio, Italy	Captain
Jack R. Junek	WI	Aug. 16, 1945	757th Railway Shop Battalion	Netherlands	Private
Clarence Dale Karren	UT	May 8, 1944	725th Railway Operating Battalion	India	Technician 5th Class
Harry S. Keith	PA	June 14, 1943	727th Railway Operating Battalion	Carthage, Tunis, Tunisia	Private
Joseph P. Kennedy	MN	Feb. 25, 1944	713th Railway Operating Battalion	Rome, Italy	Private
Harry L. King	ME	Apr. 20, 1945	746th Railway Operating Battalion	Netherlands	Private
James A. King	IL	June 24, 1945	720th Railway Operating Battalion	Germany	Captain
Harold Kleinberg	NE	Oct. 12, 1945	790th Railway Operating Company	South Pacific	Lieutenant

NAME	STATE ENLISTED	DATE OF DEATH	UNIT	PLACE OF DEATH	ARMY RANK
Orel Lee Lance	IL	Dec. 27, 1944	740th Railway Operating Battalion	Belgium	Private
George A. Layman	WA	Sept. 20, 1945	735th Railway Operating Battalion	France	Private
Donald R. LePell	NM	Apr. 6, 1945	750th Railway Operating Battalion	Unknown	Lieutenant
Arthur C. Lewis	NY	Dec. 27, 1944	740th Railway Operating Battalion	Belgium	Technician 5th Class
Gurnie Lindsay	IN	June 2, 1945	740th Railway Operating Battalion	France	Sergeant
Harmon Lindsey	AL	Dec. 24, 1944	741st Railway Operating Battalion	France	Private
Drenzellee Lindstrom	TX	Sept. 1, 1944	715th Railway Operating Battalion	Nettuno, Italy	Private
Vincent A. Lipira	NY	Apr. 21, 1945	746th Railway Operating Battalion	Belgium	Private
Eugene Lopez	TX	Apr. 10, 1944	716th Railway Operating Battalion	Fort Sam Houston, TX	Technician 5th Class
Jack W. D. Mann Jr.	MA	Apr. 11, 1945	756th Railway Operating Battalion	Germany	Technical Sergeant
Clarence H. Marshall	IN	July 25, 1945	740th Railway Operating Battalion	France	Technician 4th Class
Michael H. Massaro	NJ	Dec. 24, 1944	741st Railway Operating Battalion	Belgium	Private
John M. McGillis	MN	Dec. 25, 1944	755th Railway Shop Battalion	Belgium	Private
Kenneth E. McGilvray	WA	July 8, 1945	734th Railway Operating Battalion	Netherlands	Sergeant
William Gage Miles	NJ	Apr. 18, 1945	723rd Railway Operating Battalion	Netherlands	Technician 5th Class— Crew Dispatcher
Alfred R. Mitchell	AL	Oct. 31, 1944	711th Railway Operating Battalion	Carthage, Tunis, Tunisia	Master Sergeant
Mervin Sanford Moore	NY	Aug. 19, 1945	741st Railway Operating Battalion	Netherlands	Private

NAME	STATE ENLISTED	DATE OF DEATH	UNIT	PLACE OF DEATH	ARMY RANK
James L. Mullin	AL	Dec. 27, 1944	740th Railway Operating Battalion	Belgium	Technician 4th Class
Merlin P. Murnan	AL	Aug. 22, 1945	724th Railway Operating Battalion	Belgium	Technician 5th Class
Harold R. Myers	CA	Apr. 13, 1944	719th Railway Operating Battalion	Nettuno, Italy	Corporal
Harold J. O'Brien	MN	Dec. 24, 1944	741st Railway Operating Battalion	Belgium	Private
Luke O'Brien	CA	Apr. 5, 1945	718th Railway Operating Battalion	Belgium	Technician 5th Class
Clarence Orr	NJ	Sept. 26, 1943	719th Railway Operating Battalion	Carthage, Tunis, Tunisia	Private
Clinton C. Ostrander Jr.	UT	Apr. 30, 1945	737th Railway Operating Battalion	Central Luzon, Philippines	Private
Roman G. Padilla	NV	Sept. 27, 1945	732nd Railway Operating Battalion	France	Technician 5th Class
Louis A. Proulx	MA	Feb. 12, 1945	743rd Railway Operating Battalion	Belgium	Private
Frank Rallo	NY	Dec. 27, 1944	740th Railway Operating Battalion	Belgium	Technician 5th Class
Benjamin Reiss	MI	Dec. 24, 1944	741st Railway Operating Battalion	Belgium	Private
Roy M. Ricketts	N/A	June 20, 1945	713th Railway Operating Battalion	France	Private
Nicholas Romanchak	NY	Jan. 25, 1946	734th Railway Operating Battalion	Unknown	Unknown
Herbert W. Rowland	IA	Nov. 4, 1945	746th Railway Operating Battalion	Unknown	Unknown
Philip E. Sargeant	PA	Feb. 1, 1945	743rd Railway Operating Battalion	Netherlands	Captain
George F. Saylor	MI	July 3, 1944	715th Railway Operating Battalion	Nettuno, Italy	Technician 5th Class
Melvin D. Shaffer	OH	Dec. 7, 1944	722nd Railway Operating Battalion	France	Private
James W. Schrock	OH	Apr. 12, 1944	719th Railway Operating Battalion	Nettuno, Italy	Private

NAME	STATE ENLISTED	DATE OF DEATH	UNIT	PLACE OF DEATH	ARMY RANK
Robert C. Sealock	NE	Apr. 23, 1945	746th Railway Operating Battalion	Germany	Sergeant
Melvin D. Shaffer	OH	Dec. 7, 1944	722nd Railway Operating Battalion	France	Private
Joseph J. Shuboney	NJ	Dec. 24, 1944	735th Railway Operating Battalion	Belgium	Technician 4th Class
Charles S. Smith	IL	Apr. 28, 1945	746th Railway Operating Battalion	Germany	Unknown
Joe C. Spencer	KS	Nov. 25, 1945	746th Railway Operating Battalion	France	Private
Gilbert F. Stride	OR	July 31, 1945	718th Railway Operating Battalion	France	Private
Charles L. Surface	OR	June 26, 1943	730th Railway Operating Battalion	Carthage, Tunis, Tunisia	Private
Leo Taft	IL	June 16, 1944	719th Railway Operating Battalion	Nettuno, Italy	Technician 5th Class
Robert M. Thomas	IL	Sept. 20, 1944	722nd Railway Operating Battalion	France	Captain
Edwin J. Thompson	RI	June 12, 1944	729th Railway Operating Battalion	England	Technician 5th Class
George A. Trimmer	VA	Oct. 19, 1944	716th Railway Operating Battalion	France	Private
John R. Valentine	MT	Dec. 10, 1944	723rd Railway Operating Battalion	France	Technician 5th Class
Arthur Allen Van Kleeck	WI	Dec. 27, 1944	740th Railway Operating Battalion	Belgium	Medic— Medical Unit
Francis Waldbillig	MI	June 28, 1944	727th Railway Operating Battalion	Nettuno, Italy	Technician 5th Class
Emil H. Wiese	IL	Dec. 24, 1944	741st Railway Operating Battalion	Belgium	Private
Wayne Wingenroth	PA	Aug. 16, 1945	757th Railway Shop Battalion	Netherlands	Technician 4th Class

NAME	STATE ENLISTED	DATE OF DEATH	UNIT	PLACE OF DEATH	ARMY RANK
James H. Yarbrough	IL	Aug. 6, 1944	719th Railway Operating Battalion	Unknown	Technician 5th Class
Edward Yohr	NY	Aug. 25, 1945	735th Railway Operating Battalion	France	Technical Sergeant
Robert B. Youngs	NY	Aug. 15, 1945	757th Railway Shop Battalion	Kassel, Germany	Technician 5th Class

ACKNOWLEDGMENTS

Rarely is an author as grateful to his researcher as I am to Nancy Cunningham. I came across her by accident at the start of this project, and she has been an invaluable source of material for the book, providing details of incidents from sources I would never have known about, let alone found, on my own. She has given texture to this book in a way that would have been impossible without her knowledge and her library.

Nancy is a librarian, and both her father, Major William "Bill" M. Griffin, and her uncle, Lieutenant Colonel Laurence B. Griffin, worked for the Illinois Central Railroad in Chicago when they were enlisted into the railroad company–sponsored army units in 1943. During World War II, William served in Antwerp, Belgium, with the 743rd Railway Operating Battalion, and Laurence in Liège, Belgium, with the 741st Railway Operating Battalion, two cities that feature prominently in this story. Both went on to serve in rail units in the Korean War and beyond. Nancy has maintained contact with many servicemen and their families for decades and is now helping inform their descendants about the activities of these veterans. Nancy contacted the three daughters of Emerson Itschner, one of the heroes of this story, and they provided personal information, so I give additional thanks to Gail, Ann, and Carol.

Nancy has researched the Military Railway Service for almost 40 years and has maintained a blog and web page to chronicle the history of the railway units to ensure that their unique contributions to the war effort and the sacrifice of the men who served are not forgotten. What started as a small personal web page quickly developed into a large blog, where veterans from all rail units and their families could share their stories and personal photos. The site now has had over two million visitors and contains more than 2,000 posts. Nancy told me: "The entire purpose of my websites and blogs for the past 25 years has been to collect and share the amazing work of the US Army rail units of WWII and Korea and I now hope this book will help to share this information." The site is at https://militaryrailwayservice.com and the Twitter handle is @MilitaryRailway.

I owe much to many others, of course. Numerous people with military experience were helpful, most notably Major General (Ret.) Mungo Melvin CB OBE, the historian of the Corps of Royal Engineers, who provided me with much information and read the manuscript as well as having kindly provided me with a superb foreword. My longtime friend and running partner, Liam Browne, undertook an immense amount of research on the British side and uncovered some gems. Others who helped include, in no particular order: Rob Bayliff, the longtime secretary of the Military Railway Study Group; Alex Hamilton, who is particularly adroit at digging up documents; the British Overseas Railways Historic Trust; Clem Maginnis; Nicolas Aubin; Lord Dannatt; Phil Kennedy; Giles Milton; Patrick Kelly; Ted Inman; Lieutenant Colonel Matthew Whitchurch; the Royal Engineers; and finally, the librarians at the Imperial War Museum and the National Archives.

I would also like to thank my publishers and, in particular, my agent, Toby Mundy, of Aevitas Creative, who made me work hard—but successfully—to develop this concept. And my gratitude as ever to my wife, Deborah Maby, for her support and ideas.

NOTES

INTRODUCTION

1. Carlo D'Este, *A Genius for War* (New York: HarperCollins, 1995), 605.
2. Emerson Itschner, speech to engineer conference, Fort Leonard Wood, Missouri, May 6, 1989.
3. *Military Engineer* 36, no. 336 (December 1944): 408.
4. Office of the Chief of Transportation, European Theater of Operations, *Historical Report of the Transportation Corps in the European Theater of Operations*, Vol. 5, Pt. 1 *October, November, December 1944* (Paris: Office of Chief of Transportation, European Theater of Operations, 1944), 35, https://alu.army .mil/library/special_collections/Documents/Transportation%20Corp%20 V.%205%20Part%20I.pdf.
5. "Tracks to Victory," *Classic Trains*, special edition, 2019, 54.
6. "Tracks to Victory," *Classic Trains*, special edition, 2019, 55.
7. Both quotes: Don DeNevi, *United States Military Railway Service: America's Soldier-Railroaders in WWII* (Toronto, ON: Stoddart Publishing, 1992), 7.
8. David Matthew Wilkins, "The L&N's Battalion: The Story of the 728th Railway Operating Battalion, Sponsored by the Louisville and Nashville Railroad Company During the Second World War" (unpublished PhD thesis, University of Western Kentucky, 2002), iv.
9. Andrew Grant, *The Saga of the 708 Grand Division* (Hassell Street Press, 2021), 6.

CHAPTER 1: THE BIGGEST TASK

1. Max Hastings, *Overlord: D-Day and the Battle for Normandy 1944* (New York: Simon & Schuster, 1984), 23.
2. Brigadier R. F. O'D. Gage, "The Army Transportation Service" (lecture), Joint Services Staff College, April 21, 1947, published in *Royal Engineers Journal* 61 (1947): 322.

3. Quoted in Chester Wardlow, *The Transportation Corps: Responsibilities, Organization, and Operations* (Washington, DC: Office of the Chief of Military History, United States Army, 1951), 10.

4. Lieutenant Colonel Clem Maginniss, "Overload to Overlord," *Royal Logistics Review*, 2004, 59.

5. Alfred M. Beck, Abe Bortz, Charles W. Lynch, Lilia Mayo, and Ralph F. Weld, *The Corps of Engineers: The War Against Germany*, United States Army in World War II: The Technical Series (Washington, DC: United States Army Center of Military History, 1985), 7.

6. Quoted in Beck et al., *The Corps of Engineers*, 23.

7. Joshua Schick, "Operation Jubilee: The Raid at Dieppe," National WWII Museum, October 8, 2021, https://www.nationalww2museum.org/war/articles/operation-jubilee-dieppe-raid-1942.

8. Both quotes in Wardlow, *The Transportation Corps*, 1.

9. Quoted in Wardlow, *The Transportation Corps*, 159.

10. Hastings, *Overlord*, 26.

11. Cable from Churchill to Roosevelt, October 23, 1944, quoted in Hastings, *Overlord*, 26.

12. Wardlow, *The Transportation Corps*, 17.

13. There is a remarkable YouTube video on how to sabotage a railway that was produced by the Army at the railway in March 1944: Charlie Dean Archives, "Army Experiments in Train Derailment & Sabotage—1944—CharlieDeanArchives/Archival Footage," YouTube video, 7:16, https://www.frrandp.com/2020/05/an-experimental-military-railway.html.

14. J. H. Joiner, *One More River to Cross: The Story of Military Bridging* (Barnsley, UK: Reprinted by Pen & Sword, 2006), 153.

15. *Railway Age* 116, no. 23 (June 3, 1944).

16. "World War 2 Bailey Bridge," Halling Historical Society (HHS), HugoFox, https://www.hugofox.com/community/halling-historical-society-18475/world-war-2-bailey-bridge/#.

17. Kenneth Oldham, *Steam in Wartime Britain* (Stroud, UK: Alan Sutton Publishing, 1993), 94.

18. John Westwood, *Railways at War I* (Oxford: Osprey, 1980), 207.

CHAPTER 2: DESTRUCTION

1. "*Les cheminots dans la guerre et l'occupation, temoignages et recits*," *Revue d'Histoire des Chemins de Fer, Hors Serie* 7 (November 2002): 131, Associations pour l'histoire des Chemins de fer en France (author's translation).

2. Quoted in *"Les cheminots dans la guerre et l'occupation,"* 70–71.
3. Quoted in *"Les cheminots dans la guerre et l'occupation,"* 74.
4. Marcel Péroche, *Pacific Senator: A Train Driver's Life*, trans. Roland Wilson (Glendaruel, UK: Argyll, 2005), 168.
5. AAF Evaluation Board in the European Theater of Operations, *Effectiveness of Air Attack in the Battle of France* (Washington, DC: US Army, June 1945), 4.
6. Cécile Hochard, *Les cheminots dans la résistance* (Paris: La Vie du Rail, 2011), 37 (author's translation).
7. Gordon A. Harrison, *United States Army in World War II: The European Theater of Operations, Cross-Channel Attack* (Washington, DC: United States Army Center of Military History, 1950), 204.
8. Hochard, *Les cheminots dans la résistance*, 28.
9. Don DeNevi and Bob Hall, *United States Military Railway Service: America's Soldier-Railroaders in WWII* (Toronto, ON: Stoddart Publishing, 1992), 8.
10. Reproduced in Hochard, *Les cheminots dans la résistance*, 140.
11. Giles Milton, *D-Day: The Soldier's Story* (London: John Murray, 2014), 30.
12. All these quoted in Milton, *D-Day*, 30.
13. Quoted in Sébastien Albertelli, *Histoire du Sabotage* (Paris: Perrin, 2016), 389.
14. Cited in Milton, *D-Day*.
15. Translated by the author from accounts published on "6-7 mars 1944: 1 260 tonnes de bombes sur Trappes," l'Histoire en rafale, 20 février 2021, http://lhistoireenrafale.lunion.fr/2014/03/06/6-7-mars-1944-1-260-tonnes-de-bombes-sur-trappes/.
16. Letter from Churchill to Eisenhower, April 3, 1944, FO/954/18, UK National Archives, Kew, London.
17. Letter from Eisenhower to Churchill, April 5, 1944, FO/954/18A.
18. *Saturday Evening Post*, June 15, 1946, 116.
19. Solly Zuckerman, *From Apes to Warlords, 1904–1946: An Autobiography* (London: Hamish Hamilton, 1978), 247.
20. Zuckerman, *From Apes to Warlords*, 249.
21. Richard G. Davis, *Carl A. Spaatz and the Air War in Europe* (Washington, DC: US Government Printing Office, 1993), 403.
22. Quoted in Winston Churchill, *Closing the Ring* (London: Penguin Classics), 467.
23. Zuckerman, *From Apes to Warlords*, 256.
24. AAF Evaluation Board, *Effectiveness of Air Attack in the Battle of France*, 86.

25. The Overall Air Plan for Operation Neptune, in "Forward Echelon Communications Zone for Neptune," Annexes 8–26, 260, US National Archives, Washington, DC.

26. Jean-Charles Foucrier, *La Stratégie de la destruction: Bombardements alliés en France, 1944* (Paris: Vendemiaire, 2015), 349 (author's translation).

27. Jonathan Trigg, *D-Day Through German Eyes: How the Wehrmacht Lost France* (Stroud, UK: Amberley, 2020), 161.

28. Trigg, *D-Day Through German Eyes*, 147.

29. Jean Quellien, "*Les bombardements pendant la campagne de Normandie*," *Cahiers du Centre d'études d'Histoire de la Defense* 37 (2009): 68 (author's translation).

30. Harrison, *United States Army in World War II*, 204.

31. AAF Evaluation Board, *Effectiveness of Air Attack in the Battle of France*, 99.

32. AAF Evaluation Board, *Effectiveness of Air Attack in the Battle of France*, 111.

33. Quoted in Albertelli, *Histoire du Sabotage*, 390 (author's translation).

34. Quoted in "*Les cheminots dans la guerre et l'occupation, temoignages et recits*," 171 (author's translation).

35. Péroche, *Pacific Senator*, 178.

36. Péroche, *Pacific Senator*, 183.

37. Péroche, *Pacific Senator*, 183.

CHAPTER 3: FIRST TRACKS

1. Brigadier R. F. O'D. Gage, "The Army Transportation Service" (lecture), Joint Services Staff College, April 21, 1947, published in *Royal Engineers Journal* 61 (1947): 322.

2. Alfred M. Beck, Abe Bortz, Charles W. Lynch, Lilia Mayo, and Ralph F. Weld, *The Corps of Engineers: The War Against Germany*, United States Army in World War II: The Technical Series (Washington, DC: United States Army Center of Military History, 1985), 299.

3. *Transportation by Rail, Second Military Rail Service* (pamphlet), chap. 4, 2.

4. Roland G. Ruppenthal, *The European Theater of Operations: Logistical Support of the Armies*, Vol. 1, *May 1941–August 1944* (Washington, DC: United States Army Center of Military History, 1995), 315.

5. "Railway Operation on the Cherbourg Peninsula," 1, US Army, US Forces, European Theater, Historical Division; Records, 1941–1946, National Archives, Washington, DC.

6. "Lt. Col. Harvey Gives Rotarians Account of War," *Medford Mail Tribune*, August 14, 1946.

7. All references from *Historic Report US Army Corps*, A. D. Harvey, Diary, Appendix 12, US National Archives.

8. All these quotes taken from Becker's papers at the University of New Orleans, Administrative History Collection Historical Section, ETOUSA Folder, Cherbourg Notes Psychological Warfare ADM NR 492Q, National Archives, https://www.archives.gov/research/guide-fed-records/groups/498 .html#498.1.

9. *Railway Age* 118, no. 21 (May 21–27, 1945): 865.

10. "Railway Operation on the Cherbourg Peninsula," 72.

11. "Railway Operation on the Cherbourg Peninsula," 72.

12. Gordon A. Harrison, *Cross Channel Attack* (Washington, DC: United States Army Center of Military History, 1993), 441.

13. Both quotes from "*Les cheminots dans la guerre et l'occupation, temoignages et recits,*" *Revue d'Histoire des Chemins de Fer, Hors Serie* 7 (November 2002): 236, Associations pour l'histoire des Chemins de fer en France (author's translation).

14. "Railway Operation on the Cherbourg Peninsula," 3.

15. The quotes from Monsieur Vosluisant are all taken from "*Les cheminots dans la guerre et l'occupation, temoignages et recits,*" *Revue d'Histoire des Chemins de Fer, Hors Serie* 7 (November 2002): 240–241 (author's translation).

16. "Railway Operation on the Cherbourg Peninsula," 5.

17. "Railway Operation on the Cherbourg Peninsula," 5.

18. "Railway Operation on the Cherbourg Peninsula," 6.

19. "Railway Operation on the Cherbourg Peninsula," 10.

20. "Railway Operation on the Cherbourg Peninsula," 11.

21. "Railway Operation on the Cherbourg Peninsula," 12.

22. *Railway Age* 118, no. 3 (January 20–26, 1945): 194.

23. *Railway Age* 118, no. 3 (January 20–26, 1945): 195.

24. *Railway Age* 118, no. 3 (January 20–26, 1945): 195.

25. "Railway Operation on the Cherbourg Peninsula," 16.

26. My previous book provides numerous examples: Christian Wolmar, *Engines of War: How Wars Were Won and Lost on the Railways* (New York: PublicAffairs, 2010).

27. Roland G. Ruppenthal, *The European Theater of Operations: Logistical Support of the Armies*, Vol. 1, *May 1941–September 1944* (Washington, DC: United States Army Center of Military History, 1995), 547.

28. "Railway Operation on the Cherbourg Peninsula," 14.

29. "Railway Operation on the Cherbourg Peninsula," 14.

30. All these quotes from the Brothers of Locomotive Engineers and Trainmen
document posted on the *Galveston County Daily News* website, October 23,
2003. https://www.galvnews.com.
31. "Railway Operation on the Cherbourg Peninsula," 15.

CHAPTER 4: THE GREATEST CHALLENGE

1. Alfred M. Beck, Abe Bortz, Charles W. Lynch, Lilia Mayo, and Ralph F.
Weld, *The Corps of Engineers: The War Against Germany*, United States Army
in World War II: The Technical Series (Washington, DC: United States Army
Center of Military History, 1985), 399.
2. US Army, *The Transportation Corps in the Battle of France*, Vol. 4, *July–
September 1944* (Washington, DC: United States Army, 1946), 1.
3. Geoffrey Perret, *There's a War to Be Won* (New York: Random House, 1997),
345.
4. Robert Allen, *Drive to Victory* (New York: Berkley Publishing, 1947), 27.
5. Allen, *Drive to Victory*, 17.
6. Allen, *Drive to Victory*, 19.
7. Allen, *Drive to Victory*, 20.
8. Martin Blumenson, *Breakout and Pursuit*, United States Army in World War
II: The European Theater of Operations (Washington, DC: United States
Army Center of Military History, 1993), 432.
9. Roland G. Ruppenthal, *The European Theater of Operations: Logistical Support
of the Armies*, Vol. 1, *May 1941–August 1944* (Washington, DC: United States
Army Center of Military History, 1995), 482.
10. US Army, *The Transportation Corps in the Battle of France*, Vol. IV, *July–
September 1944* (Washington, DC: United States Army, 1946), 1.
11. Ruppenthal, *The European Theater of Operations*, 1:546.
12. "History of the 347th General Service Regiment" (unpublished document
owned by Nancy Cunningham, available through her personal digital archive
https://drive.google.com/file/d/1xQ3FpPwH4lWIem6qufycuMj1BNBi9
VvR/view?usp=sharing), 20.
13. Historical report US Army Corps of Engineers, European Theater of
Operations, *Railroad Reconstruction and Bridging*, Report no. 12, Liaison
Section, Intelligence Division, Office of the Chief Engineer, August 1945, 52,
US National Archives.
14. "History of the 347th General Service Regiment," 21.

15. ADSEC, *Communications Zone*, Vol. 4, *Operational History, Oct 1943–July 1945* (Washington, DC: Advanced Section Communications Zone European Theater of Operations, United States Army, 1945), 97.

16. All quotes from Order No. 7, August 13, 1944, Engineer Section, Advance Section Communications Zone, APO 113, US Army (in Nancy Cunningham's personal collection).

17. Robert Allen, *Drive to Victory* (New York: Berkley Publishing, 1947), 74.

18. David Matthew Wilkins, "The L&N's Battalion: The Story of the 728th Railway Operating Battalion, Sponsored by the Louisville and Nashville Railroad Company During the Second World War" (unpublished PhD thesis, University of Western Kentucky, 2002).

19. US Army, *U.S. Forces European Theater Historical Division Records 1941–1946* (Washington, DC: United States Army, 1946), 437.

20. Order No. 7, August 13, 1944, Engineer Section, ADSEC.

21. *Engineering News Record*, April 19, 1945, 67.

22. Order No. 7, August 13, 1944, Engineer Section, ADSEC.

23. *Railroad Reconstruction and Bridging*, Report no. 12, 55.

24. *Railroad Reconstruction and Bridging*, Report no. 12, 56.

25. *Railroad Reconstruction and Bridging*, Report no. 12, 56.

26. Robert Lerouvillois, *32 Trains pour Le Mans, 1944, Cherbourg, Porte pour la Liberté* (Cherbourg: Isoète, 1994), 131 (author's translation).

27. *Military Engineer* 36, no. 230 (December 1944): 408.

28. *Military Engineer* 36, no. 230 (December 1944): 408.

29. "History of the 347th General Service Regiment," 28.

30. "History of the 347th General Service Regiment," 29.

31. "History of the 347th General Service Regiment," 29.

32. "History of the 347th General Service Regiment," 33–34.

33. 91 Cong. Rec. (January 3–February 23, 1945).

34. Lerouvillois, *32 Trains pour Le Mans*, 134 (author's translation).

CHAPTER 5: ALL ABOARD TO PARIS

1. John Livingstone, *740th Railway Operating Battalion* (New York: Carlton Press, 1981), 56.

2. Randolph Leigh, *American Enterprise in Europe: The Role of the SOS in the Defeat of Germany* (Frankfurt: United States Forces European Theater, 1947).

3. The regimental histories contain somewhat conflicting accounts about the precise timing of these early trains and whether the first train was carrying any supplies. There is no doubt, however, that the first train arrived on the seventeenth and that further trains started arriving soon after that, taking the French railway staff by surprise. Accounts also vary about the precise number of trains, with between 31 and 36 being suggested.

4. All quotes from Robert Lerouvillois, *32 Trains pour Le Mans, 1944, Cherbourg, Porte pour la Liberté* (Cherbourg: Isoète, 1994), 134–135 (author's translation).

5. "History of the Second Military Railway Service," 48.

6. John Livingstone, *740th Railway Operating Battalion* (New York: Carlton Press, 1981), 61.

7. Livingstone, *740th Railway Operating Battalion*, 56–57.

8. Leigh, *American Enterprise in Europe*, 69.

9. Livingstone, *740th Railway Operating Battalion*, 59.

10. Livingstone, *740th Railway Operating Battalion*, 57.

11. *United States Army Railway Grand Division, 706th* (Frankfurt: Pennsylvania Railroad, 1949), 26.

12. Livingstone, *740th Railway Operating Battalion*, 71.

13. All these quotes: Livingstone, *740th Railway Operating Battalion*, 72.

14. Livingstone, *740th Railway Operating Battalion*, 82–83.

15. "History of the 347th General Service Regiment" (unpublished document owned by Nancy Cunningham, available through her personal digital archive https://drive.google.com/file/d/1xQ3FpPwH4lWIem6qufycuMj1BNBi9 VvR/view?usp=sharing), 32.

16. "History of the 347th General Service Regiment," 32.

17. Sébastien Albertelli, *Histoire du Sabotage* (Paris: Perrin, 2016), 390 (author's translation).

18. Memo from Roosevelt to Churchill, No. 537, May 11, 1944, UK National Archives.

19. Solly Zuckerman, *From Apes to Warlords, 1904–1946: An Autobiography* (London: Hamish Hamilton, 1978), 273.

20. Vincent Cuny, *Les Trains de la Victoire, le rôle du chemin de fer dans la libération de la France, 1944–1945* (Paris: La Vie du Rail, 2015), 50.

21. Roland G. Ruppenthal, *The European Theater of Operations: Logistical Support of the Armies*, Vol. 1, *May 1941–August 1944* (Washington, DC: United States Army Center of Military History, 1995), 547.

22. Livingstone, *740th Railway Operating Battalion*, 72.

23. John Latta, *A Thousand Letters Away: One Man's War* (CreateSpace, 2012), 216.

24. Latta, *A Thousand Letters Away*, 218.

25. Latta, *A Thousand Letters Away*, 218.

26. Quoted in Nicolas Aubin, *Liberty Roads: The American Logistics in France and Germany, 1944–5* (Paris: Histoire et Collections, 2014), 93.

27. Ruppenthal, *Logistical Support of the Armies*, 1:564.

28. Ruppenthal, *Logistical Support of the Armies*, 1:571.

29. Aubin, *Liberty Roads*, 104.

30. "Red Ball Express Hauled Critical Supplies for American Troops," *FreightWaves Classics*, February 10, 2021.

31. Both quotes: "WWII Driver Recalls the Red Ball Express: World at War," *Cleveland Metro*, September 27, 2009.

32. Both quotes from "Road to Victory," *Times-Picayune* (New Orleans, LA), September 11, 2000.

33. "Road to Victory," *Times-Picayune* (New Orleans, LA), September 11, 2000.

34. Both quotes in Aubin, *Liberty Roads*, 100.

35. Aubin, *Liberty Roads*, 108.

36. Ruppenthal, *Logistical Support of the Armies*, 1:571.

37. Ruppenthal, *Logistical Support of the Armies*, 1:571–572.

38. Ruppenthal, *Logistical Support of the Armies*, 1:572.

39. Ruppenthal, *Logistical Support of the Armies*, 1:583.

CHAPTER 6: RAILWAYS EVERYWHERE

1. 21 Army Group, Royal Engineers, *Bridging Normandy to Berlin* (British Army of the Rhine, 1945), 25.

2. 21 Army Group, *Bridging Normandy to Berlin*, xii.

3. Alfred M. Beck, Abe Bortz, Charles W. Lynch, Lilia Mayo, and Ralph F. Weld, *The Corps of Engineers: The War Against Germany*, United States Army in World War II: The Technical Series (Washington, DC: United States Army Center of Military History, 1985), 403.

4. "History of the 347th General Service Regiment" (unpublished document owned by Nancy Cunningham, available through her personal digital archive https://drive.google.com/file/d/1xQ3FpPwH4lWIem6qufycuMj1BNBi9 VvR/view?usp=sharing), 35.

5. "History of the 347th General Service Regiment," 36.

6. "History of the 347th General Service Regiment," 36.

7. "History of the 347th General Service Regiment," 37.

8. "History of the 347th General Service Regiment," 41.

9. Clair Bowman, "Normandy to Paris" (unpublished memoir, interviewed by Edwin Coker, 1945).

10. "History of the 347th General Service Regiment," 41.

11. "History of the 347th General Service Regiment," 46.

12. "History of the 347th General Service Regiment," 48.

13. Roland G. Ruppenthal, *The European Theater of Operations: Logistical Support of the Armies*, Vol. 1, *May 1941–August 1944* (Washington, DC: United States Army Center of Military History, 1995), 485.

14. Ruppenthal, *Logistical Support of the Armies*, 1:488.

15. *The 706th Railway Grand Division* (Frankfurt: n.p., 1945), 37.

16. Emerson Itschner, interview by Dr. Schubert, 26, Emerson C. Itschner Papers, Box 36, Folder 10, 1918–1974, US Army Heritage and Education Center, Carlisle Barracks, Pennsylvania.

17. Ruppenthal, *Logistical Support of the Armies*, 1:551.

18. Office of the Chief of Transportation, European Theater of Operations, *Historical Report of the Transportation Corps in the European Theater of Operations*, Vol. 5, Pt. 2, *October, November, December 1944* (Paris: Office of the Chief of Transportation, European Theater of Operations, 1944), chap. 4, 8, https://alu.army.mil/library/special_collections/Documents/Transportation%20Corp%20V.%205%20Part%20I.pdf.

19. Major K. Henderson RE, "Impressions of Railway Sabotage in France During a Visit There in December 1944" (unpublished manuscript, 1945), 2.

20. Henderson, "Impressions of Railway Sabotage," 2.

21. All these quotes from: Officers and Men of the 713th Railway Operating Battalion, *History of Company A 713th Railway Operating Battalion* (Austin, TX: n.p., 1946).

22. All these quotes from: Officers and Men of the 713th Railway Operating Battalion, *History of Company A 713th Railway Operating Battalion*.

23. Both quotes from "Army Railroading from D- to V-E Day," *Railway Age*, May 26, 1945, 944.

CHAPTER 7: LIFESAVERS — BUT NOT ALWAYS

1. John Livingstone, *740th Railway Operating Battalion* (New York: Carlton Press, 1981), 79.

2. "The Hospital Train in the E.T.O. 1944–1945," WW2 US Medical Research Centre, https://www.med-dept.com/articles/the-hospital-train-in-the-e-t-o-1944-1945/.

3. Letter by Robin Wilson (unpublished).

4. Roland G. Ruppenthal, *The European Theater of Operations: Logistical Support of the Armies*, Vol. 1, *May 1941–August 1944* (Washington, DC; United States Army Center of Military History, 1995), 551.

5. "An Avoidable Tragedy," originally published in *World War Two* magazine in 2001, and HistoryNet Staff, "Russell C. Eustice Recalls the Troop Train 2980 Tragedy at St. Valery-en-Caux During World War II," HistoryNet, June 12, 2006, https://www.historynet.com/russell-c-eustice-recalls-the-troop-train-2980-tragedy-at-st-valery-en-caux-during-world-war-ii/.

6. HistoryNet Staff, "Russell C. Eustice Recalls the Troop Train 2980 Tragedy," https://www.historynet.com/russell-c-eustice-recalls-the-troop-train-2980-tragedy-at-st-valery-en-caux-during-world-war-ii/.

7. "*Mémoire de la Seconde Guerre mondiale: la catastrophe ferroviaire de Saint-Valery*," *Le Courrier Cauchois*, July 25, 2014.

8. HistoryNet Staff, "Russell C. Eustice Recalls the Troop Train 2980 Tragedy," https://www.historynet.com/russell-c-eustice-recalls-the-troop-train-2980-tragedy-at-st-valery-en-caux-during-world-war-ii/.

9. HistoryNet Staff, "Russell C. Eustice Recalls the Troop Train 2980 Tragedy," https://www.historynet.com/russell-c-eustice-recalls-the-troop-train-2980-tragedy-at-st-valery-en-caux-during-world-war-ii/

10. These quotes from Bill Jones, "The 1945 Train Crash in France That Killed 89 Soldiers," *Tribune Democrat* (Johnstown, PA), January 12, 2008.

11. HistoryNet Staff, "Russell C. Eustice Recalls the Troop Train 2980 Tragedy," https://www.historynet.com/russell-c-eustice-recalls-the-troop-train-2980-tragedy-at-st-valery-en-caux-during-world-war-ii/.

CHAPTER 8: WAITING FOR ANTWERP

1. Emerson Itschner, interview by Dr. Schubert, 26, Emerson C. Itschner Papers, Box 36, Folder 10, 1918–1974, US Army Heritage and Education Center, Carlisle Barracks, Pennsylvania.

2. US Army, *The Transportation Corps in the Battle of France*, Vol. 4, *July–September 1944* (Washington, DC: United States Army, 1946), 25.

3. Office of the Chief of Transportation, European Theater of Operations, *Historical Report of the Transportation Corps in the European Theater of*

Operations, Vol. 5, Pt. 2, *October, November, December 1944* (Paris: Office of the Chief of Transportation, European Theater of Operations, 1944), chap. 4, 10, https://alu.army.mil/library/special_collections/Documents/Transportation %20Corp%20V.%205%20Part%20I.pdf.

4. Roland G. Ruppenthal, *The European Theater of Operations: Logistical Support of the Armies*, Vol. 2, *September 1944–May 1945* (Washington, DC: United States Army Center of Military History, 1995), 8.

5. All these quotes from Ruppenthal, *Logistical Support of the Armies*, 2:3–4.

6. Nicolas Aubin, *Liberty Roads: The American Logistics in France and Germany, 1944–5* (Paris: Histoire et Collections, 2014), 53.

7. "MRS in France Drafted Railroad Men," *Railway Age*, December 2, 1944, 854.

8. *History of the 706th Grand Division, 25 October 1943–9 May 1945* (Frankfurt: n.p., June 1945).

9. Ruppenthal, *Logistical Support of the Armies*, 2:148.

10. "History of the 347th General Service Regiment" (unpublished document owned by Nancy Cunningham, available through her personal digital archive https://drive.google.com/file/d/1xQ3FpPwH4lWIem6qufycuMj1BNBi9 VvR/view?usp=sharing), 50.

11. "History of the 347th General Service Regiment," 76.

12. John Livingstone, *740th Railway Operating Battalion* (New York: Carlton Press, 1981), 85.

13. Livingstone, *740th Railway Operating Battalion*, 90.

14. Livingstone, *740th Railway Operating Battalion*, 93.

15. Livingstone, *740th Railway Operating Battalion*, 94.

16. Livingstone, *740th Railway Operating Battalion*, 96.

17. Livingstone, *740th Railway Operating Battalion*, 127.

18. Livingstone, *740th Railway Operating Battalion*, 128.

19. Sergeant Joseph R. Ives, "Buzz Bombs on the Rails," *Army Transportation Journal* 1, no. 8 (September 1945): 70.

20. Nicolas Aubin, *Liberty Roads: The American Logistics in France and Germany, 1944–5* (Paris: Histoire et Collections, 2014), 130.

21. Steve R. Waddell, *United States Army Logistics: The Normandy Campaign 1944* (Westport, CT: Greenwood Press, 1994), 99.

22. Aubin, *Liberty Roads*, 136.

23. Quoted in Aubin, *Liberty Roads*, 137.

24. Major Andrew Grant Gregory, *The Saga of the 708th Railway Grand Division* (Baltimore: Baltimore and Ohio Railroad Company, 1947), 6–7.

25. Mark S. Womack, interview by Rebecca Patterson, Mark S. Womack Collection, second video, 30:50, February 19, 2003, Library of Congress, https://www.loc.gov/item/afc2001001.06054/.

26. "Louisiana Man Heads Antwerp, Eisenhower's Biggest Port," *Times-Picayune* (New Orleans, LA), August 12, 1945, 4.

27. "Louisiana Man Heads Antwerp, Eisenhower's Biggest Port."

28. "Louisiana Man Heads Antwerp, Eisenhower's Biggest Port."

29. Aubin, *Liberty Roads*, 139.

30. Aubin, *Liberty Roads*, 139.

31. Brigadier R. F. O'D. Gage, "The Army Transportation Service," *Military Review*, September 1948, 106.

32. Joseph Bykofsky and Harold Larson, *United States Army in World War II: The Technical Services: The Transportation Corps: Operations Overseas* (Washington, DC: United States Army Center of Military History, 1957), 344.

CHAPTER 9: HITLER'S LAST THROW

1. Chief Information and Education Division, *American Enterprise in Europe* (Paris: Chief Information and Education Division, USFET, 1945), 74.

2. Antony Beevor, *Ardennes 1944: Hitler's Last Gamble* (New York: Viking, 2015), 97.

3. Beevor, *Ardennes 1944*, 86.

4. Beevor, *Ardennes 1944*, 97.

5. Reproduced in "Trains Go to War," *Classic Trains*, 2019, 61.

6. Major Jeffrey W. Decker, *Logistics and Patton's Third Army: Lessons for Today's Logisticians* (March 20, 2003), https://www.airuniversity.af.edu/Portals/10/ASPJ/journals/Chronicles/decker.pdf.

7. Decker, *Logistics and Patton's Third Army*.

8. Yuri Bezmenov, "718th Railway Operating Battalion, Headquarters Company, Camp Claiborne, 1944," US Militaria Forum, October 23, 2022, https://www.usmilitariaforum.com/forums/index.php?/topic/377876-718th-railway-operating-battalion-headquarters-company-camp-claiborne-1944.

9. Bezmenov, "718th Railway Operating Battalion," https://www.usmilitariaforum.com/forums/index.php?/topic/377876-718th-railway-operating-battalion-headquarters-company-camp-claiborne-1944/.

10. Mitch Williamson, "Railways of WWII Part I and Part II," Weapons and Warfare, June 19, 2020, http://militaryrailwayservice.blogspot.com/2024/01/railways-of-wwii-part-i-and-part-ii.html. (These articles were on the Weapons

and Warfare website, which no longer exists: https://weaponsandwarfare
.com/2020/06/19/railways-of-wwii-part-i/.)

11. *The 706th Railway Grand Division* (Frankfurt: n.p., June 1945), 56.

12. *The 706th Railway Grand Division*, 56.

13. US Army, "The Soldier-Railroaders' Story of the 716th Railway Operating Battalion," *Regimental Histories* 35 (1946): 58, https://digicom.bpl.lib.me.us /ww_reg_his/35/.

14. US Army, "The Soldier-Railroaders Story of the 716th Railway Operating Battalion," 59.

15. All these quotes from Emerson Itschner, interview by Dr. Schubert, 22–23, Emerson C. Itschner Papers, Box 36, Folder 10, 1918–1974, US Army Heritage and Education Center, Carlisle Barracks, Pennsylvania.

16. Major Andrew Grant Gregory, *The Saga of the 708th Railway Grand Division* (Baltimore: Baltimore and Ohio Railroad Company, 1947), 23.

17. Both quotes: Gregory, *The Saga of the 708th Railway Grand Division*, 23.

18. *The 706th Railway Grand Division* (Frankfurt: June 1945), 160.

19. John Livingstone, *740th Railway Operating Battalion* (New York: Carlton Press, 1981), 154.

20. Livingstone, *740th Railway Operating Battalion*, 153.

21. Livingstone, *740th Railway Operating Battalion*, 157.

22. Gregory, *The Saga of the 708th Railway Grand Division*, 22–23.

23. Gregory, *The Saga of the 708th Railway Grand Division*, 22–23.

24. *Yank*, July 22, 1945. The archive is available here: https://tomharperkelly .com/the-yank-magazine-archive.

25. Hugh M. Cole, *The Ardennes: Battle of the Bulge*, United States Army in World War II: The European Theater of Operations (Washington, DC: United States Army Center of Military History, 1993), 662.

26. Cole, *The Ardennes*, 662.

27. Cole, *The Ardennes*, 663.

28. Cole, *The Ardennes*, 664.

29. Cole, *The Ardennes*, 664.

30. Cole, *The Ardennes*, 664.

31. Cole, *The Ardennes*, 665.

32. *The 706th Railway Grand Division*, 57.

CHAPTER 10: TAKEOVER

1. Chester W. Nichols, *Bridging for Victory* (Self-published, 1983), 342.

2. US Army, "The History of the 341st Regiment Engineer Regiment, July 29, 1942–March 2, 1946," *Regimental Histories* 188 (1946), https://digicom.bpl .lib.me.us/ww_reg_his/188.

3. US Army, "The History of the 341st Regiment Engineer Regiment."

4. Nichols, *Bridging for Victory*, 341–342.

5. Nichols, *Bridging for Victory*, 341.

6. Nichols, *Bridging for Victory*, 343.

7. Reproduced in "Trains Go to War," *Classic Trains*, 2019, 63.

8. Colonel E. Paul Semmens, *The Hammer of Hell* (El Paso, TX: Fort Bliss, 1990), 23.

9. Emerson Itschner, interview by Dr. Schubert, 21, Emerson C. Itschner Papers, Box 36, Folder 10, 1918–1974, US Army Heritage and Education Center, Carlisle Barracks, Pennsylvania.

10. Andrew Grant Gregory, *The Saga of the 708th Railway Grand Division* (Baltimore: Baltimore and Ohio Railroad Company, 1947), 33.

11. Roland G. Ruppenthal, *The European Theater of Operations: Logistical Support of the Armies*, Vol. 2, *September 1944–May 1945* (Washington, DC: United States Army Center of Military History, 1995), 403.

12. Itschner interview, 24.

13. Both quotes from Itschner interview, 24.

14. Brigadier R. F. O'D. Gage, "A British Bridge Across the Rhine," *R.U.S.I. Journal*, November 1945.

15. Lieutenant A. W. Gillitt, memoirs during NW Europe Campaign 1944–1945, *World War Two Railway Study Group Bulletin*, March–April 2003.

16. Various accounts differ on the precise date because inauguration of the service was delayed for lack of demand.

17. George Pillette, "Toot Suite Express," *Army Transportation Journal* 1, no. 3 (April 1945): 10–12.

18. *Yankee Boomer* 2, no. 43 (July 26, 1945): 1.

19. Joseph Bykofsky and Harold Larson, *The Transportation Corps: Operations Overseas* (Washington, DC: United States Army Center of Military History, 2003), 351.

20. Bykofsky and Larson, *The Transportation Corps*, 351.

21. Antony Beevor, *Ardennes 1944: Hitler's Last Gamble* (New York: Viking, 2015), 47.

22. John Livingstone, *740th Railway Operating Battalion* (New York: Carlton Press, 1981), 169.

23. "735th Op Bn Now Operates at Hamm," *Railway Age* 118, no. 25 (June 1945): 1064.

24. Colonel John H. Wheeler, "German Railroads at the End of the War," *Railway Age* 118, no. 26 (July 1945): 1138.

25. Christian Wolmar, *Engines of War: How Wars Were Won and Lost on the Railways* (London: Atlantic Books, 2010), 259.

26. Wolmar, *Engines of War*, 260.

27. Wolmar, *Engines of War*, 261.

28. Don DeNevi and Bob Hall, *United States Military Railway Service: America's Soldier-Railroaders in WWII* (Ontario, Canada: Stoddart Publishing, 1992), 7.

29. Jonathan Trigg, *D-Day Through German Eyes: How the Wehrmacht Lost France* (Gloucestershire, UK: Amberley, 2020), 162.

EPILOGUE

1. Major Andrew Grant Gregory, *The Saga of the 708th Railway Grand Division* (Baltimore: Baltimore and Ohio Railroad Company, 1947), 44.

2. US Army, "The History of the 341st Regiment, July 29, 1943–March 22, 1946," *Regimental Histories* 188 (1946), https://digicom.bpl.lib.me.us/ww _reg_his/188/.

3. Stuart Van Leer Bradley Jr., *Photo History of the Black 95th Engineer General Service Regiment in World War Two*, Vol. 2 (Alexandria, VA: Railway Station Press, 2017), 3.

4. Maggie Hurst and Chris Elliott, *Show Me the Way to Go Home* (Farnborough, UK: Medloc Enterprise, 1995), 15.

INDEX